D1553270

A Ballet for the Ear

A Ballet
for
the Ear

Interviews, Essays, and Reviews

JOHN LOGAN

Edited by A. Poulin, Jr.

Ann Arbor   **The University of Michigan Press**

Copyright © by The University of Michigan 1983
All rights reserved
Published in the United States of America by
The University of Michigan Press and simultaneously
in Rexdale, Canada, by John Wiley & Sons Canada, Limited
Manufactured in the United States of America

1986   1985   1984   1983   5   4   3   2   1

I wish to thank the State University of New York at Buffalo
for a sabbatical leave during which the final work on this book
was completed.—John Logan

Library of Congress Cataloging in Publication Data

Logan, John, 1923–
  A ballet for the ear.

  (Poets on poetry)
  Includes index.
  1. Logan, John, 1923–   —Interviews.
2. American poetry—History and criticism—Addresses,
essays, lectures.   3. English poetry—History and
criticism—Addresses, essays, lectures.   4. Poetry—
Addresses, essays, lectures.   I. Poulin, A.
II. Title.   III. Series.
PS3523.0344B34   1983   811'.5'09   82-23883
ISBN 0-472-06336-7 (pbk.)

For my father
James B. Logan

Acknowledgments

Grateful acknowledgment is made to the editors and publishers of the following journals and books for permission to reprint copyrighted materials:

Allegany Poetry for "A Conversation with Helen Ruggieri and David Perry," *Allegany Poetry* 1, no. 2.

Boa Editions for the foreword to *Eggs in the Lake,* poems by Daniela Gioseffi. Copyright © 1979 by Daniela Gioseffi and John Logan, reprinted by permission of Boa Editions.

The Brockport Writers Forum for permission to reprint "A Conversation with Anthony Piccione and A. Poulin, Jr." and "A Conversation with William Heyen and Gregory Fitz Gerald." The first article was edited from a transcription of a videotape produced by the Educational Communications Center on February 15, 1972; the second from a videotape produced by the Educational Communications Center on April 21, 1970. Both were sponsored by the Brockport Writers Forum, Department of English, State University of New York, College at Brockport, Brockport, New York. Copyright © by the State University of New York. All rights reserved. Not to be reprinted without permission.

Chicago Review for "*The Sorrows of Priapus* by Edward Dahlberg," *Chicago Review* 12, no. 3 (Autumn 1958).

Commonweal for the following reviews: Richard Wilbur, "Things of This World," volume 64 (August 10, 1956); W. S. Merwin, "Green with Beasts," volume 65 (December 28, 1956); Karl Shapiro, "Poems of a Jew," volume 68 (September 19, 1958); Karl Shapiro, "In Defense of Ignorance," volume 73 (January 20, 1960); Galway Kinnell, "What a Kingdom It Was," volume 73 (November 4, 1960).

Dryad for reviews of *In the Sleep of Rivers* by Joseph Stroud and *Sailing Too Far* by Milton Kessler.

Dustbooks for John Logan's foreword to *Night Conversations with None Other* by Shreela Ray.

Ecco Press for poems from *Only the Dreamer Can Change the Dream*.

Epoch for "Josephine Jacobsen, *The Animal Inside*," *Epoch*, Fall 1966.

Hudson Review for "John Gruen's Settings for Wallace Stevens," *Hudson Review* 9, no. 2 (Summer 1956).

Iowa Review for "A Conversation with Thomas Hilgers and Michael Molloy."

Liveright for the foreword to *White Buildings* by Hart Crane, 1972 edition.

Minnesota Review for "Psychological Motifs in Melville's *Pierre*," *Minnesota Review* 7, no. 4 (1967):325–30.

The Nation for a review of *Northfield Poems* by A. R. Ammons, published April 24, 1967; and for a review of *Body Rags* by Galway Kinnell, published September 16, 1968.

Poesia for "A Conversation with Michele Riccardelli," originally published in Italian in *Uomini E. Libri*.

Prologue Press for "Poetry and Change: Interview with John Logan" by Dan Murray, *Prologue* 3, no. 1. Copyright © 1968. Reprinted by permission of Prologue Press.

Sewanee Review for "The Poetry of Isabella Gardner," *Sewanee Review* 70, no. 2, (Spring 1962).

Trace for "A Conversation with Marvin Bell."

Voyages for "On Poets and Poetry Today," *Voyages* 4, nos. 3 and 4.

Windsor Review for "*Changing the Windows* by Jerome Mazzaro," *Windsor Review* 8, (Fall 1972).

Every effort has been made to trace the ownership of all copyrighted material in this book and to secure permission for its use.

Contents

Preface as Prelude

John Logan's critical prose is pleasurable because it sounds like his poetry. In fact, it is a necessary extension of his poetry: the subjects are often the same, the themes are parallel if not contiguous, even the language of his criticism is marked by that resonant lyricism characteristic of Logan's poems.

Logan is also an ideal poet-as-critic. He knows that the critic's primary role is to elucidate and evaluate the text and, as reviewer, occasionally to exhort. He knows that the good poet-critic's observations are informed by solid critical principles and arise from a complex of *poetics* that directs his critical judgment as much as it serves as the intellectual wellspring of his own poetry.

Logan further knows that a sensitive response to one genre of art is an implicit response to all genres. Poetry, music, dance, fiction, painting—all art is the composite image of the human mystery at a given moment of history cast in interdependent media. Thus, what Logan has to say about Melville's fiction, Beckett's drama, the poetry of Crane, Cummings, and Thomas, about poets and poetry today and his own early poems, as well as about the inarticulate as hero—all of it is an essential part of his more encompassing *poetics* in the comprehensive Aristotelian sense of that word.

Logan's essays on Crane, Cummings, and Thomas, then, are natural extensions of his poems about those and many other poets, from his early poem, "The Death of Southwell" (*Cycle for Mother Cabrini,* 1955) to his more recent poems about

Yeats, Thomas, Joyce, and Hemingway (*The Bridge of Change: Poems 1974–1980,* 1981). His vibrant concern for the nature of human love and sexuality in some of his essays is Logan's further exploration in prose of themes that are central to his poetry, from an earlier poem like "Lines to His Son on Reaching Adolescence" (*Ghosts of the Heart,* 1960), through the very title of his book, *The Anonymous Lover* (1973), to a recent poem like "Lines for an Unknown Lover" (*The Bridge of Change*). The range of his intellectual search for clues to illuminate the human spirit in his essays is the inner mirror of his wide-ranging search for epiphany in his poems, from "Cycle for Mother Cabrini," through "A Trip to Four or Five Towns" (*Ghosts of the Heart*), "Three Moves," and "The Search" (*The Zigzag Walk,* 1969), "Poem for My Friend Peter at Pihana" (*The Anonymous Lover*), to "Poem in Progress," "Traveling," and the last lines of the concluding poem in *The Bridge of Change:*

> Well, I am still a traveler and I don't know where
> I live. If my home is here, inside my breast,
> light it up! And I will invite you in as my first guest.
> —"Believe It"

In short, what John Logan has to say in his critical prose and in his poems are equally essential parts of what he has to say about all *poetry,* about the human species as maker and lover.

As the title of this book suggests, John Logan's poetics also arise out of a profound anthropological view of poetry. That is clear in his insistence that poetry is a natural extension of dance, song, and ritual, as well as in his expectation that art offer its own redemptive, albeit momentary, peace. Logan's all-consuming effort in his poetry to bridge those factors that exile one human being from another also becomes one of the primary themes of his critical prose. His preoccupation with religious themes—which has been misunderstood by so many critics of his poetry—is as much a fundamental human theme as it is an ostensibly religious one. What Logan demands from all art, all poetry, is no more and no less than a full awareness of the human species' essential bid for some measure of transcendence.

And John Logan is a generous spirit. While editing this book I had several disagreements with him over whether or not he should include some of his earlier, more exacting reviews of his contemporaries' work. But if some of his remarks seem harsh, they are so only in so far as he recognizes his responsibility to challenge his contemporaries to be as fully human as they are accomplished in their craft. And in the process he raises important questions about the nature of poetry and of the critical process.

Reading John Logan's critical prose, I find myself wishing that he'll continue writing much more—provided, of course, that such criticism doesn't rob us of his wonderful poems.

A. Poulin, Jr.
Athens, Greece
Summer, 1982

I

Interviews

A Conversation with Marvin Bell

(1961)

Are you a "religious poet?"

I think the essential impulse to poetry—the desire to hold in one's arms the beauties not yet created, as Stephen Daedalus puts it—is religious. In this sense all poetry is religious. I agree with John Crowe Ransom that "poetry is the secular form of piety," and I find three or four marks of what might be called "natural religion" in poetry: natural creation (making something new); natural miraculism (making something happen unaccountably in the world of the reader); natural resurrection (bringing alive again the dead relics and ghosts one finds within oneself); natural grace (the bringing of what Dylan Thomas called "a momentary peace" to one's audience.) Also, there is a certain quality of annunciation and conception to the origin of poetry within the poet. ("True song demands a different kind of breathing," Rilke writes; "A calm. A shudder in the god. A gale.")

There is a more specific sense of religious poetry, having to do with the use of religious figures, motifs, and doctrines within the poem. In the earlier part of my career, I was far more a "religious poet" in that sense than I am now. However, I have never confined my subjects to religion, nor lost my interest in religious "story."

What is the significant difference between your books?

There is a sequence from the treatment of the lives of the dead saints in the first book through dead classical heroes, of whom there are a few in the first book, and in the first part of the second book, to the treatment of the lives of dead artists (no saints). The turning point came when, after writing about Heine and Rimbaud (I wrote about Byron, Shelley, James Joyce, and Hart Crane later), I became faced concretely with the problem of dealing with a live artist—myself. I came to feel that if one had constantly to adopt successive masks in his poems, avoiding the reality of his own living situation, then one was using his art more to escape from himself than to face himself, and this was dissatisfying. It was in some profound sense boring. So I wrote "On the Death of the Poet's Mother Thirty-Three Years Later," which was the hardest poem I had written to date, and which was also the first poem in which I tried to work directly with my adult feeling. In the last poem of the second book, I broke away from set principles of composition entirely and used a free form, writing about myself and my friends and acquaintances. It was the best poem. "A Trip to Four or Five Towns."

What is your attitude toward the Index of Forbidden Books—with or without direct reference to your own Catholicism?

I always had worse sins to worry about than that of reading banned books. Beyond that, I came to believe that imaginative literature was incapable of heresy, because it does not by its nature hold up for affirmation or denial any scientific (including theological) truth. The statements of poems are always qualified by the living dynamics of feeling which surround them, and feeling itself cannot be wrong (though it can be perverse or hidden). A poem comes into existence like an apple, and an apple cannot be mistaken. It can't be right either. The purposes of censorship are not well served by poetry.

So far as the problem of obscenity is concerned, it is important to remember that this is more complex than the problem of diction. I am inclined in fact to see the truly obscene as the truly mediocre, and vice versa. Then, there is the fact that obscene art bypasses the condition of fine art and approaches that of rhetoric, through the characteristic of its moving one to some further action (which Lawrence analyzes as fundamentally masturbation), rather than restoring one to his own inner resources of human refreshment, or to some form of lucid contemplation and savoring. Nevertheless, every word in the language and every feeling in the book of the heart are fit material for poetry, for they are colors on the palette the poet brings to his task. He has a right to its completeness. There is a special rhetoric to the short Anglo-Saxon words we carry over from our childhood as names for parts and functions, and this rhetoric can easily scuttle a poem in incompetent hands. But that is no reason for throwing out the adult with the baby.

What makes a good poetry critic?

My first impulse is to answer "love." However, I'm afraid half of my audience would think I'm simply quoting St. Paul, and the other half would think I'm quoting Rilke. So, I'll take another tack (and quote Nietzsche): A good poetry critic is someone who is able to detect "the vision generated by the dance," and to perceive that in the best poetry, there is no vision apart from the dance of words, whereas at the same time there is no dance of words which fails to issue in a vision. If it sounds like I am talking about the relationship of the spirit to the flesh, I can only say it sounds that way to me too.

Do you differentiate between "prose" and "poetry"?

Poetry makes use of the line as a unit and thus sets up new periods not available to the prose artist. The effect of this is a more complex counterpointing of the rhythms and musics of language, which raises the whole product to a new level of existence. The shortcoming of this is a certain tendency toward angelism: i.e., poetry tends to leave the earth and emulate the gods (whom the poets named). Nevertheless, this is also its strength. The true image of the poem is seen in the *tension* between Jacob and the angel—the *balance* of the two as they dance ("wrestle" is the vulgar word to describe what they were doing.) Jacob corrects the timid and anarchic impulse to flight, while the angel exorcises the earth-bound impulse of Jacob. The result is a poem. In some poems, one is more aware of the unearthly shine brushed off from the angel onto Jacob. In others, one is more aware of the sweat brushed off from Jacob onto the angel. The poem itself is a creature "crawling between heaven and earth" like Hamlet.

What ought to be the poet's place in the economic scheme of things?

He ought to be rich.

Would you say you write by choice or by compulsion?

When a poem comes to me to write, I am compelled to write it at some time, you might say; but I have learned to choose the time. My life has been happier since I have learned how to do this. I refer to the problem that arises when a poem is ripe for writing but you have to read papers or prepare a class or load trucks or babysit. This is different from the problem that arises when a poem presents itself before it is ripe. Sometimes the poem lays around for years in the earth of your imagination, putting out white roots, perhaps even growing monstrous before it is ready for the pen. It is a point of pride with me that I always eventually get these poems written. When I first read the life of Robert Southwell, I knew I would have to write a poem about it some day. It was two years before I sat down to do it. No, I didn't sit down to do it. I got sick with pleurisy and couldn't breathe without pain and began to write the poem.

It has been nice to learn how to let ready poems hibernate until I can get to them with minimum damage to my other commitments. It's a little like being able to choose the time you'll have your baby—which is convenient.

Is the "gap" between poet and audience inseparable?

The gap between the poet and his audience is based on the gap between the poet and himself. When the one is healed, the other will be. I do not know which fracture came first; however, there is one repair which the poet has control over. And he has more than one reason for making it.

What makes a poem bad?

Intercourse with the muse is interfered with under several cases: impotence, *ejaculatio praecox,* lack of attention to fore-pleasure and afterpleasure, exhaustion, boyish fixation on masturbation. Nevertheless, celibacy is perhaps an overharsh recommendation.

What direction do you think American poetry is taking?

Seems to me that's a question for the critics, not the poets. I hope it's moving in several directions, and I think it is. When it moves in one direction only, it's dead. It's tempting to say that American poetry is growing up, that the beat movement was a late adolescence. Yet, reflection shows that movement closer to infantile regression. Certainly, the movement around Eliot was a premature aging. The joy is still ahead, at any rate. Odd that Wallace Stevens's achievement, now complete, was so baroque and gorgeous.

What qualities make you see a poetry talent in a particular student?

(1) The gift of image, showing one at home with the inventive powers of his unconscious, which intimidates a duller man. The clichés come from the back of the conscious mind. (2) The gift of intelligence, which is related to the discernment of integrity, and enables one to direct and shape and finish his poem. (3) The gift of a good ear, which , so far as the sounds of poetry are concerned—as they present themselves in the wings

of the "ivory stages" of the poem to dance—is like the gift of good choreography. (4) The will and the serenity (even if only occasional) to exercise and produce.

What effect do nine children have on your work?

They give me a distinction no other American poet has. They start in me enormous guilt feelings at the amount of time I spend with poetry instead of with them. They give hope of a later, special, enlarged, beloved audience.

What relationship is there between Bohemianism and the arts/artists?

Historical. It was an attempt to perpetuate the punishing myth that an artist must be denied the sustaining pleasures others have. "How can he deserve this too?" Well, he does.

A Conversation with David Ossman

(1963)

Having written a good deal of it yourself, how do you feel about religious poetry?

I very much dislike pious, sentimental, sticky poetry of which there is a good deal published in poor magazines, but it seems to me that religious themes need and deserve good, powerful treatment. It happens that my second book had many fewer poems on specifically religious themes in it. I made a statement for that book which I'd like to read:

> A poet is a priest or necromancer of the baroque who dissolves by the incantations of his cadenced human breath the surface of the earth to show under it the covered terror, the warmth, the formal excitement and the gaudy color-burst of the sun. This is not a chemical function. It is a sacramental one, and John Crowe Ransom is right to call poetry 'the secular form of piety.' 'Miraculism everywhere,' he says. So if some people find my subjects less religious now than they used to be, the reason is that I now think poetry itself more religious than I used to do.

By this I mean the sense of the transformation by art of the natural event into something of beauty and of an enduring transcendent quality, which brings to people a kind of secular grace. This seems to me to be very much the function of a poem. I remember Dylan Thomas talking about a poem as a

9

"momentary peace" won out of the harsh reality and this seems to me a kind of religious-like theme. That's why I like Ransom's term "a secular form of piety." So in this sense, it seems to me that every successful poem involves a kind of religious process.

Do you mean a process of belief?

No, I don't mean that so much as one in which elementary materials are transformed, in a higher way, as a result of the impact of art. Henry Miller's statement is very striking in this regard—he said something to the effect that the work of the artist was to take the sour dough of humanity and make this into bread and the bread into wine and the wine into song. And this seems to the point. It's a notion of art quite close to James Joyce's also, I think. Joyce used religious terms like "epiphany" to describe what he thought was going on in art. An epiphany is the showing forth, under a special artistic light, of a human event.

Paul Carroll told me that when he was young he used to think poetry was "telegrams from angels," but now that he's older, he no longer believes that. . . .

The idea of receiving an inspiration—an angel's telegram—is a sort of passive notion. It's a very old one, of course. That sounds like Paul talking.

How do you, as an academician, feel about the current revolt against the "academic" in poetry?

That's like your question about the religious in poetry. It has to be good and it can't be dull. If academic themes in poetry mean something pedantic, textbookish, the poem's not going to live.

I don't care how much one is against academic themes or the academic notion in poetry. I'm not against any kind of poetry that is good and I feel a pretty strong sense in some of those people who supposedly are in such revolt that they can't get into the magazines which print such poems. I do agree with Karl Shapiro wholeheartedly when he talks about the notion that poetry has to be taught in its own time. He says that our time is the first in which we've had this idea of poetry. I think that this is quite right. You have a sense sometimes that the academic poet writes the poems in order to have them taught to somebody. This is ridiculous. The sense of the creative in the poem has no such bounds upon it.

But, if getting rid of the academic in poetry means getting rid of literary allusion, for example, then I am, in some of my most recent poems, still quite academic. I don't see why we have to chop off any kind of experience or expression in poetry and say that they can't be used any more. Let's keep anything that's good. Some of my poems are academic in the sense that they use heavy literary allusion, but even when they do, I want there to be present sufficient surface feelings that the poem gets a response from the reader without whole knowledge of the pattern of allusion.

From a Conversation with Dan Murray

(1968)

I want to ask you about the idea of a poetry of communion, a poetry of reconciliation, which I think describes your poetry. Would you say something about that?

I think the ideas of communion and reconciliation are crucial to what should happen when poetry is working rightly. I suppose these are religious notions in a way, and I've already talked in some other places about my idea that poetry is a secular form of religion. It includes notions of virgin conception, of being born of a virgin, and of bringing something like grace, the momentary peace which all art brings to the beholder; and a quality of resurrection takes place in poetry, too, through the bringing to life again of the dead parts of the self: the boy one once was, for example, or the resurrection of the ghost of the parent, friend, or experience one once had. This is why poetry, it seems to me, is magical. It makes things happen in a way that cannot be accounted for in usual terms. Once you can account for what happens in poetry, you realize you are no longer in the presence of a poem that you will want to return to, probably. You have no need of it anymore, because you've surrounded it instead of its leading you on. So I think that words like "communion" and "reconciliation" take one's mind to religious notions, to secular-religious notions.

I'm not religious in any dogmatic sense at all anymore, so far as I know, but I am more interested in poetry than I ever was before. The notion of communion particularly interests me because of my idea that poetry is meant to put people in touch. In this sense it may be a little less spiritualized than the idea that "communion" usually brings to mind. I would choose the word "touch" over the word "communion," perhaps, but I know that I felt very much the rightness of expressions of contemporary French playwrights whom Wallace Fowlie wrote about, when he said that the idea of communion is central to their feeling: Giraudoux among others. The idea of uniting members of an audience to each other and to the figures in the play, and, behind the play, to the figure of the playwright; the notion that when one goes to the theater to watch a play, or goes to the auditorium to hear a poetry reading, one expects some kind of histrionic experience which one can't get in any other way. It's not a substitute for anything else that can happen; and this bringing together of people seems to be something which seldom occurs in real life. I mean that when one thinks about how this happens in real life, maybe one thinks about violent bringings together, such as riots, rather than benign comings together.

I talk about being brought together a lot closer by art in my poem "To a Young Poet Who Fled," when I speak about poetry "breaking/down the lines of lead that separate a man from a/man, and the husbands from their wives, in these old, burned glass/panels of our lives." By that I mean that one is taken out of the straightened circumstances of his own skin and situation by the experience of art, and he's left open to human encounter. Of course, he's safe from the effects of that human encounter on himself when it takes place on the stage. But the histrionic experience (and I'm referring to what happens at a poetry reading as well as at a play) has to do with exercising human feelings in a way that they really can't be exercised in real life, because of the consequences of showing human feeling in real life and the way in which commitments and reprisals result from the showing of human feelings.

Everyone likes to feel, and I don't think people are particularly happy with the unfeeling character of much of their workaday life. Art gives an occasion to exercise feeling without fear of consequences, and I'm not being naive about this; there is a real response from art that takes place inside one's self. But it's not a response that one has to adjust to somebody else, or that one is receiving from somebody else who is demanding an adjustment. Of course, when art works rightly, there's a great response that leads one toward change; I mean, something more like what the word "paradise" refers to—a level of human experience that is higher than one has known before. Art leads one to this, and Rilke's poem "Archaic Torso of Apollo" ends with the line, "You must change your life."

I've used this notion in a couple of poems: the poems on the photographs of Aaron Siskind and my poem "Three Moves," which ends with the phrase, "the hope of change." I think art works in two ways with regard to change—and by change I don't mean simply shifting; I mean movement to a higher level of existence that is more fulfilling, not simply hedonistic satisfaction, but fulfillment of the human spirit. First, it gives witness to the existence of the spirit as a work of art, of the reality of a kind of higher level than the workaday world provides. Second, it intimidates one. When a person is in the presence of the experience of art, he becomes aware of what a human being can come to as a maker of something that brings such pleasure and such hope. So I think the idea of paradise does come into poetry too.

How about the notion of prophecy?

There is that, too, in the sense that prophecy goes back to dreams; my idea is that only the dreamer can change the dream, a notion which I've thought about using as a title for my new book. Self-prophecy is one of the genuine functions of art, as far as the artist himself is concerned.

How do you feel your poetry has changed since your first book, Cycle for Mother Cabrini?

I hate to repeat myself, but as I've said elsewhere, the most obvious change is that it's become less overtly religious. The title of my first book is religious, which I didn't choose and didn't particularly want, but Grove Press did. I think Horace Gregory, who was reading poetry for them, turned on to the religious aspect of my poetry, and they chose that title themselves. I acquiesced, not realizing that poets have some rights in these matters.

From a Conversation with William Heyen and Gregory Fitz Gerald*

(1970)

(This videotaped interview begins with John Logan reading "Song on the Dread of a Chill Spring." See p. 296.)

FITZ GERALD: Mr. Logan, there's some religious imagery in that poem that seems very fascinating. How do you account for it?

LOGAN: I was thinking, really, about some lines from Rilke whom I was translating when I first started to write poetry. This is not really a cop-out answer to the question, because I was myself very involved with Rilke at the time I wrote that poem. So, the first, easy answer to your question is because I was interested in Rilke. The second, more difficult answer might involve my talking about my feelings about Catholicism and about religion in a way that I'm not prepared to do at this time of day.

*Edited from a transcription of a videotape produced by the Educational Communications Center on April 21, 1970, and sponsored by the Brockport Writers Forum, Department of English, State University of New York, College at Brockport, New York. Copyrighted © 1983 by SUNY. All rights reserved by the State University of New York. Not to be reprinted without permission.

HEYEN: I think it's a beautifully modulated poem, the way the sounds nudge in and out. Listening to you read I'm fascinated by the sound patterns, and it just occurred to me that Robert Bly has said that rhyme in our time is just plain boring. I would guess you wouldn't agree with that.

LOGAN: Well, it depends on the rhyme. I know that Bly has said that if Shakespeare sent in some of his sonnets he wouldn't publish them in *The Sixties*. I think that's because the idea of the sonnet grows out of a certain time and situation which is not our time and our situation. And most rhyme in contemporary poetry has so much echo to it of nineteenth-century work or early twentieth-century work that it's very hard to hear the voice of a contemporary poet behind rhymes which, just as rhythms and expressions, can be cliché. I've tried to use off-rhyme, slant-rhyme, musical relationships which are not full rhyme. Like other poets who are concerned with lyric poetry, musical expression of one's battle with one's self, I want a musical happening in poetry, but I do not want it to be a cliché or an echo. So I do various sorts of off-rhyme things for the most part.

HEYEN: The poem you just read is from Spring of the Thief. *I'd like to take you back right to the beginning. I wonder if you'd tell us how you began writing, when it was, how you came to it.*

LOGAN: Well, I was old enough to know better than to become a poet, which has its curses as well as its blessings.

FITZ GERALD: Exactly how old were you then, Mr. Logan?

LOGAN: I was twenty-eight or twenty-nine; I was teaching; I had a family. I hadn't thought really about being a poet, except for a kind of yearning and desire and a jealousy of poets. When I was in college I wrote a couple of poems that were published in the student magazine; they were terrible. I wrote them as much at the time because I wanted to see my name in print. To show you just how terrible they were, I can quote part of one of them, most of which I've fortunately forgotten. But is started with: "To travel out in winter time when all is cleansed with white / While fade the brilliant grays of day into the chiaroscuro of night. . . ." something like that. It was quite bad. It was a strongly rhymed, tight form. But I wasn't serious about poetry then and didn't think about it as a possibility; I was a premed student. I finished my course in premedicine, majoring in biology, but I did not go on into medicine, both because I didn't have the money and because I realized I was afraid of the flesh. (It seemed to me that a physician should not be in that position).

Of course, I had taken one course in humanities (I think it was Shakespeare) and realized there was another world besides science. But actually I began majoring in science; I was a zoology major at the University of California for a while in graduate school. I quit and started over again in the humanities and took a master's degree in English literature. I still had no idea about the poetry, which is what you asked me. I began to teach, got married, had some kids. I was interested in philosophy; actually I thought I might take a doctorate in philosophy, and in that connection with my study of German I began to read Rainer Maria Rilke. Translating Rilke sort of primed my pump, and I began to write my own poems.

FITZ GERALD: You think that Rilke was the seminal incident in your life that tipped the scales in that direction? Is that fair to say?

LOGAN: Yes, as a poet. I was working. I had a summer job in a mental hospital for Negroes in Crownsville, Maryland, which was extraordinary, miserable. I was useless, everybody was useless. I was a custodian so to speak. And the fact that I'd learned something about the line of poetry and that I was involved in a situation which I could not handle, except to try to make a poem, made me start writing poems. My first poem was published in *Partisan Review* in January of 1953; I was thirty years old. My poem was about trying to feed an insane Negro who was blind; it was called "Contagious Ward."

FITZ GERALD: And from then on it was a complete devotion to poetry, wasn't it?

LOGAN: Well, I wish I could agree that it was a complete devotion, but my mind was torn between poetry and teaching, wanting to learn something. I feel that in some ways I did not learn anything in graduate school except a kind of example of what teaching was, and I learned things that stick with me. As I began to teach—I love students and the situation of teaching— but at the same time I was working on the poems, that's why I said it wasn't really a complete devotion to poetry. They seem to go together in a special way, though.

FITZ GERALD: You wouldn't agree, then, that teaching is detrimental to the writing of poetry?

LOGAN: I hardly could do that since I was teaching before I was a poet, I still am teaching, and much of the material of my poetry has come either from preparation for classes or from relationships with students or something of the kind. Teaching turns me on to write and I probably wouldn't do any writing at all if I were not involved with teaching. At least, last year I had a Rockefeller grant, I had a whole year off from teaching, and I did very little writing as it turned out. I've done more writing since I've gotten back into teaching.

FITZ GERALD: So you feel there's a kind of stimulus in teaching that helps your creative impulses toward poetry.

LOGAN: Yes I do, indeed. . . .

(Here follows a substantial discussion on the relation of poetry to various kinds of religious attitudes and beliefs which are discussed in other interviews with John Logan.)

FITZ GERALD: You spoke of Dylan Thomas's intellectual limitations and obviously you've had an enormously interesting intellectual back-

ground yourself. You've studied philosophy, science, and literature—a very wide background. How do you reconcile these factors in the poet's temperament? To what extent do these things come in balance in your own work? It is a disadvantage to a poet to have too strong an intellectuality?

LOGAN: I can't answer that question very directly. While I spoke a moment ago about the mixed curse and blessing of being a poet, some people who become poets are overeducated. They turn to poetry because, disenchanted with the world of intelligence, they become cynics in a certain way, self-cynics, I think, primarily, and they look to the world of feeling for some kind of certainty and some position on which they can move. I do not know if they had not read so many books and looked continually in books for a moment of salvation and release, whether they would have been poets or not. I don't know that about myself.

What I'm trying to say is that poets are committed to the world of feeling which philosophy is not, except in certain high moments. We were talking about Plato earlier today. One of his most moving passages—moving in the literary sense and beautiful in Greek and even in translation, as a matter of fact—is when he exiles the poets from the Republic. There's a kind of drama that takes place as a result of Plato's gift as poet which, I think, he was not entirely prepared to deal with. So, I'm not really prepared to say that in order to be a poet one should read a lot of books and get a lot of degrees. I think it's not entirely relevant. The question is how one finds one's way into the world of feeling, and one can be catapulted into that world by disenchantment with reading. That happened to me to a certain extent. . . .

(Here follows a substantial discussion on the role of personal experiences in the poetry of John Logan, a subject discussed in other interviews.—A. P., Jr.)

A Conversation with Anthony Piccione and A. Poulin, Jr.*

Edited by S. Tobie Hewitt

(1972)

(This videotaped interview begins with John Logan reading two poems: "Mother Cabrini Crosses the Andes" and "On the House of a Friend." See p. 269 and p. 302.)

PICCIONE: Welcome to the Brockport Writers Forum. We asked you to read those two poems to show the great movement from your first book, Cycle for Mother Cabrini, *to your more recent book,* The Anonymous Lover. *And I notice that in this development you're moving from the oracular voice, the voice that stands aside and pronounces, to something that many poets have been calling for, something we learned from Neruda: loving kindness in a poem, warmth in a poem, the personal evidence of a personal life, which I think exists in "On the House of a Friend." Could you perhaps tell us a bit about what has happened in the matter of voice, in your grasp of persons during those years?*

*Edited from a transcription of a videotape produced by the Educational Communications Center on February 15, 1972, and sponsored by the Brockport Writers Forum, Department of English, State University of New York, College at Brockport, New York. Copyrighted © 1983 by SUNY. All rights reserved by the State University of New York. Not to be reprinted without permission.

LOGAN: I think it would be to the point to mention that there are a couple poems in the *Cycle for Mother Cabrini* volume which don't adopt a persona in the usual sense of, say, a figure or someone other than the author. For example, "Pagan Saturday" and "Grandfather's Railroad" (see pp. 271–74) are reminiscences of childhood in which the "I" figure is the remembered boy, myself; most of that book, however, is made up of poems about saints. But there's also "A Pathological Case in Pliny" (see p. 279) which is about heroes, and "A Dialogue with La Mettrie" (see p. 275) which takes the voice of an eighteenth-century figure. I think what happened was that I got more into writing poems directly out of my own adult experience. Actually, there's no poem in *Cycle for Mother Cabrini* which is written out of adult experience. The only direct experience of my own that's involved is that of the two childhood poems.

In the second book, *Ghosts of the Heart,* I began writing poems that also adopted a persona, in most cases that of an artist. For example, I have poems on Heine, Rimbaud, Byron, and Shelley, and there's one on Achilles. I mention the Achilles one because it's sort of the exception that proved the rule. Since this section from *The Iliad* that I chose to translate in the poem "Achilles and the King" was the first section, which ends with Achilles clinging to his mother as he moans on the shore after his harrowing encounter with Agamemnon, I began to see that I was writing poems a little closer to home—because in *Ghosts of the Heart* I was writing poems about artists. Actually, there's one in *Cycle for Mother Cabrini,* too. The last poem and I think, in some ways, the best poem, called "The Death of Southwell" (see p. 281), dovetails the artist figure (since he was a poet) and that of the more saintly figure (since he was a martyr in Elizabethan England.) That was the first poem on the life of an artist. Then there was the Rimbaud one, the Heine one and the Hart Crane. The thing which those poems had in common with the selection of a hero like Achilles was that they had to do with people whose mothers were very emotionally close to them. In another sense, particularly with somebody like Heine, they could be said to have been hung up on their mothers. And I began to see that while writing about artists instead of saints I was moving closer to myself.

At that point it occurred to me that I could use poetry to continue to avoid my own adult experience or I could use it to try to *encounter* my own adult experience, and I did the latter thing. I wrote a poem called "On the Death of the Poet's Mother Thirty-Three Years Later" (see p. 285) which is about my own adult feelings about my dead mother, and I found that to be a kind of breakthrough poem, after which I could write poems that had to deal with my looking around, out of my adult life, at relationships with students and with other people. The persona went through a kind of natural shift, therefore, and I took less and less an adopted persona of another figure.

PICCIONE: You just shifted into part of your essay called "On Poets and Poetry Today,"[1] and I wonder if you could talk a minute about this? You said that the progression in your poetry was natural, and I see that. You and others are interested in the phenomenon of finding the body, of finding the self as well. And you say it is especially true of Americans, perhaps in the Midwest, that a mother "hang-up" involves the lack of reconciling self and mother. I think it was an acquaintance of yours who said in the essay that when poets (perhaps others as well) are weaned at, say, one-and-a-half years of age, they spend the remaining years of their lives trying to come back to motherness: the mouth of the poet trying to find its motherness.

LOGAN: Yes, actually the weaning takes place earlier than that; it might take place at several months before one-and-a-half. (I changed the copy in my essay once I realize that somebody who's had as many kids as I have should remember when children are weaned). But I first took that year-and-a-half figure, which I got from a psychologist named David Bleich who I thought referred to weaning itself. When I read his essay, I found that that was not true. He was talking about the infant's attempt to *deal* with the fact of the weaning, so it covers a period of time after the weaning and involves syntax or the child's breaking into syntactical language.

---

1. Reprinted as one of the essays in this book.—A. P., Jr.

In the existence of the language itself, according to Bleich, there's a kind of oral recall of the earlier experience at the mother's breast. Poetry is, of course, only one form of language, but it seems to me that it is a form of language in which the relationship to the mother continues to be expressed for some reason that I cannot account for. I don't know enough. I know that it recurred in my own poems in my trying to deal with my mother's death. She died when I was one month old. I had thought that the poem "On the Death of the Poet's Mother Thirty-Three Years Later" in *Ghosts of the Heart* would be the last one on that subject. Let me read the last part of the poem to show you what I mean. I thought I was laying her ghost to rest:

> I do not
> Resurrect again her restless
> Ghost out of my grievous memory:
> She waits the quiet hunt of saints.
> Or the ignorance of citizens of hell.
> *And here is laid her orphan child with his*
> *Imperfect poems and ardors, slim as sparklers.*

I thought I was through with her ghost, so to speak, but I found out that the first of my "Monologues of the Son of Saul" (in *Spring of the Thief*) spoke about her again. It says: "I have thieved my father's treasure. And I cannot pay." And it continues in that vein. Then in the fifth of those monologue poems I used the phrase, "The dead ducks of poets, stretched / across a virgin lap." There's one more poem—I might as well finish this—that shows I didn't exorcise her ghost in that one poem. It's called "Lines on His Birthday," and it speaks about her death. (Logan reads "Lines on His Birthday." See p. 297.)[2]

So, at any rate, I began to talk about this question of the relationship of the poet to his mother in the essay you speak of. I thought of the sense of the word "body" to a poet, when he

---

2. In a later poem, "Returning Home," in *The Bridge of Change: Poems 1974–1980*, there is further reference to the death of the poet's mother.—S. Tobie Hewitt

talks about "the body of his work," and it occurred to me, especially in the light of Bleich's idea referred to earlier, that very shortly after weaning, children break into syntactical language and that this is a way of relating themselves back to their mothers. Thinking of that, I also thought of the fact that so many lyric poets—who sing, as a mother sings to her child—do not survive beyond midlife. Robert Southwell, whom I spoke of earlier, died at thirty-three; Hart Crane was just short of thirty-three when he died; and it occurred to me that these poets who go ahead and die in their thirties (or earlier, as Keats and Shelley did) are leaving an unfinished body of work behind them and that they may have been encountering some aspect of "body" in their work which was extraordinarily difficult for them to deal with. I also thought about the fact that if you survive to write poetry into old age, you may find yourself like Yeats writing about more sexual matters. So I developed this theory that poets build, with their words, the body, really, of their mother. The body of their work is in some way related to the body of the mother and, if one could think of the top part of the body as connected with the earlier part of the work, then the part of the work that continues to fail or that does not continue to be completed is the part of the body of work having to do with the lower part, the lower segment of the body as such: in other words, sexuality, and particularly the sexuality in the family triangle involving the mother and, of course, the father. So that was how the whole thing got started.

PICCIONE: The way you speak of the body of poems that some of our best people tragically avoid completing may sound as though you mean it to be an "external," but you mean the body of poems is an internal building.

LOGAN: It has an internal aspect to it which I think in some way is related to the image of the mother; that's my intuitive guess.

Let me say this. My friend Murray Schwartz had done an extensive study of Sylvia Plath. Murray is a colleague of mine at Buffalo, and he is absolutely convinced that what Sylvia Plath was doing with her work was building the body of her father, as the name "Colossus," which is a poem about her father, suggests. So this sort of substantiated my feeling that somehow *lyric* poetry in particular—and I stress that because of the musicality and the questions of the singing—relates to the mother figure for the male poet and perhaps to the father figure for the female poet. Many poets find that they have to deal to some extent with problems having to do with the mother. Of course, a lot of people who are not poets do also. I'm not trying to say that there's a one-to-one relationship, but the ability to produce poetry out of the pain and delight of this relationship is what distinguishes the poet's hang-ups from those of the non-poet.

PICCIONE: And so, after achieving this there will be a period of calm discovery because there's a whole being once again.

LOGAN: One would hope so, and one thinks about the old Chinese poets who wrote so marvelously and so intimately and with so little sense of hang-up in their language. They wrote about their friendships with each other and their drinking together and such; one also thinks about Yeats's late poems which have more an edge of humor as well as an edge of sexuality to them than some of his earlier poems.

PICCIONE: Another part of this is the length of time it seems to take for a man to find his whole self. Robert Bly, in some of his talk about returning to mother consciousness, indicates at least that this period is being foreshortened by what he says is a "spiritual upsurge," especially among the young. Can there be a foreshortened time then, instead of delay, in one's early twenties?

LOGAN: Indeed it could. One would be fascinated to find what influence, if any, this foreshortening has on the poetry of that generation. I do think that such a foreshortening is possible, and it should result in a different kind of content in the poetry. I know Bly himself has written extensively about a certain concept of the body of the mother, the so-called "teeth mother," a concept which he gets from Eric Neumann's *The Great Mother,* I believe, a Jungian approach. Bly's own poem, "The Teeth Mother Naked at Last," is about that one aspect of the relationship to a mother—the so-called bad mother as distinct from the good mother—as a kind of *threat* which the concept of "teeth mother" tries to represent, a threat to his strength and hence to his virility. There is a kind of castration, as a matter of fact, in the idea of the *vagina dentata* which some "teeth mother" figures have.

Consequently, Bly wrote a long poem which has to do with, among other things, the idea that the war-making impulse results from overmasculinization of the consciousness and has less of the influence of the good mother—which would move toward love. "Make love, not war" has become a common slogan, but it's certainly a part of the thesis of Bly in "The Teeth Mother Naked at Last," which is a poem against the Vietnam war. I think he believes that this addresses the younger generation—I don't know if we would properly call it "the Woodstock generation," but the event of Woodstock comes naturally enough to mind, with thousands, millions of young people coming together in a benign, gentle way to share whatever they had, their food, their experience, and their listening. There seems to be a benign quality about that which relates to things of the earth and to things of the good mother rather than to the things of the bad mother or the overaggressive father.

PICCIONE: I'd like to try to go back just a step or two to some talk of technique within the realm of this theory of balanced consciousness. In his essay, "Some Notes on French Poetry," Bly speaks not only of the voyage to the unconscious but also of that thing I keep looking for in French poetry and of which I'm not sure yet. He speaks of loving-kindness, of something our culture has felt is perhaps feminine, that warmth, that kindness. When you went to the Europeans, from Rimbaud on, was that your experience? Is that part of your connection with finally saying, Here I am, I live, I love, and I am?

LOGAN: I wouldn't say so. My moving to Rimbaud didn't give me any more feelings of a gentleness and benign quality than I had found any place else. I would say something happened to me in my reading of Trakl, whom I love very much and feel very close to. But something happens having to do with violence and the treatment of violence in Trakl's poems that astounded me. Any time an image would appear in a Trakl poem that was quite violent, the next line would cancel that feeling in some way. I can remember his poem "Grodeck," about the war. Trakl served, of course, with the Germans, and because of his war experiences found that he himself really couldn't survive and took an overdose of laudanum. He was left, I know, in a barn one night, to deal with ninety wounded men. He worked in a hospital as part of his military service and he died, a very young man, by suicide. But in his poems I've felt this kind of thing, the desire to cancel the feelings of violence and transmute them in one way or another.

PICCIONE: This brings me to the next part of this question. When you bring attention to the French Symbolists, from whom the whole European movement learns, you think of technique. When they used the creation-destruction process, as you speak of Trakl doing, it was literary theory: in order to make room for the next image, you cancel out the previous one. When Trakl does it, I'm not thinking of theory, but I'm involved in creation-destruction.

LOGAN: Yes, I was thinking of Rilke, too, who was my great poet-father, really. I still would rather read Rilke than any other poet who comes to mind, and his *Letters to a Young Poet* are absolutely essential to anybody trying to get an idea of what it is to be a poet. But Rilke, for example in the *Das Marienleben* sequence telling the story of the life of the Blessed Virgin, has much of this gentleness and repose, though also, of course, much of the agony of the passion that the Virgin went through. But I find in Rilke an extraordinary ability to identify with feminine feelings. I'm thinking of his poems relating a girl to a tree, for example, that are especially beautiful and of the poem in which he talks about being with his mother as she plays the piano.

I think I was thrown off when you suggested that the Europeans might have interested me because of the presence of more of this feminine and gentle feeling and because you mentioned Rimbaud first. I don't find this in Rimbaud, but I do find it in Rilke, and I do find the tendency, as I said, to cancel violent feeling and make the experience, therefore, a cathartic one, as in Trakl. Because if one is left with naked violence in a poem, to my mind one hasn't really read a *poem*, as such. It seems to me that the proper sphere of poetry has to do, as Dylan Thomas so aptly put it, with the breeding of "a momentary peace." At the end of a poem one should be suffused with feelings of fulfillment and of the dream come true. I think that the impulse to write poetry comes more from the benign feelings than it comes from the violent ones. I'm talking about what Aristotle would have used the word "catharsis" to describe; but if a poem doesn't contain within it the ability to calm the very passions which it has unleashed—as great tragedy does so powerfully, for which the word "catharsis" was first formed as an aesthetic term—if a poem doesn't do that, then to my mind it falls short, and I think this is another reason why I talk about the lyric aspect of poetry. Music and rhythm can have this calming effect, and to my mind a poem is not a poem unless it has an essential surface to it which is musical in character. One reason, I suppose, why I'm turned off to many of my contemporary poets is because they have no "ears." Jim Wright, Robert Bly, Galway Kinnell, to the contrary, since they are each blessed with a musical ear. But this thing of using musical and rhythmic qualities, which are really formal qualities, to calm the reader in some way, to handle the emotions one has roused in the poem, is to my mind very much a part of the vocation of being a poet. That's why overly militant figures don't strike me as poets at all, in the proper sense of the word. They are doing something else; they are doing something with language other than making poetry out of it. They may be very much needed; I'm not saying they aren't. I'm just saying that the impulse to poetry does not spring from violent feelings. It may spring partly from violent feeling, but it has more to do with touching; this is the concept I needed to bring this around full circle. Poetry, properly, is a reaching of the poet through his language, a way of touching others and bringing them together in a shared experience. Whereas violence, militancy in poetry, is divisive: therefore it is antipoetry. Poetry must bind together, not divide from.

PICCIONE: This is not just another way of saying the poet takes all his chances and wants to be loved. I'm thinking that if you said what you just said five years ago, it would not have made the sense that it now makes. We have been coming to this. Why do you suppose that there is a fifty-year timelag between the American and European traditions? It can't just be because we lacked the translation and therefore lacked some of the technical innovations as vehicles to this great life-awakening. Is there something else, do you suppose?

LOGAN: It must have to do with the whole way in which feelings are trained. American schools are so heavily overintellectualized, they forget that part of their responsibility is to train the feelings as well as the intelligence.

PICCIONE: How about restrain as well?

LOGAN: "Train" would include "restrain," but also "free." I find in my teaching very often, and in my readings, say, in the high schools, that students are hungry for the activation of feeling, the kind that comes to them through poetry. They need it. That aspect of education having to do with art and poetry has often been neglected in American schools; many of them are so technically oriented. Well, I can only think of my own experience, and I went to a very good school in Red Oak, Iowa. We won the "Brain Derby" (I think it was called) year after year, competing scholastically with other high schools around the state. But so far as poetry is concerned, I had no interest in it when I was a high school student. We had to memorize "Eldorado" by Poe and we had to memorize forty lines of "Snowbound" by John Greenleaf Whittier, I believe. There was nothing to awaken one to poetry, except for my very last year of high school when I was given some Shakespeare to read. I must have been given Shakespeare earlier, too. I think we read *The Merchant of Venice* and George Eliot's *Silas Marner* together as freshmen. But *The Merchant of Venice* didn't do much for me as a freshman. Shakespeare's use of language in the great tragedies (I think we read *Julius Caesar*) did help bring me alive to language, but I, of course, then went to college as a premedical major and had no idea that I would become a poet. I didn't start writing poetry seriously until I was about twenty-eight years old, married, had several children, and was teaching.

One other thing that occurs to me to mention before we leave this subject of mother consciousness, so to speak, is Bly's idea that it is part of the business of the poet to restore some of that lost mother consciousness to the reader. I agree with that entirely.

PICCIONE: You speak of students being hungry for feeling, and it seems that the next part of such a statement is that they are hungry for touching, for this type of restoration of humanness despite the tradition they come from. You feel that, too, despite the tradition you come from. This is all acceptable now. What makes this the time? Is it just that it would have been time no matter what?

LOGAN: I think it comes partly out of the really revolutionary attitude toward educational curricula that students have been involved in for the past few years. They have required the overhauling of curricula, they have broken away from the lycée/gymnasium idea that was the formation of so many high school concepts in this country, an idea which was heavily rational in character. I realize that here I'm getting back into another problem, because earlier, we talked about the fact that the Germans seem to have a freedom of sensibility. But I'm thinking of the kind of training that would be taken over in the German gymnasium. This European consciousness, which we were saying was more restorative than the American consciousness, must have come from some place other than the gymnasium, then, or else I'm barking up the wrong tree.

PICCIONE: Yes, I always want to say that the roughest background is

German, and then it frightens me to find so many outstanding modern and contemporary German poets.

LOGAN: It might have more to do with the fact of the European family sense than with education. The sense of the *pater familias,* for example, which the Germans have so strongly.

PICCIONE: I suppose this is a transition: I admire your Trakl translations, and I notice something that occurs in looking at other translators. I'm thinking especially of your translation of "Twilight Land." I wonder if I could read, say, the first part of a famous translator's translation and then have you read your entire translation. All right? This is part one of Michael Hamburger's translation of the poem. He calls it "Occident":

Occident
(for Else Lasker-Schüler)

I

Moon, as if a dead thing
Stepped from a blue cave,
And many blossoms fall
Across the rocky path.
Silver a sick thing weeps
By the evening pond,
In a black boat
Lovers crossed over to death.

Or the footsteps of Elis
Ring through the grove
The hyacinthine
To fade again under oaks.
O the shape of that boy
Formed out of crystal tears,
Nocturnal shadows.
Jagged lightning illumines his temples
The ever-cool,
When on the verdant hill
Springtime thunder resounds.

Now, would you read your entire translation?

(Logan reads "Twilight Land." See p. 300.)

PICCIONE: It should be obvious to anyone that there is a vast difference between the two translations. Somewhere Trakl is there, but I wonder about the business of translation. Shall we admit to America that translators use dictionaries on the side? But here's the point: the task of transforming the German to American English as poem seems caught up especially in the element of nuance. And here I'm thinking of words like "verdant hills." I mean, we don't say that.

LOGAN: Well, "verdant hills" is an archaism. I don't know why Michael Hamburger would come up with that. He's a competent person. He's a poet in his own right. I think he was trying to make it sound like a translation, that's the problem, instead of just sounding like a living poem in the other language.

PICCIONE: That's incredible, then. What is the purpose?

LOGAN: I don't know, but a number of translators definitely give this impression. I'm thinking about translations of *The Iliad,* too. It just is a general quality of translations. Some translators like to try to bring alive the quality of the poem in the new language. Others prefer to have it sound as though it has been brought over from another language; therefore, it sounds like a translation. I'm thinking about the Loeb classics (which Ezra Pound once called the Low Ebb Classics) which were mainly done, not by literary people but by people who were language specialists.

PICCIONE: I think perhaps that is the greatest single flaw in the whole business. There's the translator C. F. MacIntyre who gave me my first taste of the French symbolists. I didn't know how wrong his translation was, but now I do and now I see something.

LOGAN: He is the person who introduced me to Rilke, also, so I'm very grateful to him, even though I know that his translations are not as close to the German as Herder Norton's, for example. But I'm eternally grateful to MacIntyre because I first met Rilke through him. He apparently was a good enough man to carry something of the strength of the people he was translating, even though he made errors.

POULIN: Could the problem of translation be that matter of music you were discussing a little while ago—attempting to discover another rhythm, another music for another man's emotions?

LOGAN: It could be, indeed, the question of not having an ear that matches that of the poet in the first place, so that one is more aware of other qualities of language than the word-for-word accuracy as a quality of a translation. I think that without the essential surface, the musical surface, one doesn't get interested in plumbing further into the depths of the poem. It becomes more like reading an essay than it does like really reading poetry.

POULIN: I say that because it seems to me that your translations often read like your poems. They assume the music that your own poems assume and, therefore, the reader hears that blend of Logan and of Trakl (or of someone else.)

LOGAN: Well, that would be strongest in my Rilke poem, "Homage to Rainer Maria Rilke," where I used fragments and in some cases complete sections, complete poems of Rilke, but I included lines of my own that were turned on by him, by his writing.

POULIN: I'd like to explore that question of music a little bit more. Some critics (I believe both James Dickey and Paul Carroll) have mentioned that some of your poems become prosey at times. And yet I don't sense that. What kind of music is going on in the poems?

LOGAN: I don't know that I can answer that. I know that my development of a new line break—which all the poems in my book, *The Anonymous Lover,* use—involve broken lines, and the principle of the breaking of the line is a musical one: the relationship of assonance or a strong consonance, occasionally of a full rhyme. I'm not sure where that comes from, except my desire to make the music more explicit, which is the only thing I'm clearly aware of. It often exploits, so to speak, what would otherwise be an internal rhyme.

PICCIONE: I'd like to dare ask this. I've never had a good answer. From the musicality of the poem, according to Ginsberg, there's a way of finding the body and finding body-poems. Robert Bly and Gary Snyder also talk of body energies. And in his essay on you, "John Logan's Field of Force," Robert Bly speaks of the energy of body. Could you tell us about that?

LOGAN: I think that by body language Bly means the kind of language which images muscular, visceral, and interior feelings rather than images the five senses. There is a visceral sense, a kinetic sense as well. I can remember Randall Jarrell talking about this in his review of Robert Lowell's first book, *Lord Weary's Castle,* which is an extraordinary book. I can remember it blew my mind when I was beginning to read modern poetry. Bly quotes my "Zoo" poem when he talks about this body language—a use of language to image different stances and attitudes of the body.

PICCIONE: Is it also a matter that more of the senses are becoming legitimate? For instance, Snyder again reminds us that the sense of taste is also the province of the poet. Are we ready for more sensorial experiences to reach the page?

POULIN: Or might it be related more closely to your opening remarks that you've broken through from your more mature intellectual life to your more mature emotional life, and in the process perhaps you also broke through to this body-language and body-music?

LOGAN: I think that makes sense, yes. Though I also think that the poems in *Cycle for Mother Cabrini* have a pretty strong body-sense, too; for example, the first and second poems in the

"Cycle for Mother Cabrini" sequence. It would be hard for me to pull that sense out of my own work. Of course, Bly was talking about my more recent book, *The Zigzag Walk;* but I'm not sure that he wouldn't also find things in *Cycle for Mother Cabrini.*

PICCIONE: Bly makes the distinction in that same essay between what he means by body-sound and mental-sound, and he accuses Robert Lowell of more mental-sound, just for contrast, and perhaps parts of Cycle for Mother Cabrini *can still be accused of more mental-sound.*

LOGAN: Yes, I think that's true, but it's not so in "Pagan Saturday" and "Grandfather's Railroad." I feel I'd like to read one of those to show you what I mean.

This is "Grandfather's Railroad." It's actually the underground railroad, and it was pointed out to me by my uncle, not by my grandfather. Why I changed it to grandfather, I'm not sure. . . . It relates to the poem "The Weeping" (from *The Zigzag Walk*) a little bit. This concerns the same man for whom I had much feeling. He was actually my stepgrandfather, Thomas Morgan. But while pointing out where the underground railroad used to run (I, as a child in a little southwestern Iowa town, had never seen a Negro at the time) he told me about the running of Negroes through on the underground railroad and I fantasized them just as I fantasized a real railroad. This poem came out of it. (Logan reads "Grandfather's Railroad." See p. 273.)

I sort of wish Bly had talked more about some of my earlier poems. I think that there always has been music present in my work, and we or they are really talking more about a difference in content than a difference in music. The content is more intellectualized in *Cycle for Mother Cabrini.* I'm not convinced that it's less musical than in my more recent work.

PICCIONE: Gentlemen, we're running out of time. Perhaps we can end with some of your newer work, John, and let it stand as evidence itself.

LOGAN: Oh, sure. These are two short poems. I call them "Two Poems for Women."

(Logan reads "Two Poems for Women." See p. 305.)

From a Conversation with
Michele Ricciardelli

(1973)

What does "the mythology of the body" mean in general in your poetry and what does it mean in particular in "Big Sur: Partington Cove" in connection with William Blake's epigram: "The eyes of fire, the nostrils / of air, the mouth of water, / the beard of earth"?

"Mythology of the body" refers to ideas, difficult to summarize, deriving mainly from Norman O. Brown, particularly in his *Love's Body*. A related form of it I have heard of recently in Berkeley and San Francisco having to do with the Sufi form of meditation which "maps" various areas of the body. When Robert Bly—in his essay on my work in *Voyages* (4, no. 3–4, Spring 1971–Spring 1972)—talked about "body language" in my work, he explained to me in a letter that he was thinking in particular of the thoracic area of the body as a source of power in my work. I know that he is interested in the ideas of the displaced Tibetan Lama Choygam Trungpa (now in this country), which are perhaps related to the idea of "mapping the body" which I just referred to. I am unsure. My own interest is primarily in a uniting of the psyche to the body—I believe that poetry is of great use in healing or undoing the kind of split between psyche and body which Freud (and Marcuse) would speak of in terms of "repression," where in particular a split between the genital processes of the body and the processes of the mind are in conflict.

Norman O. Brown has a lecture on the myth of Daphne in which he speaks of this split in the Western world. In general I feel that T. S. Eliot's critical theories perpetuated a separation between the rational powers and the feeling (more bodily) powers. I think his poem, "The Love Song of J. Alfred Prufrock," beautifully expresses the fantasy (and desire for) such a split and that his criticism rationalizes it. In Eliot's aesthetics poets are not supposed to write about *their own* feelings.

In the "Big Sur" poem I am speaking of the mythology of the body in so far as (a) body and feeling are seen as a source of human reality and truth, (b) the body is seen as a metaphor for landscape and vice-versa. I became aware of the relation between landscape and body from dreams and from paintings (as in the paintings of Diebenkorn and his student, my friend James Johnson, the painter to whom the poem is dedicated.) The last section of the poem describes a sunbathing experience where the body of a companion became clearly related in my mind to the landscape around us.

Blake's quotation seems to emphasize the relation of body to elements that form landscape (earth, air, fire, water). The final lines of the poem refer to the body of Christ, absent from the grave, but (in Christian doctrine) still present in the cosmos as a source of truth. (The dogma of the Assumption of Mary has added the female body to the cosmos as a further source of truth.)

I feel the need of a new poetics based on Norman O. Brown and on the Christian doctrines of the eternity of the male and female body, united to eternal spirit (psyche). My new poem, "Middle Aged Midwesterner at Waikiki Again," speaks of this as a healing and grace-giving thing.

You have been interested in men involved in psychoanalysis and Catholicism. Why these men, and who in particular have attracted you? And what do you feel about psychoanalysis and Catholicism?

I was baptized a Catholic at the age of twenty-three and confirmed at the age of twenty-eight (which already shows some conflict) and later (at the age of thirty-three) found my orthodox Catholic beliefs interfered with by psychoanalytic therapy and doctrine. Therefore, I became interested in men who had reconciled Catholicism and analysis, such as the convert psychiatrists Karl Stern and Gregory Zilboorg, and read their works avidly.

I knew and studied philosophy at Georgetown University with Dr. Rudolph Allers who had earlier been in the department of psychiatry at Catholic University of America and who had written a book against Freud and later revised his views positively about Freud. It was in 1950 that I knew Allers and studied Renaissance philosophy with him. We did not in fact talk much about psychiatry, but I knew his book. His wife used to visit the class and she and I were Augustinians and fequently opposed Allers who was a Thomist. . . .

Would you mind saying why lately you have been using "projective verse" and the "splitting lines"?

I don't think of myself as using (Olson's) "projective verse" at all. The break in my lines is based on musical relationships which would otherwise appear as internal rhyme and which serves to help pace the line as I would like it read. So far as I know, I invented this technique. It began as a kind of free verse couplet influenced by the kind of delayed rhyming technique used by Ogden Nash.

As you know, today people often speak or write about "the death of art," "the death of poetry," etc. What do you think of the "death of poetry"?

People speak of the death of poetry in connection with the development and expansion of visual media. (I am thinking of Marshall McLuhan especially.) We need to remember that poetry existed long before print was invented and it is not dependent on it. The use of color or film or song (the latter also ancient) in connection with poetry is a development which can enhance poetry and which I am interested in but have little experience. I am pleased that my son John has made two guitar settings for two of my poems and sings them in his programs. I am not knowledgeable about multimedia settings for poetry, such as those experimented in by Daniela Gioseffi in New York. I am opposed to electronic and computer experiments with poetry *to the extent* that they interfere with the basic function of poetry as an expression of interior life of the human being in touch with other human beings. Otherwise I am not opposed to them.

So far as "the death of art" is concerned in a more general sense, it would imply the death of man as man, whose *nature* it is to be creative. (There is a theory, which I think is false, that a fully psychoanalyzed society would have no need of art.)

Should you judge American poetry in general, which ones to you are the most vital poetic experiences of the last ten years? And speaking of such experiences, how would you classify your own type of poetical research?

I would *not* classify my own type of "poetical research." I am not so interested in classification and categorization and schools in literature as I am in the *uniqueness* of the art work—which at the same time appeals to something deep, common, and essential to the mystery of man himself. Classification implies abstraction and leads us to science and its function rather than to art. Comparativeness at the heart of art is based on *feeling* rather than on ratiocination.

The most important poets of the last ten years I believe to be Galway Kinnell, James Wright, Robert Bly, James Dickey (his early work), A. R. Ammons, Isabella Gardner, Carolyn Kizer, W. S. Merwin, Allen Ginsberg, Gary Snyder, and Robert Creeley. (I have not put them in a ranking order.) The list could be extended twice as long; and friendships, of course, do (perhaps should) influence judgment.

In what direction do you believe American poetry is going?

American poetry is going in *several* directions, which I think is healthy. It is a huge and diverse country which is also assimilating its own primitive poetry (through Indian translations as by Jerome Rothenberg) and the poetry of its neighbors (through translations of Italian, French, German, and Spanish poetry by Bly, Wright, Knoepfle, Gardner, et al.) I have qualified my interest in avant-garde electronic and computer poetry in my last answer.

At the end of your poem, "To a Young Poet Who Fled," you write: "I'd rather be a swineherd in the hut, understood / by swine than a poet misunderstood by men." From this I conclude that you believe the poet has a mission. What do you think is the main mission of the poet?

The quotation at the end of "To a Young Poet Who Fled" is from Kierkegaard. The mission of the poet, as I see it, is to put man in touch with himself and with the deeper mystery of mankind itself, "the riddle of the sphinx," through extending the world of created things in the animal world of breath and the human world of language-music.

A Conversation with Helen Ruggieri and David Perry

(1975)

You teach at the State University of New York at Buffalo?

Yes, I started the graduate workshop in poetry there about five years ago; they had never had one before, and I'm still teaching it, although next term it looks like I may be going to Hawaii as an exchange professor, so somebody else will take that class.

Is SUNY at Buffalo still a stronghold of Black Mountain poetry?

Yes it is, because Charles Olson was there for a time. That was just before I came. He was a powerful influence. I came in 1966 and I believe he left that year. One of his proteges, John Clarke, a poet, still teaches there and writes, as does Robert Creeley, of course. And there is a strong cult which developed around Olson's personality and gift which lives on through his disciples, so to speak.

What's your view of Buffalo as a place to live and work?

Buffalo has some very strong points in its favor. The state university is one of the best universities in the country; the English department is one of the best; and *SUNY* has always had a strong name in medicine, psychology, and law. But, besides the university, there is also a superb art gallery; some people claim the Albright Knox Museum is better than the Museum of Modern Art in New York City for modern works. There's a good repertory theater called the Studio Arena, and the symphony is getting better and better under Michael Tilson Thomas. There are some beautiful old sections of town, too.

Also, the cemetery is quite astonishing. Have you ever been in the cemetery in Buffalo? It's called Forest Lawn, the original one before Hollywood took it up. It's got some famous graves, including Millard Fillmore's. One of the projects that my students and I did last year was agree, all of us, to write a poem about Forest Lawn Cemetery. I've done this sometimes; we all write about the same painting in the gallery or we all write a poem about the feeling of autumn. This time we decided to write a poem about the cemetery. It was the last assignment for the year and it was pretty successful. You get these various views, and the poem I wrote I like well enough to keep.

I called it "Five Preludes for Buffalo's Own Forest Lawn." There's a statue of Chief Red Jacket just at the entrance of the cemetery. Since Red Jacket was a native Indian and not a Christian, there were several attempts to convert him. At one point he said: "I say instead of white men converting us, let's watch him, and if there is any difference to be seen, then we will listen for his white god." Chief Red Jacket was buried in a native burial ground and then his body was moved to the Christian cemetery, along with those of several of his fellows. He was a very great orator—Red Jacket; he had a natural gift of speech. (Logan reads "Five Preludes for Buffalo's Own Forest Lawn." See p. 307.)

When I was reading your poems, I noticed one had an epigraph from A. A. Brill: "Years ago I came to the conclusion that poetry is nothing but an oral outlet." And in your essay in Voyages *("On Poets and Poetry Today") you seem to reinforce that Freudian theory of art. Do you believe that poetry is nothing but an oral outlet?*

What I was trying to do was to use the Brill quotation ironically.

In the Voyages *essay you spoke of the male lyric poet building the body of the mother in his poetry. In the same essay you make the point that you must conjure the vision of the mother and make her sing. The two statements are so apart, one Freudian, the other Jungian. They seem incongruous to me.*

I think that Freud's vision was rather limited and needed to be supplemented. I also think that Jung is a very good supplement, in the sense that he gives a place for higher feelings of man, for spirituality, and has a notion of the universality of certain, what he calls, archetypes which are shown forth in myths and in sculptures of all races. I've learned a lot from Freud, but I'm not reductive about poetry in the way that many Freudian critics are. The critics use his conclusions to destroy the notion of creativity and of poetry, whereas Freud himself said that creativity remained a mystery which he admitted he didn't understand.

Anyway, the poem that has those epigraphs is called "On the Death of the Poet's Mother Thirty-Three Years Later." There are two epigraphs. The first one is from St. Augustine: "The tongue fits to the teeth and the palate by Number, pouring forth letters and words." The other one you mentioned is from Brill. Now, I intended my poem to use that epigraph ironically. It is clear from the reading of the poem that the writer of it doesn't think that poetry is nothing but an oral outlet; but he thinks of it as a way of showing feeling about his dead mother. And similarly in the essay; it has a kind of psychoanalytic orientation to it, but I believe it goes beyond that. At least I intended it to.

I was struck by the poem you read last night with references to your father ("Poem in Progress"). How do you create out of your family background without being sentimental?

I think that one can use anything out of his own experience, including his relationships with members of his family in poetry, so long as he does it in a way which connects with the deeper experience of many people. You say you were moved by the poem, which shows that in some sense there is something inside yourself that resonated to it, even though not in a literal way; but everyone has siblings or people in their lives whom they think of as brothers or sisters. I think it was Emerson who said that the deeper we go into our own feeling the closer we come to the depth of the feeling of others. We find a kind of common bond at the depths of feeling which becomes a transcendent experience and rises above the personal connotations of the psychological history of the poet himself. And I've had this transcendent experience on a number of occasions. One of them I was talking about in the last poem I read last night ("Grace"), which ends with the statement: "*you*/too will taste this apple with us/for we all have the same mother, and her name is Grace."

That poem actually grew out of some experiences I had while taking LSD with a therapist. I'd never taken LSD before. I was with a therapist whose name is Gregory Calvert.[1] The strange thing was that at one point on the LSD trip, which is why I use the word "voyage" in the poem, I said, "You know, my mother's name is Grace." And he said, "Well, you know, so's mine." Then he said, "We all have the same mother and her name is Grace." And so I'm really quoting him in the poem. I sort of stole his line, but it's curious how it works. There is a communal bond which poetry is about that goes beyond personality and is concerned with something which is, or which you might call, the higher unconsciousness. It's very different from the Freudian unconscious. Jacques Maritain had a phrase he called "the musical unconscious," out of which poetry and art come.

As an epigraph for that poem, "Grace," I use a statement

---

1. The poem was originally entitled "Prose Poem for My Brother and for My Teacher Gregory." But after it was rewritten as a syllabic poem, Logan also changed the title and called it simply "Grace." (See p. 311.)—A. P., Jr.

from a psychiatrist named Robert Assagioli, who spoke about how men tend to repress the sublime—by the sublime he means the higher unconscious—which would give them a sense of this common experience in the transcendence of ordinary personal encounters and disappointments. And I think that it's one of the functions of poetry to use that common bond. When I read my poem yesterday afternoon, "To a Young Poet Who Fled," I spoke about this fact. I think of poetry as a kind of sharing and a kind of reaching which forms a bond that comes back to the poet from the audience. That's why I called my book *The Anonymous Lover*, because I used to tell my students that poetry is a kind of anonymous loving which occasionally becomes personal when there are those present who care to listen.

Do you think that the anger that comes out in a great deal of poetry is because the poets want so badly to reach out and touch in some way, and at the end of that touch is air, because the other person has moved away?

There's a resentment of rejections, certainly. This isolation of the poet from his audience is a modern phenomenon. As you know, poets used to read Homer by rote while playing the lute to large numbers of people; and in other cultures there's a greater appreciation of the poet—in Italy or in France, for example. But that isolation from the audience becomes useful to the poet in another way. Because everybody is isolated in some way; through the thickness of the skin, so to speak, people are separated from each other like those figures in Rouault's paintings by black lines like lead. This separation can happen by religion, by color, by neurosis, but to a certain extent everybody is in exile. Paul Tillich uses this feeling of being alienated as his definition of original sin. So that the poet can make use of the alienation he feels in order to reach other people, and when other people realize that alienation is a common experience, then they are not alone in the same way they were before the realization occurred.

I think that poetry and love are the two places where this awareness of a common bond beyond alienation is found.

Dylan Thomas talks about this (the crotchetiness of poets) a little bit in "In My Craft and Sullent Art." The word "sullen," of course, comes from the Latin "solus," and although it means crotchety in modern language, its root meaning is "alone, to be in solitude." And there's a connection between the crabbiness of sullenness and the sense of isolation. But in Thomas's poem that is related to love, and essentially solitude is related to the making of an artwork itself, because everyone does his creating by himself. Even if he's in a crowd, he has to be within himself at the moment of creation. I think Thomas's poem talks about this so beautifully. He's saying that, even if the audience pays no attention, he's still writing for them.

Is he one of your "masters"?

Not in craft so much, though perhaps some. He had such a great musical gift. I believe music and rhythm are essentially important.

You read beautifully. There's something in the rhythm of your reading that calls him to mind.

Good. That's important to me and I suppose Thomas has influenced me in that because he's one of the greatest readers that we've ever had. In fact, he almost singlehandedly brought poetry back to the spoken word in this country.

How did you earn your necklace of Bad Mother's teeth? Or, what's your relationship to the feminine archetypal powers?

This may not answer your question, but I think the giving aspect of poetry is a kind of feminine quality related to creativity. That's why the muses are all figured as feminine. I can remember when I'd had a long dry period and I wrote a poem one day. The occasion of my writing the poem was that my wife was upstairs in the hospital having our fourth child. The poem is an affirmation of life, a poem complaining about Hart Crane's suicide and his becoming overwhelmed by his problems, instead of continuing to stay alive to write his own work. I couldn't miss the sense of a certain kind of competition between the poet and the mother, because we were both busy at the same time making something, so to speak. I think that there's a maternal generative quality in poetry which relates to the gifts of the feminine side of our nature.

Do you believe, as Graves does, that no woman can be a great lyric poet?

No. I don't think that's true. Sappho comes to mind first, of course.

Do you set specific goals? Do you set a marker to move toward? Do you find yourself changing those markers?

Life is not static. Poetry is related to the way in which the poets are alive. Their art grows naturally out of their living. Therefore, the poems change. I've had five books of poems and I've had five different publishers.[2] The editors wanted me to keep writing the same poems in the same way I had done in the book they edited. But I didn't, so I've had to keep hunting for publishers. That seems to be changing now, because the editor of my book at Dutton, *The Zigzag Walk,* later moved to Liveright and asked me to move there with him. So the fact that the last book, *The Anonymous Lover,* was published by Liveright doesn't mean that there wasn't that change. But in the other cases it was true. Each publisher had rejected the subsequent manuscript.

Do you have anything scheduled for publication soon?

You'll be interested in a book of mine which is just being published by Abbatoir Editions (The University of Nebraska at

---

2. In 1981 these figures are revised to ten books of poetry and ten different publishers.—A. P., Jr.

Omaha). It is called *The House That Jack Built: Portrait of the Artist as a Young Sensualist*[3] and is a long autobiographical memoir from earliest memories to about age fourteen. Much of my early life was spent on a farm, because my stepmother's sisters and brother were in the farming business in a small town, Red Oak, Iowa.

---

3. Originally issued in a hand-printed, limited edition, *The House that Jack Built* is being re-issued in a trade edition by Slow Loris Press in 1983.—A. P., Jr.

A Conversation with Thomas Hilgers and Michael Molloy

(1979)

We want to congratulate you on the recent award of the Guggenheim Fellowship, John.

Thank you. I'm looking forward to a whole year off in which to write new poems and collect older poems, perhaps in a new selection.

Do you have any particular plans?

Well, I hope to return to Europe. I have several poems based on places in Europe, and I seem to be turned on to write by new situations.

Do you find that particular locales lend themselves to your producing particular types of poems? What is the relationship between where you are and what you write?

It varies a good deal. I can't answer that question directly, except that very often there are other people involved, other people whom I'm visiting or traveling with, who get involved with the landscape somehow.

I'm interested in your evolution as a poet. I know that I read somewhere that you began your college career by majoring in biology, and in fact began your professional career by teaching biology. Can you tell us something about how you began to write poetry?

That was a number of years after I began teaching. I had been working on the German poet Rilke, translating him—I was actually working on a degree in philosophy and was studying German for that. The translation work was very satisfying. The nature of the German language is such that the meat of the sentence comes toward the end, and Rilke's poems are such that there's a change of key quality in them toward the end of the poem. Not knowing German very well, I found it especially satisfying to do the translating, and it sort of primed by own pump. I also got some practice in the iambic pentameter line, the line which most of the Rilke poems I was translating—the early ones—used.

Then things were happening in my life which were difficult to handle emotionally. I was teaching at a—excuse me, I was not teaching, I was working—at a hospital for insane Blacks in Crownville, Maryland, and I was sort of moved to write as a kind of prayer or incantation for them because there seemed so little that could be done. The first poem I published, in *Partisan Review* in January of 1953, was about feeding a blind and insane tubercular old man his dinner.

Was there a gap of years between your beginning to write and your first publication?

I wasn't eager to leap into print. I wanted to be sure of what I was doing. I worked mainly alone, at St. John's College in Annapolis, Maryland. I began writing around 1949–50, at least three years before the first poem was published.

How did you begin to write? Did you simply work out what you wanted to say, or did you depend a great deal on poetry that you had read?

Actually, one of the first two poems of mine that were published was based on reading—it was based on a text from the Roman author Pliny, from his *Natural History*. I had been reading that in connection with my work in biology classes at St. John's College, and was very much taken by one story that Pliny relates. It has to do with a very heroic man who is very dangerous and has killed a number of the enemy, but who can not be caught himself. When he is finally caught, they throw him to the ground and open his heart. They find his heart covered with hair. That strange quality of the hairy heart, in connection with the courage of the man, made me interested, and I wrote about it in my poem "A Pathological Case in Pliny."

Had you read many other poets whose style you learned from or tried to imitate?

No, not really, I had read a good deal of poetry, but I wasn't aware of influence outside of Rilke. I think in my third book, *Spring of the Thief*, there are a couple of poems that show his influence.

What do you think it was about Rilke that so attracted you?

It's his great gift of image and his own commitment to poetry. He has this marvellous group of letters published in a book called *Letters to a Young Poet*, in which he talks about the necessity of becoming one's own best critic and not continually taking one's work around to various people. One can always find somebody to approve it. It's a book I would recommend for all young students of poetry.

Some teachers of novice poets believe that in order to really become a poet you have to go through some sort of apprenticeship where you learn traditional forms. What do you do with your students?

There are two schools of thought on this. One of them, a traditional school, to which people like Milton and the contemporary Theodore Roethke belonged, encouraged writing in imitative forms at the beginning. But I have found with contemporary students that the big problem is to get them to believe in their own voice and to stop echoing other people. So I don't usually use strict forms at the beginning. I try to get them to write a good deal, and to find what is unique in themselves. But I have them read a lot. Then I believe in using forms somewhat later, in order to structure what one is doing once one is free of imitative material.

You've written a prose work, The House that Jack Built, *which I've heard you refer to as a "fictionalized autobiography." We don't often hear those two words put together. Yet a lot of your poetry has an autobiographical "ring of truth" about it. Some people today might call it "confessional poetry." How does your life fit into your poems?*

Very often it's not really, historically, "out of life," but the gift of the poet has to do with making it seem as though it were. The important thing is not whether it happened in the life of the poet, but whether it is somehow shared in the life of the reader. That's one of the reasons I don't like the notion of "confessional poetry." I don't really believe in it, because what one talks about is not primarily himself as a poet. If he has any power, he is talking about the reader too. So what is "confessed" is what is in the reader, in a sense—as much as what is in the author. An example might be my poem "Picnic." There never was, actually, such a girl as Ruth and a particular school picnic. I should perhaps not say that, because it disappoints people. It's a product of imagination. I of course went on a number of picnics, but "Picnic" is not about any particular happening. (See p. 290.)

And yet the moment of awakening you describe in "Picnic" is something that happens at one time or another to all of us.

Indeed.

Are you conscious of the reader as you write?

Oh, yes. The first audience is the listening part of yourself.

When do happenings in your life make for good poems?

Very often, it's an anxiety state, which one works through by writing through it. Poets have what I call the occupational hazard of poetry, which is that they don't know what's happened to them until they find the words to express it. Once you find the words, the experience is altered. If the poem works well, it brings what Dylan Thomas calls "a momentary peace," a temporary end to anxiety. This is something very much like what in religion is called "the state of grace." I think the natural equivalent of grace is the peace, or catharsis, to go back to the old term—refreshment of the inner spirit—that comes from art.

I've particularly enjoyed your poem "Shore Scene," and I wonder if we might use it to talk more specifically about how your poems come into being. Could you read it for us?

Sure. (Logan reads "Shore Scene." See p. 292.)

What do you remember about its evolution—did it have many other versions? Where did the incident in it take place, if it took place at all?

Well, this one did take place. It happened that I was visiting with a couple of my children and a friend named Pat Sweeney (who later taught at Lone Mountain in San Francisco) and his young brother, Tim, in the sand dunes on Lake Michigan, I think the park that's called "Tower Hill." At any rate, I have difficulty sometimes in scenes with the sea and the sun. For one thing, I am very fair-skinned and I burn easily. I often don't enjoy myself as much as one would expect on an outing. But this day I was determined to enjoy myself. We unpacked the car; the kids went to this hill of sand, "The Tower," and were falling down. We made some peanut butter and jelly sandwiches, and the first thing I did was to bite into a sandwich and there was a bee in it! Actually, it was a yellow jacket, not a bee. It stung my tongue. It worried me a good deal, because I thought some people were very sensitive to yellow-jacket bites. I was expecting my mouth to swell up or swell shut or something.

Then I describe some scenes that took place on the beach that day: the girl building the canals which she then opens to let the lakewater in; the child who was tricked into being sanded into a pit. The last part of the poem—"My own shadow followed then, until / I felt the cold swirling at the groin"—reflects something about the anxiety of the scene, I suppose, but actually it describes the experience of slowly walking out into the water until the cold water reaches the level of the groin.

That's the literal basis of it. You always hope that there's more richness in the actual images and rhythms as they come out than in the literal story.

I take it, then, that what you've just said is an illustration of what you meant earlier when you talked about poems growing out of the poet's anxiety. Is the anxiety here the anxiety of a yellow-jacket bite, or do you think there's something more?

As I've said, a beach scene generally is an anxious one for me, partly because of the fear of sunburn, partly because of the Puritan inhibition about sensuality which is so present in a beach scene, and which I think it takes quite a while to get comfortable with—but not for people here in Hawaii who are so used to the constant scene. But when you have only a couple of months a year when you can visit the beach and see the lightly clad bodies, there's sometimes some anxiety associated with that.

How much after the incident was "Shore Scene" written?

Pretty shortly. I don't remember exactly.

Why did you think that this would be a good subject for a poem?

It seemed to me it had a kind of element of experience that could be shared. There's something archetypal about a beach experience, and about some of the details—the attraction of the boy trapped in the sand. I thought it had a number of details that would touch other people.

"Shore Scene" is constructed of ten-syllable lines. Why did you pick that particular form?

The syllabic form gives you a kind of minimum discipline for revising a line and for reaching ahead to discover new images. Of course, a ten-syllable line has been used in a lot of poetry—I don't use it anymore because it tends to break down too easily into iambic pentameter. That's now a sort of cliché rhythm in English poetry. But sometimes one notices that some of his best lines are in a certain number of syllables, and it seems to make sense to choose to write other lines with the same number, if you can.

How do you know when a poem is finished, John?

William Butler Yeats said that you know when a poem is done because it "shuts, like the click of a box." I don't seem to have any difficulty recognizing when a revision is done.

Do you test your poems with friends before they reach final form?

Often, sure. With university colleagues. Or I often bring them into workshops that I teach, and discuss them with the students.

Your poems have many children in them. While that's perhaps not unusual, it's not all that common either in contemporary American poetry. Is there any reason beyond your experience with your own children that brings so many children into your poems?

There's the constant sense of life in the play of children—constantly refreshing and constantly ancient like games and dances that are paradigms of play. Their naivete, their direct-ness, if they haven't been stepped on when they were too young.

What kinds of things are you writing now, John?

Of the most recent poems I've done, one is about a visit to

Hemingway's house in Key West. I had known Hemingway's son Gregory, in fact had taught him at St. John's College. It was rather moving to be in the presence of his father's overwhelming marks—the furniture, which is gigantic, from Spain; the cases full of memorabilia, which they have at this house which is now a kind of shrine. I knew that Gregory had left there when he was a young boy, just after grammar school. You can see his bed, broken down, and the cases of his father's work, filling his room. It touched me, it made me think very strongly of him, so I wrote a poem about it.

There's another one. I made a visit recently to Salisbury, Maryland, to the eastern shore where there's an island called Assateague, about which there are some myths. There are herds of wild ponies there still, and I was very taken with them, and I knew that they were rounded up yearly and the herds decimated and taken away from their wild place. I thought of this in connection with a couple I went with who were in love, with a kind of yearning that we all have for love relationships and which the yearning of ponies for their home seemed to be a metaphor for, after they had been rounded up. Let me read you "Assateague." (Logan reads "Assateague." See p. 309.) I hope some magazine will be interested in that. I haven't had it accepted yet.

You must have a much easier time having your poetry accepted now, though, than you did twenty-five years ago, when you were just beginning.

Well, yes. There were many rejections in those early years. Everybody has to get used to rejection in order to make it into a mature writing scene. *The Zigzag Walk,* my fourth book, was turned down by eight New York publishers before I found one.

I know one of the important things in your life is music. How would you describe the relationship between poetry and music?

I would quote Ezra Pound, whom I agree with, who (paraphrasing Walter Pater) said that poetry approaches itself as it nears the condition of music. And then (this time paraphrasing Yeats) he adds that music approaches itself as it nears the condition of the dance. So the notion of the dance is the general one there, and it makes me think of Nietzsche's notion of art as "the vision generated by the dance." Without the dance, which refers to some kind of sensual movement, you don't have the vision. That's one of the paradoxes about art.

I think that the surface music in poetry is very important. I've therefore called poetry "a ballet for the ear." I think without that surface beauty, one is not really taken into it to study it, understand it, look up references, follow it out. Poetry is like an extension of personality that way. We can fall in love with a person; then we want to know everything we can find out about him or her. But you don't fall in love with someone unless there is a kind of response that could be described as toward the sensual, the surface, whatever that might mean in terms of human beauty.

There's something Rilke talked about too—the connection between poetry and human response and feeling. Just as we can't ignore people, we can't ignore poems: we have to respond to them with feeling. So Rilke said, "Poetry is nothing so little to be reached as by criticism. Only love can securely grasp and judge it." I think by "love" he means simply "feeling," whether that be negative feeling or positive.

The surface sensuality comes through very much to me in your reading. In fact, I find myself sometimes so taken by the music of your reading that I forget that I'm listening to something with verbal content also.

That's all right. Because one can then look at it a second time. But without the music one might not be interested in going back to it.

Have you worked a lot on how you read a poem?

I'm constantly reading poems aloud as I write them. I recommend that to all. Think of music. Remember that the thing that makes poetry *poetry* is something it shares with music and painting and other arts, because it's an art before it's an art of language. We tend to forget this.

Your own reading is to me almost incantatory. When I hear you reading, I think of the notion of the poet as the person in touch with the world beyond, the frenzied prophet. Except, you also give me a feeling of serenity. Have you always read like that?

Well, I guess I got better!

What do you get out of being on the poetry circuit?

There's a lot of satisfaction in connection with the sharing that the poetry brings, and especially the sharing involved in the reading. The title of one of my books, *The Anonymous Lover,* comes from something which I used to tell my students: "Poetry is a kind of anonymous loving, which occasionally becomes personal when there are those present who care to listen." So the listening occasion is the occasion for sharing that I especially am interested in.

Isn't that idea of yearning, searching, used in some of your poems?

Oh yes. The poem called "The Search," from *The Zigzag Walk* ends this way:

> . . . I must not be alone
> no matter what needs be done,
> for then my search is ended.
> So now the panicked thumbs of my poem pick
> through the grill. They poke
> the lock
> and put out a hand and then an arm.
> The limbs of my poems
> come within your reach.
> Perhaps it is you whom I seek.

II

Essays

Dylan Thomas and the Ark of Art

(1960)

I suppose the easiest part of the production of art is the suffering. Artists have not minded pain so long as they could keep it from killing them and get their work done; so long as the madman—the beast and the angel Dylan Thomas found in himself or the boy, the man, and the woman James Joyce found in himself—did not crack the china skull in which they sprouted so dangerously together.

Dylan Thomas's pain, like that of Keats and that of Hart Crane, grew to the point where, without help, he had to pay attention to it, and at last it interested him more than the construction of his art, and he stopped writing and died. While he lived he saw his art as an ark, rescuing the building Noah from the floods of destruction he found in himself. "The moonshine drinking Noah of the bay" he calls himself in perhaps his last major poem, the "Author's Prologue" to his book of collected poems. The book itself he thought of as an ark, and the ark as the flower of the spring of the sea, the cloth woven out of the sea-deep, sea-rich pain of Penelope as she waited for love. Thomas finally lost patience with the waiting and stopped weaving. His cloth was not a shroud for his father, as was hers, but one for himself.

We learn in the first of Thomas's three birthday poems, "Twenty-four Years," that from birth "crouched in the groin of the natural doorway" he thought of the poet as a tailor "sewing a shroud for a journey/By the light of the meat-eating [man-eating] sun." When he wrote another poem on his birthday at thirty called "Poem in October," he asks hopefully that his "heart's truth" might "still be sung/On this high hill in a year's turning." He was still singing five years later in "Poem on His Birthday" which ends with the statement, "I sail out to die." In another five years, when it was time for a fourth birthday poem at forty in October of 1954, he had already been dead a year.

Everyone who knows anything about Thomas knows that he was continually dying, except in his poems where he kept himself alive. In the poems he used inward fire to fuse and mold like Hephaestus his gorgeous shield of Achilles, or to melt the pitch used to build the ark. "Song is a burning and crested act," he says in this same poem, "Author's Prologue," "The fire of birds in/The world's turning wood,/For my sawn, splay sounds." But in his life he let this inward fire burn him up as it did the child in one of his most beautiful poems, "A Refusal to Mourn the Death, by Fire, of a Child in London." Substitute New York for London and you see that it is himself for whom he said he would not grieve, though he did, as he does in that poem, making of himself, of his dissolving body melting in its grave, the elemental tears, "The zion of the water bead," "the salt seed," which kills the fire that kills the man that built the ark that Dylan built.

The image of the ark which Thomas uses in his prologue poem is saying something general about the nature of art, namely that it rescues from the flood, and the flood—though in that poem it is also the flood of tide by the poet's house, the flood of autumn and winter, the flood of middle age—is primarily the flood of self-destruction that emerges out of the "fountain-head of fear:"

> I build my bellowing ark
> To the best of my love
> As the flood begins,
> Out of the fountainhead
> Of fear, rage red, manalive . . .

This ark of Noah is also the rescuing whale of Jonah, where the artist comes to know himself and to return to his responsibilities, and it is the Ark of the Covenant which takes him out of himself, putting him into touch (the correct word) with other living people by a pledge which he seals with his own internal blood, a pledge to which he is loyal despite its continuing risks and public exposures. The artist has no catacomb in which he can hide. If he enters the shark for awhile it is so that he can recover himself and emerge into the sunlight of the city and shore to "sing at poor peace to you strangers." The artist's place of exile is in the open among crowds. His love is lonely because it must show itself in poems and because he must write the poems by himself, when he might be making love if he were somebody else, as Thomas says in his poem "In My Craft or Sullen Art;"

> In my craft or sullen art
> Exercised in the still night
> When only the moon rages
> And the lovers lie abed
> With all their griefs in their arms,
> I labour by singing light. . . .

I have not made up the idea that Dylan Thomas struggled with self-destructive forces and that his poems are a record of his fight, showing the sweat and strain of the crippled Jacob ambiguously trying to throw out from him, or to contain more comfortably within him, his blazing, erupting angel. I've seen it in the poems. But one can read it more directly in comments of his. He says someplace that the poems were "the record of struggle upward from darkness into some measure of light," and in another place that "Each poetic image holds within it the seed of its own destruction . . . the central seed is itself destructive and constructive at the same time . . . out of the inevitable conflict of images, inevitable, because of the creative, recreative, destructive and contradictory nature of the motivating centre, the womb of war, I try to make that momentary peace which is a poem."

I believe the "momentary peace" which Thomas found in making a poem is brought to the reader in the reading, through the calm of beauty, whatever the violence of style or subject, and that the love we feel for Thomas in his art has about it something of the delight of the greeting of The Dove. The artist's ark rescues us too, for a while:

> Huloo, my prowed dove with a flute!
> Ahoy, old, sea-legged fox,
> Tom tit and Dai mouse!
> My ark sings in the sun
> At God speeded summer's end
> And the flood flowers now.

The tension between destruction and construction, or between death and life, which makes both the artist and the audience need rescuing as Dylan Thomas supposes, is even more general than human kind for him. He talks about the two forces as earth- and heaven-wide, and as allied to the same forces in the poet:

> The force that through the green fuse drives the flower
> Drives my green age; that blasts the roots of trees
> Is my destroyer.
> And I am dumb to tell the crooked rose
> My youth is bent by the same wintry fever.

For Thomas the force of destruction is indissolubly bound up with that of construction. Death is the result of life's continuing. Birth is the first moment of death. In "Twenty-four Years" the crouched fetus is a tailor sewing a shroud. The title of one of his books, *Deaths and Entrances,* reflects this association of ideas.

I use the term constructive as opposed to destructive purposely in its several meanings, the alliance of art to life, more particularly to love, being a constant juxtaposition to Thomas. Love, like art, puts two together to make one, building a higher unity. They make one out of many, instead of fracturing one into many, a devilish activity against which Plato warned.

It is of the nature of art that every poem is an act of love, a virgin conception, and its completion is a virgin birth. Only one individual is involved, abandoning himself with love and energy to the visitation of a creative spirit, which is associated in Thomas's imagery with the musing "October wind," the wind of the month in which he was born and which gave him in an obvious way the three birthday poems, which are among his finest. He writes about the poetry-generating power of this "wind" in one of his best early poems, "Especially when the October Wind:"

> Especially when the October wind
> With frosty fingers punishes my hair . . .
> My busy heart who shudders as she talks
> Sheds the syllabic blood and drains her words.

The implied alliance of the artist figure with the figure of the Virgin is a far reaching concept which makes me want to digress a moment to Rilke. Rilke uses annunciatory language in his lines about the poet from *The Sonnets to Orpheus:* "True song demands a different kind of breathing. A shudder in the god. A gale." The concluding line of his beautiful "Annunciation to Mary" is "Then the angel sang his melody." A melody is a song, a poem.

Rilke agonized after each poem, afraid that he was now impotent, that he would be unable to produce another. Was this why Joyce, after finishing *Ulysses,* after his long "labor" of ten years, cried like a child at the top of his voice? Was it because he felt like a boy again, no longer fruitful? I am sure this feeling of the impotence to create is the source of Rilke's empathy into the situation of the Pietà about which he writes in his poem of that name:

> Now is my misery full, and namelessly
> it fills me. I am stark, as the stone's
> inside is stark . . .
> Now you are lying straight across my lap,
> now I can no longer
> give you birth.

Rilke ironically has several poems about being unable to write poems, at least one of which uses the image of the sterile womb. One thinks of Thomas's image for the generating point of poetry, "the womb of war."

Thomas also has a poem on the situation of being unable to write, and in a context directly relevant to the situation of virgin birth, using an image of false pregnancy, "the big purse of my body" and identifying it androgynously with an image of masculine sterility: "the blind shaft." The poem is "On no Work of Words":

> On no work of words now for three lean months in the
> bloody
> Belly of the rich year and the big purse of my body
> I bitterly take to task my poverty and craft:
>
> To take to give is all, return what is hungrily given
> Puffing the pounds of manna up through the dew to heaven,
> The lovely gift of the gab bangs back on a blind shaft.

The image of the Pietà, with the dead Christ in his mother's lap, across her womb and just outside of it, points up the connection between "deaths and entrances," between Good Friday and Christmas, between death and birth, which is so important in Thomas and which I want to comment on in connection with imagery of the incarnation and of the crucifixion.

That Thomas thought of the writing of poetry as a kind of incarnation is consistent with his idea of art as virgin conception and birth, and it gives us a specific image in his poem about creation, "In The Beginning":

> In the beginning was the word . . .
> And from the cloudy bases of the breath
> The word flowed up, translating to the heart
> First characters of birth and death.

As incarnation, the poem mirrors the whole man through the word into which the poet breathes his own life, particularly when he reads his own poems aloud, and by means of which the father poet (if he is a good one, a powerful father) descends into the world of created things immortally. Thomas said in an interview with James Stephens that every new poem, through coming into existence, altered the whole of the world of created things by the new relations it brought to them. One is put in mind of Maritain's remark that it is the vocation of the saint to complete the work of the Passion and the vocation of the artist to complete the work of the Creation.

A poem is a kind of Christ child as well as a kind of dove of peace. And for Thomas each birth brought a Christ, as in his long poem about the birth of his own son, "Vision and Prayer," or the poem about his own conception and birth, "Before I Knocked."

Now note that the situation of the Pietà is emotionally similar to that of the Nativity, after birth. The pain in realizing one is unable to give birth again is like the pain *of having given birth,* particularly when in the latter case the other parent is a spirit, unreliable in its fathering visits.

Seeing the artistic exhaustion after the birth of a poem as analogous to the situation of the Pietà enables one to telescope the feeling of having given birth and the feeling of grief, and to see them as different facets of the same act, as Thomas tended to see them. He describes this exhaustion at the end of "Especially when the October Wind."

> The heart is drained that, spelling in the scurry
> Of chemic blood, warned of the coming fury.

Now this phrase "the coming fury" takes us to a new point. I have said that the poem quoted here deals with the process of making a poem. The "October wind" is the wind of inspiration. The draining spoken of at the end of the poem is then the draining of birth felt at the completion of the poem, and at the same time the draining of the Pietà, the grief stemming from the unreliability of the spirit to visit again as lover; and at this level "the coming fury" is death, the final exhaustion. Now the birth draining makes reference to a feeling in the poet on completion of his poem, but the subject matter of this poem being about the conception of a poem, the draining at the literal level of the poem, is the exhaustion of the conceptual process itself, the exhaustion of intercourse, and "the coming fury" at this same level of the poem is birth. The fury of conception (sexual fury *or* Rilke's "gale"—it is hard to know whether Thomas takes the biological or the artistic as prime) is thus allied to the fury of birth and the fury of death, characteristically. And the drainage of the conceptual process, the act of love, is allied to the drainage of the conceptual process, the act of love, is allied to the drainage of giving birth and at the same time to that of grief or dying. The blood of violent dying and that of birth, allied in so many poems of his, particularly "Vision and Prayer," is related also to the blood of the agent of conception, the blood of the semen as he images it in several poems, among them "The Force that through the Green Fuse Drives the Flower," and "This Bread I Break." In the latter poem the semen/blood is seen as wine given to the beloved:

> This flesh you break, this blood you let
> Make desolation in the vein,
> Were oat and grape
> Born of the sensual root and sap;
> My wine you drink, my bread you snap.

Two ideas, that of sacrifice and that of consummation, enable us, given these juxtapositions, to see how in Thomas's imagery the act of conjugal love (issuing in conception) and behind or before it the artistic process, are both seen as crucifixions. A poem is a crucifixion involving agony, sacrifice and a giving up of the spirit—like an act of love—after which the poet can say with the lover, *consummatum est.*

The masculine side of Thomas's use of Christian imagery for the nature of the artistic process emerges most clearly at this point. It is somewhat blurred in his incarnation imagery where the image of the virgin mother still plays such a dominant role over that of the "Christ child" poem. Thomas carries the masculine Christ imagery so far in its connection with creative potency that in a couple of poems, "I See the Boys of Summer" and "If I Were Tickled by the Rub of Love," he actually identifies Christ and the phallus—using the phrase "Merry squires nailed to a tree" in the former and "My jack of Christ born thorny on the tree" in the other, both in unmistakably sexual contexts. One can detect behind the partly blasphemous, partly Rabelaisian qualities of these images, something of the same agonized whistling in the dark about sexual love which emerges in Thomas's letters and in so many of his poems—in connection with homosexuality in "I See the Boys of Summer," auto-erotism in "My Hero Bares His Nerves," and with intercourse in numbers of poems, particularly "All All and All the Dry Worlds Lever" among early poems and the great, bawdy, melancholy "Lament" among later ones. No doubt to some extent the heat he found so destructive was the one everybody struggles with, the Carthaginian flame of St. Augustine, the fire St. Benedict tried to quench by throwing himself into a bush of brambles. Particularly in the less artful early poems (Thomas's "Inferno") one has a glimpse of the horror he tried to shape, and one has a sense of what Trilling meant when he said the artist shapes the pain we all have. Construction after all takes no more energy than destruction. It is as though Thomas again and again tried to convince himself of this, and after a while failed to do so.

In the poem "Before I Knocked," many of the themes I have referred to come together. It is a poem about existence prior to conception, about the child as Christ existing, even loving and suffering, godlike, before his incarnation and anticipating his crucifixion, which in this poem is associated with the act of conception, so that the expiration of the father's breath in the act of love at conception is used to image the expiration of breath at the death of Christ. From the idea that birth is a dying, a crucifixion, Thomas in this poem moves back one more step: conception is a dying:

> I was mortal to the last
> Long breath that carried to my father
> The message of his dying christ.

This poem also contains imagery of conception as artistic or virginal: "I was born of flesh and ghost" and imagery identifying conception or visitation with birth, speaking of the double-crossing of the womb. He could, with his identifications, which I maintain find their unity in him as different facets of the artistic process, have spoken of a triple-crossing of the womb by the spirit: one in the visitation and incarnation, one in the birth or nativity, one in the pietà where the husk of spirit lies across the womb. Furthermore the poem uses imagery identifying members of a trinity of father, son and ghost, and relating them, as a number of his poems do, to an archetypal trinity of father, mother and child. For all of this it is unfortunately not a good poem, except as a virtuoso summary of themes touching Christian imagery as employed in Thomas's early work.

One other poem about genesis called "I Dreamed My Genesis" gives us a final theme of Christian image in relation to the nature of art, namely resurrection: "the second rise of the skeleton," as that poems speaks of it "and the robing of the naked ghost." This is also an early poem, but in some of his most mature, lasting beauties, "After the Funeral," "Poem in October," and "Poem on His Birthday," one sees the force of art as resurrecter and the meaning of the poems, each a kind of elegy, lies in this. Not only does one feel this recreative effect in the poems. It is also a part of the subject matter. The poem "After the Funeral" describes itself as a living monument: "this monumental/argument of the hewn voice, gesture and psalm."

The poem "On His Birthday" so far tries this resurrecting that though it begins in the fall (October) the last stanza extends to spring. The beautiful "Poem in October" gives us again "The true joy the long dead child," and we see that it is an elegy for a dead part of the poet. A student pointed out to me how this poem, which resurrects the dead boy in the poet, puts one in mind of a parable of the raising of the dead from the Old Testament: "And I *rose* in rainy autumn and *walked* abroad in a shower of all my days."

We have the impression that in some way every poem resurrects, giving long life magically to what is gone. Elegies give us again what we don't have and want. We know they are not for the dead. They are consolations for the living. Poems are resurrecting acts, recreative, saving or perhaps damning the members of the poet's own internal, mystical family, the parts and people he finds in himself, some of them really dead, such as the boy he once was or the mother he once had, all of them dead or below surface in him as relics of himself which he resurrects in his poems, putting them into relations of peace or violence he wants for them, though ultimately if we follow Thomas the poem itself is a peace, a paradise which delights and in which tensions are resolved and everything is changed into the beautiful and the lasting, into a promised land where the ark docks, where the cycle of time, a destructive thing for Thomas, is telescoped, and visitation, conception, nativity, Good Friday, are simultaneous with each other and issue at once in an Easter. For Thomas as I read him, the Christian images find their unity not only in the liturgical year and in the life of the Holy Family but also in every event of art.

Psychological Motifs in Melville's *Pierre*

(1967)

In Henry Murray's long, windy, repetitious, uneven introduction to *Pierre* (Hendricks House Edition), which itself reads like a nineteenth-century novel, occasionally brilliant, he sees Isabel as the Jungian "anima," the essential feminine image which every man finds within himself (its origin partly racial and partly individual) and the incarnation of which one seeks in a love object—a search which often leads to his destruction for the reason that, according to Jung, the feminine image in the man is a mirror image of himself, or, put more accurately, possesses opposite, complementary qualities; this is also the case with the corresponding "animus" or masculine image which the woman finds within herself. The "anima" image is related to the *other* side of the man, the shadow side, the destructive side, the side possessing forces which Freud would have called *thanatos.* Thus the person who embodies the "anima" or soul image of the man is often a femme fatale. One sees in the Jungian psychology a kind of built-in theory of tragedy in the relations between men and women: The man is compelled to seek his ideal feminine complement, as in the figure of Aristophanes' myth in Plato's *Symposium,* but this desired complement often embodies elements which in their oppositeness are destructive to the man.

To put the "anima" figure into a literary context around the character of Isabel, one would not be apt to think of Jung's own prime example, the "She" of Rider Haggard, because few serious people read that bad book. But we can think of the sirens of the ancient literature and of Kafka, the La Belle Dame Sans Merci of Keats, the Lorelei of Heine, and in recent fiction a few figures come easily to mind: the girl of Maugham's "Of Human Bondage" and of John Cheever's "Torch Song," and she of F. Scott Fitzgerald's "Winter Dreams," though in the latter cases the hero gets a good deal closer to the woman in question than he is usually allowed to do in literature, and in the last case (Fitzgerald's) the encounter is fatal not to the hero but only to the hero's happiness.

Another Jungian feature of Murray's analysis, which like the first may be read about abstractly in Jung's "Two Essays in Analytical Psychology," is his seeing Pierre's condemnation of others as exclusively a projection of the shadow side of himself—thus Pierre's incestuous inclinations are worse than the sexuality he condemns in his father; his deceptions exceed those of his father; his pride outdoes his mother's; his rationalizing exceeds Plinlimmons's; his heartlessness is worse than the cab driver's; he is more hostile to Glen than Glen is to him, etc., so that Pierre's negative vision of the world actually is a vision of the contents of his own unconscious. His hatred is primarily self-hatred and his suicide is consistent with this.

Murray makes direct connections between Pierre and his problems and Melville and his problems, finds counterparts in Melville's life for all of the main scenes and props of the book (including the fascinating Rock of Memnon) and for all of the main characters. Mrs. Glendinning is modeled on Melville's mother, whose wishes for upper class splendour are gratified by Melville in this book; Lucy is modeled on his wife (whom interestingly enough Pierre fails to marry in the book) and Isabel is modeled on his cousin, although some of her characteristics derive from those of his sister, who had the same name as the figure in a celebrated nineteenth-century incestuous affair, i.e., Augusta, the sister of Byron.

As clinical witness of Melville's own incestuous attachment

to his mother Murray cites the fact that on the birth of his son Melville committed the slip of signing the birth register with his own and his mother's name as parents.

Regarding what might be called the tragedy of Pierre, Murray offers several provocative epigrammatical renderings, the most satisfactory of which I find the following, "The tragedy of Pierre is that of illusion, in which eros is confused with agape." Pierre's feeling for Isabel is based more on masculine response than on charitable impulse, and given the truth of this it is nearly a direct assault upon his psyche for him to place himself in such an intimate relationship with her when he intends no consummation (or, indeed even if he does intend one).

Pierre is playing with fire, and at his first meeting with Isabel after his decision is made he extends to her a burnt hand, result of the first of his self-punishments. One of the fascinating psychological turns of the book not noted by Murray is this one, particularly in its connection with the attack on the portrait of his father, an assault which bears all the marks of a classical transformation of the Oedipus syndrome but involves a representation of a father rather than the father himself. What Pierre does is to murder the image of his father, his hatred reinforced by the energy of the love he had previously felt, after he discovers in himself an emotional attachment to the woman associated with that particular image. Pierre transfers his infantile attachment from his mother to his sister. The most positive side of his action so far as his own health is concerned is specifically that it frees him from the similar bond he has established with his mother, a bond which was more crippling because the incest barrier was greater and because he was the passive figure. The lessened barrier with his sister allows his erotic feeling to flow more unimpeded, and the embrace between the two after Pierre tells Isabel of his desire to be thought married to her is unmistakeable in its significance.

After all it is not an extraordinary path toward adulthood for a young man to allow his emotional loyalty for a sister near his own age to serve as transition between the infantile love of his mother and the mature love of a woman not a member of the family. But it can hardly work this way when one sets up a public image of marriage to the sister in question. On the contrary, as Pierre himself rightly understood, this action removed from the realm of forseeable possibility the idea of really marrying Lucy or anybody else. One may therefore consider whether this is not what he wanted, a desire more closely related to the frustration of eros than to the exercise of agape, despite the ingenious quality of his rationalization concerning the latter. The destruction of Pierre follows his choice.

Murray does not himself see the attachment between Pierre and Isabel as strongly incestuous for the reason that Pierre is moved by her before he knows who she is and falls in love with her without ever knowing her as a child so that the bond is not an infantile fixation. Good as this reason is psychologically (and even given the literary support which Murray does not himself adduce—namely the presence in the book of a powerful, longstanding brother-sister attachment which this one can be measured by, the relationship between Lucy and Fred) I still find Murray's argument weak here for the following reason: the reader in his unconscious makes no more distinction here than in the case of Oedipus who also did not know his mother in earlier life. The fact still remains that to the reader the relationship given literary treatment here is palpably incestuous. The degree of disguise present in the fact of earlier ignorance alone makes the situation bearable, paying concern to the reader's own unconscious anxieties so that he is not disgusted or struck with a quality of ugliness rather than of beauty.

Murray does not dwell sufficiently on one of the most striking examples of the true erotic investiture of Pierre's action as contrasted with his supposed charity—I refer to the series of assaults on the women who love him. With all the grace of Hamlet in his progress from the distracted Ophelia, caught in her chamber, to the distracted Gertrude, caught in hers, Pierre first sends Lucy into a dead faint, fallen against his chest, her heart fluttering weakly through her nightgown, then catapults his modest mother into a towering bedroom rage. As a result of his cruel action Lucy leaves him by fainting and his mother leaves him by ordering him off the place, two standard feminine reactions. The final inevitable assault is on the person of Isabel; this one cannot take place in the bedroom for the good reason that Pierre is himself in prison, but the veiled erotic character of it is seen from the description of Pierre "tearing her bosom loose" to gain the poison, that which he had himself predicted Isabel might bring into his life. Isabel leaves him by dying, and indeed all three of the women who had loved him now lie dead. As for Pierre, the milk from his mother's breast, which he had loved too long and too well, turns at last into the death he drains from his sister's breast. To the extent that Pierre confuses eros and agape he indeed lies to himself and so is justly charged by the two men, Glen and Fred.

Seeing these workings out of Pierre's tragedy, together with others which I shall shortly set forth, I nevertheless find the book to be primarily melodrama for the reason that Pierre undergoes no *anagnorisis,* no self-understanding which would raise his final moments from the purely destructive activity of the melodramatic hero to the finally constructive and cathartic action of the tragic hero. Pierre disintegrates the lives of a number of people, including his own. He destroys in the usual fashion of the hero every crippling bond of love which exists in his life—in the classical fashion of bringing about the death of the other individual involved in each case; this, however, does not free him to form a higher, healthy bond of love, whether with a woman (as in the case of Raskolnikov), a state (as in the case of Oedipus), or with God and the ghosts of his own dead, or the ghosts of his living charges left behind (as in the case of Hamlet).

Pierre shatters everything, with one exception: he has kept intact his own purity. "There shall be no marriages," Hamlet says. Again, we may ask whether this is not what Pierre really wanted. I judge the answer to be "yes" but with one qualification: one part of Pierre did want a relationship of tender love with a woman, a relationship which would lead to fatherhood. After all he did court Lucy, and we can sense the yearning behind his final remark to Isabel that her breasts cannot bear milk for his children. And we sense also the terrific masculine frustration behind the scenes of his deterioration where he is living celibately with *three* young women, one of whom (Delly) is known to be a lady of easy virtue, so to speak, while the two others both respond physically to him, Isabel, at first quiescent, coming alive in the presence of Lucy as though competing with her.

This situation with the three women in the apartment is clearly a punishing situation to Pierre; for this reason I want to pause over it a moment to play out one strain of the tragedy of Pierre which Murray stresses insufficiently, and which he partly misunderstands. I refer to the practice of self-damage in Pierre and its relation to homosexual conflict. Pierre gives the impression of having a terrific need for punishment, as though he were making some kind of atonement. This shows in his giving up Lucy in the first place, in his fantasizing about the danger of the Memnon rock as he crawls under it, in the burning of his hand, in his self-exile and self-impoverishment (he knows that he will lose his inheritance), in the sexually torturing situation in the city apartment, and in his own eventual suicide. It is he himself who makes himself in his own words a "neuter being"; that is, he castrates himself. Why?

I believe that the central issue here is not guilt over his own erotic nature; although that this is indeed present I have been at pains to point out. In other words, the incestuous themes are secondary to another one; even after his mother's death, Pierre's need to destroy himself cannot be arrested, although after that time he would be more free to form a conjugal relation with a girl without unconscious incestuous guilt. I also think that the homosexual issue is not the central one; although it is true that, as Murray points out, a conspicuous feature (Murray calls it the *most* conspicuous feature) of the deterioration of Pierre's personality is the homosexual component of his conflict, the normal shift from his boyish love of Glen Stanley to the adult love of a woman of his own age not having been successfully accomplished. The relationship of the homosexual component to the incestuous one is clear enough, for the retreat into homosexuality is a defense against the terrific incestuous guilt which a conjugal relation would set up.

In this connection one ought not to miss the significance of the proposal that Pierre spend his honeymoon (whether with Lucy or Isabel) in Glen Stanley's cottage. And Pierre's exclamation before he shoots Glen has more erotic overtones than almost any one of his speeches to the women: "Oh Glen! Oh Fred! Most fraternally do I leap to your rib-crushing hugs." It is also precisely at this point that the feature of self-damage emerges most strongly, and we see that the homosexual component as well as the incestuous one are secondary to this one. Pierre's open attack on Glen (one more case where a person who had loved him is attacked) in the city street leads directly to his imprisonment, and the attack on Isabel in prison willfully instruments his own death.

Pierre does not really seek either homosexual gratification or incestuous gratification in his actions. What he seeks is a self-damage, atonement. Again we ask, for what? What is his crime? In my opinion Pierre is atoning not for a crime at all, but for the fact of his anointing. Pierre is atoning for his own actual superiority as a writer, denying himself the natural human delights, paying for his gift. The intensity of his need for self-damage obviously parallels the actual adoption of his vocation as writer with its possibility, if he will allow it, of his becoming a giant among men. The inner meaning of the book is clarified in the dream of Enceladus, with whom Pierre identifies himself, at the end: The vision of oneself as a titan is tolerable only if one accepts the punishment of maiming. And if the titan cannot get others to maim him he must, in the modern phrase, do it himself. Suicide is the ultimate self-mutilation. Artists are famous for their suicides or early dyings, or self-mutilations. Keats, Shelley, Wilde, Van Gogh, Hart Crane, and Dylan Thomas come easily to mind. And there are some artists who allow themselves to remain alive only if they commit the partial suicide of killing the artistic power in themselves. Rimbaud who gave up his brilliant career at twenty and lived to be nearly forty is the clearest case in point.

It is worth asking whether Melville does not injure himself in the seat of his power after the truly magnificent, splendid achievement of *Moby Dick,* not because he had written himself out, which is easy to say, but because he had written too well. He had achieved more than a guilty man can allow himself to achieve. Looked at another way, perhaps Melville's own need to pay is lessened by the proxy payments of the Ahab side of himself and the Pierre side. Still I don't see how anyone can read *Pierre* without almost a sense of dying fall after the wealth of *Moby Dick*. At any rate what I want to emphasize is that the character of Pierre as hero, and Pierre's tragedy, is tied to the character of the artist as hero and to the artist's tragedy. The role of art is brought into the book not only through the writing motif, but also through painting—three portraits figure importantly; his father's, his own and an "unknown portrait" viewed with Isabel. The book belongs in the context of such autobiographical novels as those by Butler and Joyce and Thomas Wolfe. I will suggest one other direction of the conflict of the artist as hero which I believe is relevant to the reading of *Pierre* but which I will not here analyze; I refer to the competition between artistic creators and natural creators which is sometimes felt on both sides by artists and by women. In Bernard Shaw's "Man and Superman" we find the following statement: "There is no antagonism so great as that between the artist man and the mother woman." Perhaps this idea sheds further light on the apparent cruelty of our hero to the women in his life.

A Note on the Inarticulate as Hero

(1969)

*This essay is dedicated with love to my senior students
in Literary Criticism, 1963, for whom it was originally written.*

Reading Faulkner's *The Sound and the Fury* recently and finding
myself as stirred by it as the first time I read it, I found myself
wondering why it is we are so deeply moved by a figure who is
incapable of speech. I am thinking of course of Benjy whose
interior monologue we are given in the first section of the novel
and who reappears in crucial ways throughout the book. Now,
there are special reasons in the context of Faulkner why Ben-
jy's inarticulateness is important, if I read the book aright. But
at this time I want to get some perspective on him by consider-
ing Benjy in relation to a recurring figure in literature and
art—in an attempt to shed some light on the general emotional
resonance we find around such a figure. The total mute like
Benjy is surely very rare as a character in literature, though we
find him occasionally as in Carson McCullers's *The Heart is a
Lonely Hunter.* However, the partial mute or the simply inar-
ticulate character is not so rare. Here are six examples that
occur immediately: the hero of Poe's short story "The Man
Who Lost His Voice." Billy Budd, the stammerer in Melville's
novel named for him. The man with the injured tongue who is
the central figure of Joyce's short story "Grace." The Phi-

lomena figure of Greek mythology, of Ovid, and of Eliot's "Wasteland." The prophet in Ionesco's play *The Chairs*. The boy in Steinbeck's *A Flight* who at the conclusion of the story tries to speak but, because of his dying, thickened tongue, cannot. Six figures in films who are mute or partially mute also come to mind; one is the girl in an older film, *Johnny Belinda* (the part played powerfully by Jane Wyman), a mute and deaf girl who is brutally raped. A second female figure is the character representing Helen Keller in the film, *The Miracle Worker*, where the muteness is again combined with deafness. (I wish to emphasize that I am not speaking of Miss Keller herself and her problems but of the artistic figure made from her story who moved us so deeply as part of a drama.) Four other figures are males: one is a singer whose part was played by Frank Sinatra in the film *The Joker is Wild*. This man is attacked by vengeful hoodlums and his throat slashed so that he can no longer sing. He loses his voice totally for a time. Two others are characters in works by Ingmar Bergman: The Magician in the film of that name and one of the three rapists in *Virgin Spring*. The final one I wish to mention is the figure of the prizefighter played by Anthony Quinn in *Requiem for a Heavyweight*, who, like classical heroes generally, is made to suffer through the very thing he is excellent at, through his particular virtue: for this man partially loses his power of articulation as a result of blows to the voice box suffered in the ring, the place where he is a prince.

Now if one will assume with me that these figures have a peculiar power to move us in the art works of which they are a part, we ought to try to find out why, and indeed it is likely that there are different reasons for our being moved in the different works. It is hard to suppose, for example, that the magician and the rapist in Bergman's two films move us for the same reasons. But let us explore the material a little and see if there are any relations among them. Let us, that is, put ourselves in the position of students observing a teacher who is himself unsure of what he wants to say and is struggling (as I am at this moment) and who is therefore himself one of the types of the inarticulate—whether heroic or not in this case clearly remains to be seen. We remember that there is also a type of the inarticulate as buffoon, fit object for kicks in the behind. Let us see.

It seems to me we can begin here: There is a part in each of us which responds to the inarticulate for we are all throughout our lives somewhat in the position of Socrates' slave boy in *The Meno* who did not *know* and who therefore or for that very reason could not say—he became and we become articulate only as the result of prodding and response, as the result of willing ourselves away from the direction of the vegetable, which (or who) is the absolute inarticulate in some sense. The struggle to articulate, I mean, is related to the struggle to become educated, to *Paidea,* to use Werner Jaeger's title, which title reminds us that the central concept of education for the Platonist Greeks was the notion of being led outside oneself— being moved toward another state than that which one finds oneself in and toward the higher inarticulateness of ecstasy. Plato's esoteric doctrines, he tells us in his *Seventh Epistle,* are not to be found in his writings: they are present as flames in the minds of listeners fanned to brightness by the dialogues which themselves are thus seen necessarily to lack full articulation. The importance of effort and labor and discipline in the auditor is crucial here, and I feel sure that one of the reasons we respond to the partially inarticulate hero like the prizefighter I spoke of or Billy Budd or even the standard Marlon Brando mumbler is that we are all *born* mumblers, while only through trying and effort as Plato considered it, do we come to wisdom. The true inarticulate in Plato's *Meno* is not the ignorant slave boy but the facile Meno, who paradoxically has much speech, who has learned definitions and passed many examinations and taken, we feel sure, several degrees; Meno, who can repeat, but who finally strikes us like Polonius does as a figure of impotence despite his flow of words because his words are out of touch with his self.

A logorrhea or torrent of words of the kind released by many students in oral examinations or by many teachers as well as students in seminars or by many inferior poets in their work or by many preachers in their sermons or by the character of

Lucky in Beckett's *Waiting for Godot* strikes us not as a sign of power but as a sign of powerlessness, so that there is finally no very profound connection between inarticulateness and powerlessness, for the apparently articulate director of flows of words can strike us as equally powerless. The question is this: to what extent is the power of articulation in touch with the root of the man, with his own self—or to take a physical figure paraphrasing D. H. Lawrence, to what extent is a man's penis the instrument of his speech? Lawrence said in *Lady Chatterly's Lover* that unless a painter paints with his penis the work has failed. Lawrence believed the same for the writer or reader. Now, don't misunderstand me. I am not simply saying some reductive, psychoanalytical thing about the connections in the unconscious between semen and ink and between pens or brushes and phalluses and the equivalence of these to power, nor was Lawrence doing so. These things perhaps are true but they are half truths. They are heresies. Faulkner points up their heretical nature, the false equating of penis and power, by making Benjy in *The Sound and the Fury* both mute and castrated while at the same time allowing him power and righteousness and perceptivity of an almost godlike kind. He is thus contrasted to two other castrated figures: the hero, if one may call him that, of Hemingway's *The Sun Also Rises,* who lacks power, and Clifford Chatterly in Lawrence's novel whose outward, castrative war injury strikes one as an outward symbol of his actual inner powerlessness and inhumanity. Thus I am speaking now not so much about the organs themselves and their presence or absence; rather, I am speaking of the powers or spirits (in the ancient phrase of Galen, "the faculties") *behind* organs, and I am suggesting that as the flesh of the larynx (or Adam's apple as it is so perfectly called) is contiguous with the flesh of the arm and the abdomen and with the flesh of the genitals so the power or spirit behind the larynx is contiguous with the power or spirit behind the genital, behind the organ of the man as man or the woman as woman, so that a failure in one is felt as a failure in the other through the very integrity or spiritual (I prefer *personal*) unity of the human being. Now we seem much more willing to see the larynx as the organ which marks the man than to see the penis so, for the larynx houses the word, the word is sacred for it has been made flesh, and speech connected to the rational part of man is much more his mark than the penis, which is an instrument he shares with animals and its power a power he shares with them, we smugly say. In my opinion there is about as much sense to the idea that the human genital serves the same function as the genital of an animal (say the rabbit) as there is to the idea that the human voice box serves the same function as the voice box of the rabbit—who by the way is capable of an eerie scream that rakes the heart to the bone. Remember that a rabbit doesn't *care* about Billy Budd, Benjy, the injured prizefighter, or Poe's man who lost his voice or any of the castrated figures I mentioned— and not simply because he is unable to perform syllogisms. To say that a rabbit, or whatever, is an animal is simply to say that he possesses no organ of love *whatsoever* and at the same time no power of love. The thing which makes a man a man is his ability to love; if a man's reason is not in the service of his powers of love but is used to defend himself against love or on the other hand to commit offenses against it as in the calculated seduction scene which fails to take into account his person as a man and his partner's person as a woman, then his rationality is not a human rationality at all. Reason can be inhuman. Only love cannot be.

What has this to do with the inarticulate as hero? Precisely this: that which every man primarily wants to articulate is this very fact that he is first of all a lover. We feel such blows as the slashing of the vocal cords of the figure in Frank Sinatra's film or the raping of the girl in the Jane Wyman film, or such failures as Billy Budd's in Melville's story or that of the man who lost his voice in Poe's story very deeply not because of the universal fear of literal castration as some would hold but because these blows and failures strike us at the very heart of our own inarticulateness, the inarticulateness of ourselves as lovers, and thus they make us feel our boyishness. For who has uttered his love totally or succeeded in separating his love totally from hatred, ending the ambivalence of youth? The struggle of Anthony Quinn in *Requiem for a Heavyweight* to express his love for his girl or his feeling for his friend is simply symbolized by the injury to his voice box. The reality of his struggle goes far deeper and joins with the reality of our own isolation and of our own pathetic but, God willing, our increasingly successful attempts to turn ourselves further into lovers of our wives, of our girls, of our parents, of our students, of our friends. It is only to the extent that we can make ourselves lovers that we can make ourselves men, for the part that hates is the part that is not a man.

I must say this seems to me to be a religious idea, a religious interpretation of the fact that we are moved by inarticulate heroes. There is a further development of my interpretation which I also believe to be religious. It is this: Only when we have begun to make ourselves men through the articulation of our love (the step dealt with in the tragedies of the young—as of Hamlet or of Raskolnikov) can we then begin to make ourselves saints and seers and oracles (the step dealt with in the tragedies of the aged as of Lear and Oedipus at Colonnus). It is in this second stage, the stage of the superman or oracle (I prefer to call him saint) that we see the further positive meaning of our response to the inarticulate hero, for the utterance of an oracle, like the parables of Christ, is highly inarticulate, related to the sounds of the wind and to the keenings of the Greek choruses, except for him who in the words of the New Testament "has ears to hear." The greatest moment of articulation of the fullest man we find is a moment of silence. "The rest is silence," of the end of *Hamlet* is such a moment. There is another at the end of St. Thomas's work where he says that all he has done is as nothing and there is still another at the end of Wittgenstein's *Tractatus* where he says, "Wovon mann nicht sprechen kann daruber muss mann schweigen."* These silences are very different coming as they do at the *ends* of profound works. The silences at the *beginnings* of works are the ones of which we should beware. In the tenth book of his

---

*See footnote number one in Logan's essay, "On Poets and Poetry Today" in this book. —A. P., Jr.

Confessions Augustine says of the work he has done, "In sound it is silent; in affection it cries aloud." There is such a moment in the silent ecstasy of "St. Theresa in her wild lament" caught by Bernini, of St. Augustine in his loud repose caught brilliantly by Botticelli in a fresco over the inscription "St. Augustine so lived that he does not yet know he is dead." I am speaking of the unique moment of articulation or inarticulation—one hardly knows which to say—to which we are directed by the Bible: "Be still and know that I am God." The quiet of a saint or the obscure utterance of a seer, which is like an image of silence, is very different from the silence of Iago at the end of his tragedy. The saint shuts up so that he can hear better the ineffable Voice. Iago shuts up as a natural result of his own self-castration and so that he will not have to give an account of himself.

The first problem of a man is to learn how to utter his love, which is the articulation of himself as a person; the second problem is to learn how to shut up, which is the articulation of himself as a saint. Therefore both in the struggle to speak and in the active quietness of the inarticulate hero we see ourselves in depth, and we reaffirm our hope of change and we experience through them, these superb incompetents, what Nietzsche so beautifully called "metaphysical solace." It is these factors more than the factor of apparent loss of power (superficially real as it is) which moves us in these heroes. My proof is this: we are really more or less prepared to deal with the feeling of the loss of power or the lack of power, for we have been familiar with it since infancy and have lived with it as children who could not have what we wanted or as masturbating adolescents or as adult neurotics, so that it is a feeling which is not finally very moving—we are, that is, at home with it. However we are much less prepared (and much more afraid) to tap in ourselves the feelings related to our painful articulation of our human love or the speechlessness we feel in the presence of God. And it is these feelings, not those of the impotent boy but those of the powerful man and the oracular saint which the inarticulate hero calls into our minds and hearts and which he, through the art of his creator, articulates.

Poor, mute Benjy gives us our voice as poor, drunken, dead Faulkner gave Benjy his. I believe Faulkner himself is more closely identified with Benjy than with any other character, though all his characters come out of him, for the artist is an idiot, a mad man, the poet in Shakespeare's phrase lets his eyes "roll in a fine frenzy," and the word "nothing," in "A tale told by an idiot full of sound and fury signifying nothing," source of Faulkner's title, gains meaning as we see this and as we begin to reflect on the positive meanings of the concept of "nothing" like the positive meanings of the concept of silence. "Nothing" in this phrase as it applies to Faulkner's novel is I believe related to Stephen Daedalus's "Nothung!"—the oath he uttered as he struck the chandelier with his cane in the brothel scene of *Ulysses,* ending his hallucinations and his illusions, and freeing himself. For Stephen this apparently inarticulate noise, this ejaculation, was not an end to meaning. It was a beginning.

The Organ-Grinder and the Cockatoo
An Introduction to E. E. Cummings

(1970)

"Because only the truest things always are true because they can't be true." This is the meaning of the stars proffered by a Fourteenth Street organ-grinder's assistant, Mr. bowing Cockatoo, who presents "with his brutebeak / one fatal faded . . . piece/of pitiful paper." The fortune on the piece of paper offered by the bird in poem no. 25 of E. E. Cummings's *95 Poems* (1958) is as enigmatic as the message engraved on Keats's Grecian urn: "Beauty is truth, truth beauty,—that is all / Ye know on earth, and all ye need to know." It is enigmatic because it is written on the hidden heart, but must be read in the open eyes. Such reading requires the paradigms of love as well as those of language. The meaning of the cockatoo's remark is the meaning of the poem in which it is found. The nature of truth, the nature of art, the nature of love, and the paradox of the *via negativa*—all resonate about it. But the cockatoo is a figure of the poet, and the "pitiful paper" he offers is the whole meaning of the life's work of one of the most gifted and most prolific poets of our language.

Cummings published more than a dozen volumes of poetry between 1923 and his death in 1962. His monumental *Poems 1923–1954* (1954) contained more than six hundred poems and received a special mention from the National Book Awards Committee. It was followed by *95 Poems* and the posthumous *73 Poems* (1963). Their combined titles represent an odd, uninventive conclusion to a series of books whose art and fun usually began with the names Cummings selected for their spines. His first poems were called *Tulips and Chimneys* (1923), which meant girls and boys. Later, one met the algebraic poetics of *1 × 1* (1944) and *is 5* (1926), the first suggesting the multiplication which results in love as a product and the second suggesting the product of an extraordinary and inventive multiplication of 2 × 2. *No Thanks* (1935), said another of his books, speaking the name given it as a tribute to the fourteen publishers who had refused to bring it to birth and whom Cummings names vindictively in "dedication." *XAIPE!* (Rejoice!) commands the cover of his 1950 volume. In addition to these books of poems, Cummings published a novel of World War I, based on his experiences in a prison for technical offenders in France, *The Enormous Room* (1922); a journal of a visit to Russia, *Eimi* (1933); two plays, *Him* (1927) and *Santa Claus: A Morality* (1946); a collection of his drawings and paintings, *CIOPW* (1931); a collection of his six addresses given at Harvard University under the Charles Eliot Norton Professorship, *i: six nonlectures* (1953); and more. George Firmage's *E. E. Cummings, A Bibliography* (1964) lists twenty-eight titles or "persons" in the Cummings canon, and it is indeed proper from Cummings's point of view to think of these books as "persons." He said once in conversation that he hoped *Him* would exist in the way that people do and agreed with Rainer Maria Rilke that "works of art are of an infinite loneliness and with nothing to be so little reached as with criticism. Only love can grasp and hold and fairly judge them."

Thus, the long-laboring (grinding) musician of Cummings's poem is also a figure for the poet, and in presenting us with an oracular white cockatoo, the poet holds out to us himself. However, as the poem makes clear, the organ-grinder will not tap the creature's cage unless we ask him to. We seldom ask. I think it is because even if we understand this—that if we let him, the poet, gives us himself—still we may not understand the truth behind: that what the poet offers us is not so much himself (who cares, we may say), but by a self-transcendence, *ourselves.*

But nearly everyone cares about that. If we really knew the truth of this we would be more interested in poetry. One's first impulse is to think, "Nonsense. What mysticism! It can't be true. No one can give us ourselves." Well, let us agree. What I have said can't be true. Still, as Cummings writes, "the truest things always are true because they can't be true."

My father used to tell me that you have to take a Dutchman for what he means, not what he says. All poets are Dutchmen. Why can't you take a Dutchman for what he says? Because, my father insisted, "They can't speak splain for splutterin'." To shift the image, paraphrasing a Hindu poem, the poet is the lover who "utters senseless sounds out of the fever of his love." We have to listen to poetry with that little-known, almost vestigial organ, the inner inner ear (in contrast to the outer inner ear, known to anatomists, which is made of bones). I believe it was bequeathed to us by our prehuman ancestors, who perhaps were cockatoos. We ourselves are the faded pieces of "pitiful paper" they brought forth. Yet in us is the meaning of the stars! It is Hamlet's dilemma, the mystery of the creature crawling between heaven and earth. It is the puzzle of the Incarnation. There is sadness to it. There is grief and loss. Like the fortune seeker of Cummings's poem we weep, and Fourteenth Street disappears as our vision blurs. The organ-grinder vanishes. The cockatoo is gone. But not only are our eyes full of tears, our "tears are full of eyes," and in these many-surfaced mirrors we ourselves appear, gesturing perhaps with love, hatred, frustration, awe, praise. The poet, whom I have already described as Dutchman, lover, organ-grinder, and cockatoo, I now assert is one who weeps with tears full of eyes. Do I make him sound like a tragic hero? Well, it is true the organ-grinder is a "melancholy fellow." But when one of us says, "I want a fortune," he stops grinding, and he smiles. One of the refreshing things about Cummings is that so many of his poems are in the role of the organ-grinder *anticipating* that we shall ask him for our fortune. He is, therefore, a profoundly optimistic poet, more so than any other American poet of stature, and he is certainly the funniest poet who ever lived. But he laughs with tears in his eyes in his tears.

The gaunt, melancholy face, somewhat arrogant with the sense of a long labor well done, brilliantly transformed by a smile, was Cummings's own. He was personally a vivacious, quiet, charming, solemn, funny, serious man with the look of a gentle skull about him. He was bald, and the bones of his face were high and very symmetrical, set for the most part with a certain hauteur, which his wife, Marion Morehouse, has caught in a number of famous portraits. A man with an immense gift for story telling, Cummings was a total delight as a conversationalist, and his talk was formed both with an extraordinary comic gift and with a blessed compassion, which his nervous companion felt as the easing gesture of the great, of the natural nobleman. A Cummings tea was a memorable, cockle-warming human joy. Mrs. Cummings, gracious, startlingly young (she is a former fashion model), pouring at table—Cummings nimbly hopping about, alternately the seer and the pleased small boy, serving his guests cake and jam and brandy for their tea and telling his riotous stories, as of the 1929 Ford which he used to drive around his summer home in New Hampshire.

The Ford was one of Cummings's few concessions to our mad age. He felt that machines had destroyed man's sense of himself, had by some heartbreaking rhetoric usurped to themselves as objects the energies by which man was meant to relate to other human beings. Furthermore, in order to develop machines man had exalted the values of technology and science-making over those of feeling:

> (While you and i have lips and voices which
> are for kissing and to sing with
> who cares if some oneeyed son of a bitch
> invents an instrument to measure Spring with? (no. 23)[1]

---

1. Unless otherwise identified, the numbers I cite refer to *100 Selected Poems* (New York: Grove Press, 1959). Cummings himself made this remarkable selection, which includes work through *XAIPE!* (1950)— J. L.

Cummings did not own a TV or radio and would not use the telephone—although it was the Cummings home in Cambridge which sported the first telephone in that city! It is the kind of paradox one comes on again and again looking at the man and his work.

In that huge, three-story home which still stands on Irving Street in Cambridge, Massachusetts, Cummings was born on October 14, 1894. His father was a Unitarian minister and an instructor at Harvard, where the poet himself later took a master's degree in classics (prior to his war experience as an ambulance driver). Contrary to current fashion (Cummings was a rebellious fellow), he freely claimed to have had a happy childhood and to have loved *both* his parents. He has written a number of poems about both, including the famous elegy, "my father moved through dooms of love" (no. 62), which he included in every public reading. One of Cummings's poems for his mother placed her in "a heaven of blackred roses" (no. 31). Considering the number of roses in his poems, we may wonder whether Cummings was not trying to construct such a heaven himself—or perhaps to recreate the "garden of magnificent roses" which he tells us flourished beneath one window of his room.

In the first critical biography of Cummings, *E. E. Cummings, The Magic Maker* (1957), Charles Norman quotes a completely winning memoir of Cummings's childhood, written by his sister Elizabeth Qualey. Here we learn of the toolroom on the third floor where the children played, of the roof with a railing where the boy mounted a windlass for his box kite, and of the tree house built by himself and his father, complete with porch, bunk, stove, where he went to be alone and frequently in summers to spend the night. Mrs. Qualey tells of the local balloon man who came in the spring, to stay forever in one of Cummings's best-loved poems (no. 4), and of the circus whose animals and performers he never ceased writing of. We get in this memoir a glimpse of the spirit of the boy, Cummings, who, during a whooping-cough epidemic formed a Whoopers Club of which he was president and whose paper he edited! Members had to be veterans of the illness and were required to write stories. "We had badges and mottoes too," Mrs. Qualey writes, "and we all played together and had so much fun that children tried to get exposed to whooping cough so they could join." In the work, Norman quotes correspondence relevant to every major event in Cummings's career, his incarceration during World War I, the publication of his books, his appointment to the Charles Eliot Norton Professorship in 1952, his sad, hilarious, ironic part in the Boston Arts Festival in 1957, for which he originally wrote, but was not allowed to deliver, the strong poem for the Hungarian Revolution entitled "Thanksgiving (1956)"; it concludes with the lines

> so rah-rah-rah democracy
> let's all be as thankful as hell
> and bury the statue of liberty
> (because it begins to smell)

Norman publishes some magnificent photographs of Cummings's paintings, his work sheets, and of Cummings himself, the last series beginning in 1918 uniform and finishing with a marvelous photograph by Mrs. Cummings, taken at his house in the Village. Norman writes occasionally with verve, especially about the Village in the twenties and thirties and its legendary folk, such as Joe Gould, of whom Cummings drew a portrait in verse (no. 39). He writes always competently and *con amore*, telling the story of Cummings and his novels, plays, poems, painting. He shows intelligence and feeling about the poems, is a good defender on points where Cummings comes under fire. One is grateful for many aspects of the book and for the fact of celebration (long overdue) which its happy existence implies. But it is true that the words of the book which stick best are those of other people, and not only of Cummings: Pound's squib about Cummings's Russian diary, *Eimi;* Carl Sandburg and Marianne Moore on the *Collected Poems;* Cummings's sister's account of their childhood; Burton Rascoe's fine report on a chilly fall afternoon in Paris in 1924 when Cummings visited the Archibald MacLeish's.

But perhaps the best existing introduction to Cummings's

poetry is his own *i: six nonlectures*. Certainly one comes from it with a heightened respect for both the Cummings rhetoric and the poetry. One will not forget in reading the book that it is the work of one of the greatest lyric poets in our language; it is a master's examination of himself and his writing, done when he was over sixty years old. And this is the most exciting possible kind of book. It begins with a wonderful yarn about a child of remarkably loving, remarkably intelligent, and remarkably heroic parents. It tells of his education in "cerebral Cambridge" and "orchidaceous Somerville" (Massachusetts), and in the "little barbarous Greenwich perfumed fake," where he says he first breathed, and in Paris ("love rose in my heart like a sun and beauty blossomed in my life like a star"). It is the story of his first friends, such as Harvard's Professor Royce, his first books, and his first singing. In the last group of three lectures, since for the adult Cummings "The question 'Who am I' is answered by what I write," we are given his own selection of his poems and prose (largely from *XAIPE!, 1 × 1, Eimi, Him,* and *Santa Claus*) with his comments on them. The whole is supplemented, as were the last fifteen minutes of each of the "nonlectures" when they were given at Harvard, by his own selection of the poetry which has formed him.

The book, which is marked by the poetry of the inner inner ear, is also about it. It is about it because it is about self-transcendence, which is why it is called *i*. I suspect that it would also have been called *i* if it had been about selfishness, but this would be less accurate, and Cummings is, well, careful with words. As proof of both Cummings's care and preoccupation, he writes in the fifth of his six "nonlectures":

> Let us make no mistake: Him of the play so named is himself and nobody else—not even Me. But supposing Him to exemplify that mythical entity "the artist," we should go hugely astray in assuming that art was the only self-transcendence. Art is a mystery; all mysteries have their source in a mystery-of-mysteries who is love . . . nor could all poetry . . . begin to indicate the varieties of selfhood; and consequently of self-transcendence.

Later, to stress this self-transcendence, Cummings closes the "fifth lesson" with the great serpent scene from *Antony and Cleopatra* and the hymn to the blessed Virgin, composed by Dante to open the final canto of the *Divine Comedy* (I translate the first two verses to show Cummings's point):

> Virgin mother child of your son
> More low more high than any creature
> Fixed end toward which all plans run
>
> Your self transcended human nature
> So well its maker did not shun
> To take His self its shape and feature.

One may add little on the possibilities of selfhood in the high sense. However, we may note the connection between the notion of transcendence ("climbing over") oneself and the notion of ecstasy ("standing outside"); the one follows the other, and without both, there is neither love nor art. Thus Cummings gives us a sixth and final lesson whose subjects are "ecstasy and anguish, being and becoming; the immortality of the creative imagination and the indomitability of the human spirit."

Allied to this celebration of the individual human spirit are Cummings's apparent antipatriotism and his apparent anti-intellectualism, which are large themes of *i*. Both are signs of fundamental affirmations. The apparent antipatriotism is a goad to a higher notion of self than is usual, hence a goad, as well, to a higher sense of the ends of freedom. The apparent anti-intellectualism is basically an affirmation of the *mystery* of things which Cummings believes to be more compatible with "feeling" than with knowing, supposing the latter activity to be a kind of "measuring" that excludes love. At heart, the quarrels of Cummings are a resistance to the small minds of every kind, political, scientific, philosophical, and literary, who insist on limiting the real and the true to what they think they know or can respond to. As a preventive to this kind of limitation, Cummings is directly opposed to letting us rest in what we believe we know; and this is the key to the rhetorical function of his famous language.

Resisting every kind of compromise and scornful of literary tyranny, Cummings's work contains two kinds of purity, one of art and one of the heart. The first is signified by his heroic unconcern for tyrants (such as money, "Mostpeople," various isms, and the laws of inertia as they apply to literature); the second, by the constant compassion in what he makes. The two together have always distinguished him. Thus in his first book, *The Enormous Room,* one finds the language he invented, "The Zulu . . . shoulderless, unhurried body, velocity of a grasshopper, soul up under his arm-pits, mysteriously falling over the ownness of two feet, floating fish of his slimness half a bird. . . ." One also finds an immense compassion: such a book is, in fact, best understood as an incantation, I should like to say prayer, offered for persons he loved in the war—both in hope of their well-being and as a reparation in human art for those times of inhumanity when, as another of his "criminal" and confined friends wrote, "the hoar frost grip[s] thy tent." This compassion issues in his work in a direct, feeling fashion so that one has in him little sense of the dichotomy between the artist and his art—I mean that quality whereby one senses that he writes his poems in his own voice instead of adopting a series of masks. When masks are apparent in his poems, he is using them for portraiture and still maintaining his own point of focus for selection, as in the poems which begin "rain or hail / Sam done / the best he kin" (no. 78) and "next to of course god" (no. 24).

It is this characteristic of speaking with his own voice that has put off a number of critics who, following the obiter dicta of T. S. Eliot, are embarrassed by the idea that a poet has his own feelings and that it is these which appear in his writing. It has also led to the kind of statement one often reads, that Cummings has been saying the same thing in the same way since he started to write. This is quite false. For example, he abandons quite early the Poundian archaisms which give a poem like "Puella Mea" its remarkable and exquisite flavor. Again, there are poems in *No Thanks* which, like the stunning nos. 2, 9, 13, and 48 of that volume, employ a greater range of invention than those of any previous volume. And the last three volumes of *Poems 1923–1954* contain pieces more profound than anything he wrote earlier; among them, "hate blows a bubble of despair into" (no. 83), "one's not half two. It's two are halves of one:" (no. 74), "nothing false and possible is love" (no. 80), "my father moved through dooms of love" (no. 75), "no man, if men are gods; but if gods must" (no. 92), and "i thank You God for most this amazing" (no. 95). Reading these latter poems, one smiles at the term "charming," so often applied to his work, frequently as a technique of damning. Such a term does not touch the depth of these poems or the conjugal mystique of "somewhere i have never traveled, gladly beyond" (no. 35) or "o by the by" (no. 89) (which looks as though it is about kites). And even less does such a term meet the violence, the anger, the bawdiness, the bitterness of some of his most memorable work.

The other purity of Cummings's work, that of art, has put off still others who concentrate on the craftsmanship rather than on the feeling and find themselves irritated or puzzled or intimidated by the well-known Cummings experiments with syntax, spelling, and the appearance of the poem on the page. Early a rather remarkable hostility in academic circles against the work of Cummings set in, a feeling seen archetypically in R. P. Blackmur's never altered nor recanted condemnation of Cummings's work as involving a kind of "baby talk." Much of this hostility seems to me based on a deep-laid, partly superstitious resistance to what might be called the fracturing of the word. Some of it is based on the same inveterate taboo which D. H. Lawrence and James Joyce suffered under: the banning from serious writing of certain Anglo-Saxon expressions and a feeling against the literary portraiture of certain kinds of people, such as drunks (unless they can afford it), homosexuals (whom Cummings always portrays unsympathetically), and whores (who are usually portrayed sympathetically). Their biases, of course, are far less strong in our time than they were when Cummings's earlier books were appearing. Blackmur's study, which has so heavily influenced academic critics in this country, was based on Cummings's vocabulary, which is admittedly the least imaginative aspect of his work (coinages and composites aside). The freshness Cummings has brought into the language as such has come from the unexpected qualities he has turned up in common words by shifting their usual syntactical function and by introducing various classified (viz., tmesis and grammatical synthesis) but little analyzed practices into the language of poetry. Freud's analyses of the punnings, splittings, and composings in the language of dreams and jokes provide an insight into some of Cummings's effects, which to my knowledge no student has yet followed out.

As the figure in Marianne Moore's poem "Poetry" announces, "We do not admire what we cannot understand." Fortunately, the case for understanding Cummings has improved a great deal in recent years. The promise of earlier studies by people like Theodore Spencer and Horace Gregory has been reassuringly fulfilled in Norman Friedman's *E. E. Cummings: The Art of His Poetry* (1960), which has fine, lengthy expositions of Cummings's devices and their development in his work. He has begun to be studied seriously and at length as an inventor, and there is a growing literature of Cummings research. I need only add in this connection Friedman's second book on Cummings, *e. e. cummings: The Growth of a Writer* (1964), Robert Wagner's *The Poetry and Prose of E. E. Cummings* (1965), and S. V. Baum's edition of *Cummings and the Critics: Collection of Critical Articles* (1960).

Generally we may say that Cummings's typographical inventions are instruments for controlling the evocation of the poem in the mind of the reader; they are means of mitigating the temporal necessities of language with its falsification of the different, temporal rhythms of experience itself. Cummings is a painter, of course, and most of his poems are two things, auditory art and visual art, nonrepresentational pictures whose appearance on the page is essential to the artist's intention. (His correspondence with his publishers confirms this.) There is, typically, an intimate connection between the poem's appearance and the proper control of reading rate, emotional evocation, and aesthetic inflection. Indeed, one has the sense, reading these "picture poems" (his phrase) aloud, that one is translating inadequately from one language to another, with proportionate loss to the mere listener. This is an especially striking realization when one remembers that Cummings himself read his poems memorably, indeed read his own work better than any other living poet. One wonders what the greatness would be if he could hear in Cummings's voice what is added in the eye.

It is impossible, for example, to hear what happens in the first poem of *95 Poems*. This poem achieves a simple beauty, good as anything of its kind Cummings has done, when the word "loneliness" emerges, austerely, rending the heart, simultaneously with the slow appearance to consciousness of the phrase "a leaf falls," with which it intertwines or spirals round, or is spiraled round, leaflike, falling. This small work brings about an artistic happening unique to this poet:

                    l(a

                    le
                    af
                    fa

                    ll

                    s)
                    one
                    l

                    iness

One of the most gaining tour-de-force pieces which demonstrate the importance of the visual as a determining aspect in the reading of a poem is "r-p-o-p-h-e-s-s-a-g-r" (no. 13 in *No Thanks),* where the energy of the piece is coiled in the language so as to dramatize the leap of a grasshopper, a momentary thing. For the most part, Cummings did not choose "picture poems" for his *100 Selected Poems* (1959), but visual regulation is apparent in nos. 4, 6, 17, and 20.

The problem of bridging the gap between the time qualities of language and of experience is one of the oldest which the art of poetry has had to deal with. However, the idea that the poet has a right to use visible, printed (as well as the older, auditory) means to solve this problem comes hard to some, as does the solution of another general problem of poetry, its rhetoric: that of breaking up the usual patterns of response so that the poet may exercise some direction over the way in which his materials are received. The reader must not be allowed to bask in the ease of what he thinks he knows or feels lest he be denied the reality of the occurrence of a new poem. There is a certain destructive element which enters the technique of poetry at this point, aimed at dynamiting the cliché patterns of response. Cummings's orthographical and typographical inventions are his great lingual explosives. A reader must *react* to Cummings; he cannot dismiss him willy-nilly. It happens that one of the possible reactions is hostility, or perhaps more accurately, anxiety. One has the impression that a critic like Yvor Winters is simply made very uncomfortable by Cummings's work. I wonder if there does not operate in the response of such a critic the notion I mentioned before of language as fetish, with the setting up of taboos against tampering or touching. Cummings treats words as though they were objects which could be transplanted, split, caressed, injured, brought into existence or out of it—as though they were servants subject to the feeling and control of the master, who therefore emerges as a kind of genie of language, sometimes benevolent, but possibly dangerous.

Cummings, for the most part, does not employ shapes literally related to the sense of his poems (as did George Herbert in a number of fine poems) or symbolically related ones; rather he employs shapes we would be likely to call abstract, that is, nonrepresentational. Cummings's noteworthy alternate profession as a painter is as a *modern* painter; he would no more paint a Christmas tree with its commonly acknowledged shape than he would write a poem about a Christmas tree (he has such a poem) in that shape. Now, the choice of shape, among the poets interested in them for their poems, is relevant to the general ideas of shape in the visual art of the time. I don't know enough to say which art movements influenced Cummings most, dadaism, say, or surrealism, or cubism, or. . .? Though from what I have seen of his painting, I would suppose cubism had. In any case, I am concerned here with the aesthetic of his poems, not of his paintings, and that could well be different.

What I wish to note is equally true of the three modern movements I named: they share with the baroque (which so influenced Herbert) an interest in dissolving surfaces. Applied to poems, this means that they must not look as we *expect* poems to look. The aim, of course, is different in each case; the baroque wanted to transfigure, to analyze toward mathematical and theological infinity; it had a *positive* interest in the dissolution of surface. The dadaist had a *negative* interest; he wanted not to transfigure but to disenchant, to debunk, and the cubist to disorganize (though in the best only to reorganize more perfectly). The relevance of dadaism and cubism to Cummings's poetics goes far beyond the surface of his poems; one thinks of the disenchantment of the language of the American-English lyric accomplished by his many poems reproducing the speech of prostitutes and the various idioms of working-men, or one thinks of the positive perfections of verse he achieves out of fractured forms. But I wish to emphasize here that even so far as the *appearance* of the poem is directly concerned, it is not itself the end of the interest in shape for Cummings (as it was not for Herbert): rather the language of the poem is the end of this interest, as it must be for a poet—whether or not he is also a painter.

We have still a great deal to learn about just how Cummings uses appearances to serve the ends of language art, though some studies exist, as I have indicated; my own spotty investigation has led me to three conclusions. First, the typographical inventions are instruments for controlling the evocation of the poem in the mind of the reader; they are organic and essential where they are successful and are only ornamental and precious where either the poem or the reader fails. I emphasize that Cummings's techniques of punctuation, word breaking, and word placing are means of exorcising the temporal necessities of language with its falsification of the different temporal rhythms of experience; the latter rhythms are often quicker than those of language and may be doubled, occurring simultaneously or else in some kind of conflict, on the one hand, or reinforcing phase, on the other. This is a traditional problem, and it is especially great in lyric poetry, which cannot put to use the time lag of language in the way that epic poetry can. Rhyme, counterpoint techniques like alliteration, stanza periods, and other smaller or larger units of rhythmic control are all aids for solving the problem of the disparate times between language and experience; each of them was invented by somebody.

Second, the orthographical inventions—altered spellings, irregular use of lower case, and so on—are expansions of the ancient poetic method of connotation, where a single word is pressed for richness latent in it, but unrealized in the common spelling and appearance of it. Third, the grammatical inventions (or reintroductions such as the use of Latin word orders) are designed, some of them, to break up the usual patterns of response so that the reading *can be* brought under the control of the poet, allowing him to do his work (this is a rhetorical function shared to a certain extent by typographical and orthographical inventions as well); others of them are designed to bring that possibility into act. A prime problem in accomplishing the latter is (following Pound and Fenollosa) to secure the maximum number of active verbs and to place them most effectively within the period. One of Cummings's achievements has been to gain the *effect* of the active verb, with its closeness to elemental dynamic reality, in other parts of speech (thus: "disintegrat i o n" and "stic-ky" and "onetwothreefourfive"); and again, to make verbs themselves apparently more active (thus: "SpRiN,k,LiNg" and "kIss" and ".press" and "ex:ten:ded" and "swallow)s" and "stiffenS"). Many of the examples seem exceedingly simple; that is characteristic of discovery.

I have mentioned the rhetorical function of Cummings's language. Let me add again that each of the methods above acts rhetorically to prevent the reader from resting in what he thinks he knows and what he expects; without this, poetry would be impossible, and as humans become more and more self-consciously and self-satisfiedly "knowing," as more and more they "smash . . . why . . . into because" (no. 77), the means for bringing this about will have to be more and more radical. I should say that is a central meaning of Cummings's work. He himself has described the attempt to create a dynamic and moving expression, like that of life itself or laughter, in the following anecdote: In response to an inquiry about his understanding of his own method, Cummings said, "I can express it in fifteen words, by quoting THE ETERNAL QUESTION AND IMMORTAL ANSWER of burlesk, viz. 'Would you hit a woman with a child?—No, I'd hit her with a brick.' Like the burlesk comedian, I am abnormally fond of that precision which creates movement."

The precision goes with exacting labor. In this regard, Cummings once answered a high-school editor who wrote to him: "As for expressing nobody but yourself in words, that means working just a little harder than anybody who isn't a poet can possibly imagine. Why? because nothing is quite as easy as using words like somebody else. We all of us do exactly this nearly all the time—and whenever we do it we're not poets." Cummings has set himself so satisfactorily to the task of using words in his own way that he is a despair to all young poets who could learn from him. They can't use his ways in their own ways. It is mildly consoling to discover that Pound was using some of Cummings's ways before Cummings; but then one remembers Pound was doing things most of his contemporaries do, and before them—and one despairs again.

Illustrative of the effects of this hard-worked precision in Cummings's poetry are the impressions induced by "that melancholy," the poem about the organ-grinder and the cockatoo (no. 25 of *95 Poems*). First, we observe that the poem is written in what we may call free-verse stanzas, separated by single, free lines. To say that the blocks of verse are stanzas means they follow a certain pattern of regularity, which might be signified by a set number of metrical feet and/or a recurring rhyme pattern, but which here (as often with Cummings) is limited to a fixed number of lines—so that we may call the pattern free. The single, interspersed line brings to mind the refrain or repeated line of many traditional lyric forms, and therefore the overall visual *effect* of the poem on the page is that of a traditional stanzaic construction with a refrain. This effect is reinforced by the presence of full end rhyme in the first stanza (play / say). But the facts that the stanzas are free and that actually there is no pattern of rhyme throughout and that the single interspersed line is really a repeated one make the poem a departure from tradition; that is, the traditional surface appearance disappears on examination, a characteristic one associates with the baroque, or, when it is combined with a burlesque element, the dada.

We notice, too, how Cummings's punctuation works to add movement to the poem: a meaningful disregard of grammatical rules toward this end occurs in two or three places. First, Cummings's use of a period at the beginning of the second stanza serves to anticipate the sense of the line, a stopping of the hand organ, a silence. In the reality which the poem conjures, actually the stopping would follow immediately upon the statement, "I want a fortune." Omitting the grammatical period at the end of the previous line (which a reader would *not* take expressionally) allows Cummings to juxtapose this *feeling* of stopping in a dramatic fashion when he begins the next line with a period. (".At which (smiling) he stops:"). Thus the temporal sequence of actions in the fantasy of the poem (the utterance of the statement, followed by the stopping of the organ) is caught more realistically than would be the case if grammatical propriety were observed. Again, omitting the hyphen after the divided word "pick" in the second line of this same stanza draws attention away from the two-syllable nature of the *word* "picking" and, instead, places it on the immediate, simple, or so to speak "one-syllable" character of the *action* which the word signifies. Finally, the illegal insertion of commas between the letters of "taps" ("t,a,p,s") makes use of the tentative pause signified by a comma to simulate (again, I would like to say "dramatize") the action signified by the word.

There are two places in the poem where a final *s* is separated from a word at the end of the line to be placed at the beginning of the following line. A particular ghostly quality of attenuation or stringing out (hence, *thinning* in a line containing the expression "windthin") is the functional effect of this technique in the first instance. In the second, we have a rendering of the abrupt action signified by the word "tweaks" through emphasis of the *feeling* of tweaking by collapsing it, as it were, into the one final letter capitalized to accomplish this effect, as well as separated ("tweak / S"). The special intensity provided by the use of the capital distinguishes this usage (though it appears to be so similar) from the former instance, where attenuation rather than abruptness is achieved. The treatment of the word "slowly" in the fourth stanza shows us another creative use of capitals—one of Cummings's trademarks. Here it results in the expressional deceleration of the pace of reading by drawing attention to the spelling (or literal composition) of the word as opposed to its meaning, which one perceives rapidly. Breaking the word at its middle and including it in parentheses are further delaying techniques, which expedite (paradoxical expression here!) the feeling of slowness ("SlO / wLy").

When one considers how much energy is conserved beyond that which one expects to expend in reading, in order to reconstruct from inert words the dynamic qualities of action or feeling, one is prepared to appreciate why Cummings gives so much pleasure as a writer, even apart from his extraordinary wit. This additional energy which one (working from his earlier experience as a reader) is prepared to bring to the mental activity of reconstruction, but which remains unconsumed, becomes freed and escapes as a kind of smile, or perhaps, indeed, as explicit laughter. Cummings's technique thus may be analyzed as a special case of Freud's theory of humor which is stated in terms of the economy of energy. Much could be learned by applying some of Freud's discoveries about dream mechanism as well. For instance, it is clear that what Freud calls "synthesis" and "tmesis" are operating in the following cases, respectively: "sob-cries" and "dis(because my tears / are full of eyes)appears."

Two other practices of Cummings in this poem may be commented on. First, the contraction of the elements of "fellow will" into "fellow'll" accomplishes a musical gain around the assonant sounds (chol/low'll/til) in the first stanza. Second, the printing of the name "Polly" as "Paw lee" not only recreates the effect of the name spoken with a tentative and mournful emphasis but gains through a syllabic pun (Pol-Paw) an emotional richness around the senses of "father," which resonate about the figures both of the organ-grinder and of his oracular cockatoo, to whom the speaker comes for wisdom and guidance, seeking his "fortune."

A number of the poems in 95 *Poems* show Cummings in his most virtuoso mood and consequently at his most intellectual, most abstract. The statement of "n" (no. 53), for instance, separated from its spacings and word arrangements, is simply, "Note the old almost lady feebly hurling crumbs one by one at two three four five and six English sparrows." But the words of the statement are broken up and the letters regrouped successively according to an arithmetic pattern, which issues on the page—because of the way in which the numbers of letters, and hence the lengths of lines, vary—as two proportionate isosceles triangles, or a broken diamond.

In poem no. 53 of 95 *Poems* the principle of composition has to do with the counting of letters. In many others, a syllabic principle is employed: not only the classic decasyllabic or octosyllabic line, but often a line of four syllables is employed, as in the trivial poem no. 65 ("first robin the;") and no. 79 ("whippoorwill this") or the elegant and elaborate poem no. 44 ("—laughing to find") and no. 85 ("here pasture ends—"). As one of our most accomplished masters and adapters of the sonnet form, Cummings adds here several pieces, including the sweet religious lyric poem no. 76 ("these from my mother's great-grandmother's rosebush white") and the beautiful love sonnets no. 92 ["i carry your heart with me(i carry it in"] and no. 94 ("being to timelessness as it's to time,"). One of the sonnets (no. 42) contains the lines "mind without soul may blast some universe / to might have been, and stop ten thousand stars." One is reminded of his famous lines from an earlier poem, "I'd rather learn from one bird how to sing / than teach ten thousand stars how not to dance" (no. 54 of *Selected Poems*). Having seen somewhat through the mask of his anti-intellectuality (which is actually aimed at technology with its void of feeling), I doubt that Cummings really misses the role of the astronomer as separate choreographer to the stars or the role of the poet as singing master to the birds. What would the nightingale be without Ovid and Keats? Or the robin and whippoorwill without Cummings?

The mentality of Cummings not only takes us back to the Pythagoreans and their concern with the numerical roots of language; it takes us, more than that of any other American poet, forward to the Existentialists, with their concern for catching the quality of feeling in the subject as something of greater "authenticity" than the quality of intelligibility in the object. Cummings is a scientist of the affect, a doctor of the person. He also takes us immediately, more than any other American poet except Whitman, to the idiom and subject-matter concerns of the so-called beat generation poets. The beat generation is closer to the Village mode of Cummings than to the farming of Robert Frost, the insurance selling of Wallace Stevens, the librarianship of Marianne Moore, the doctoring of W. C. Williams, the banking and editing of Eliot, or whatever it was he did, of Pound. The celebration of the body in Cummings (in such a poem as "i like my body [no. 16]) is superior to that in the litanies of Allen Ginsberg (for example, "Footnote to *Howl*"). Cummings is the least Manichaean of all the good twentieth-century poets, English and American. At the same time, the vocabulary, power of shock, and apparent antipatriotism of such a poem as "i sing of Olaf glad and big" show him peer to the beat generation in these matters, and he is far their superior in craft.

Comparing him with members of his own generation, a golden age in poetry, one finds that Stevens is more genteel and gorgeous, Eliot more reflective and religious, Williams more perfect in eye and in cadence, Marianne Moore more scholarly and prettier, Pound more versatile and outrageous, Frost more violent and pastoral. But Cummings is the most provocative, the most humane, the most inventive, the funniest, and the least understood. When Yvor Winters wrote that Cummings "understands little about poetry," he missed the point. It is not Cummings's job to understand poetry; it's his job to write it; and it is up to the critics to understand and to derive whatever new machinery they need to talk about the poems; for Cummings—cockatoo, organ-grinder, lover—is himself a father whom a whole generation of poets have already taken to themselves. Hard as he is to imitate, he has led them naturally to look for their own voices. They know he has best described in *i: six nonlectures* the subjects of the poet as "ecstasy and anguish, being and becoming; the immortality of the creative imagination and the indomitability of the human spirit." He has also best described in "no man,if men are gods;but if gods must" (no. 76) the nature of the poet:

> fiend . . . angel . . .
> coward,clown,traitor,idiot,dreamer,beast—
>
> such was a poet and shall be and is
>
> —who'll solve the depths of horror to defend
> a sunbeam's architecture with his life:
> and carve immortal jungles of despair
> to hold a mountain's heartbeat in his hand.

In the last pages of *i: six nonlectures,* Cummings quotes Keats's "Ode on a Grecian Urn" with its enigmatic close which I cited earlier. In my opinion the enigma offered by Cummings's white cockatoo casts light on that given us by Keats's urn, and a second oracular utterance of Cummings illuminates both. Speaking to the creative side in each of us, he said: "Only the artist in yourselves is more truthful than the night."

On Poets and Poetry Today

(1971)

Poets and poetry today. Yes, but where is poetry itself? Or as Cummings might ask, "Who is poetry, anyway?" Poetry is existentially first among the great genres because, thinking of poetry as lyric contrasted to tragic or epic and agreeing with Yeats that out of our quarrels with ourselves we make poetry, we can say that this thing, poetry, is the expression in literature of the narrowest or first circle of encounter, the circle of one's self, whereas tragedy is the expression of encounter with the immediate community, the community of family, and the epic is the expression of encounter with the larger community of the nation or the race. Under this view the novel is a mixed form of poetry which may be primarily lyric as in Proust, primarily tragic as in Dostoevsky and Faulkner, or primarily epic as in Tolstoy. But given this manner of definition, with its increasingly large circles of encounter, one expects the larger circles to include the smaller, so that one anticipates in tragedy certain lyric moments (as in Claudius's monologue at prayer in *Hamlet*) and one expects in epic both the lyric moment (as in Achilles' soliloquy by the sea) as well as certain tragic figurings (as that of Achilles and Patroclus in the *Iliad*).

The question arises rather naturally why lyric poets die so young—i.e., why they do not survive to surmount tragic encounters and reach the larger circle of epic involvements (or, as we might say, political involvement): Keats, Shelley, Byron,

Hart Crane, Dylan Thomas, the latter remaining a little longer, Rimbaud a little less long, having abandoned as a teenager any powerful production of words and surviving only to write domestic or business letters.

I would like to expand my definitions in a different direction to include comedy in order to say what I think about it. There are two tragic moments allied to levels of personal maturity or (looked at from inside the hero) as rites of passage: the tragedy of the young man, of Hamlet or Oedipus Rex who moves from young manhood to maturity, and the tragedy of the older man, of Lear or Oedipus at Colonus (or in a certain reading of Willy Loman) who moves from maturity to sanctity or *superior* manhood. The first is a movement embracing life as the fulfillment of youth and the other is a movement embracing death as a fulfillment of life. Oedipus must leave Thebes in order to make himself available to other states. Christ must leave us locally, he says, in order to be really with us. Hamlet died for us.

Between these two tragic moments lies comedy, which is the moment of wedding, as in *Twelfth Night,* comedy par excellence, where three couples marry at the close or in *Ulysses* which ends with Molly Bloom's powerful yea-saying to the idea of renewed honeymoon. It is at the moment of wedding where the young tragic problem is solved: the encounter with the family is reconciled by our stepping out of the family we are born into in order to found our own. But this healing action involves love and love must be learned. The source of tragic conflict is ambivalence, and the problem of learning to love is the problem of learning to exorcise the ambivalence in one's relationship with another. Language enters the discussion at this point because we are all stutterers in the face of love; all of us then are country bumpkins who must learn to speak, to utter our love without ambivalence. Thus all of us, as poor lovers, identify with the mute or inarticulate heroes, the Benjys, the jongleurs, the lonely hunters of the heart. "We fog bound people are all stammerers," O'Neill says.

The final moment of inarticulation is the moment of silence, the moment of late tragedy, as the other inarticulation is the moment of young tragedy. In the later inarticulateness one hears this: "Be still and know that I am God." It is the silence of Hamlet (who moves so swiftly from the one tragic moment to the other, combining the acceptance of life with the acceptance of death) as opposed to the self-castrating silence of Iago. "*Wovon man nicht sprechen kann darüber müss man schweigen.*"[1] As distinct from these two moments of inarticulation, the very first such moment, of which I shall speak later, is that of infancy. To say a paradox: Man's inarticulations mark the joints in his life.

Now as it is practically impossible to rid ourselves utterly of ambivalence, so at the time of wedding we still stutter and the comedy is imperfect; thus tragicomedy is the most existential dramatic form, the one closest to the truth of the human situation, and Beckett knew acutely what he was about when he used this genre.

"I suppose the easiest part of the production of art is the suffering," I have written elsewhere. "Artists have not minded pain so long as they could keep it from killing them and get their work done: so long as the mad man, the beast and the angel Dylan Thomas found inside himself or the boy, the man and the woman James Joyce found in himself, did not crack the china skull in which they sprouted so dangerously together."[2]

But many poets have chosen death rather than to continue their work, and some poets (I have mentioned Rimbaud) have been able to survive only if they did not write but committed instead the symbolic castration of the murder of the gift, the excision of power in themselves. The trauma of continued life for a poet is, I believe, allied to the problem of continuing to build what we call "the body of work" a man forms. The word body ("corpus") is important. One of my colleagues at State University of New York[3] has found that Sylvia Plath's work shows a fantasy of building the body of the father, the Colossus

---

1. Wittgenstein, "Whereof man cannot speak of this he must remain silent." (All notes in this essay are by John Logan.)
2. See "Dylan Thomas and the Ark of Art" in this volume.
3. Murray Schwartz. The title of Sylvia Plath's first book of poems was *The Colossus*.

of her title—that her poems are fragments of this body and that her suicide coincides with the inability to continue such work. This exactly corroborates for the female poet what I have suggested for the male lyric poet: that he builds in his work the body of his mother—that he wishes to give birth to her as she has done for him. In building the body of the parent of the opposite sex through his work the poet establishes a sexual relationship with his own work and dramatizes at the lyric level (the battle with himself, that is) the tragic battle (the battle with the parent). Thus he plays out within himself the primal scene, one part of himself taking the feminine role another the masculine. It is because of this fact—that one forms a body with his poetry—that we must demand of poetry a surface of sensual beauty.[4] The poet must conjure the vision of the mother and he must make her sing to him (and, in narrative poetry, tell him "a story").

The fact that so many lyric poets die young, or, in Dante's phrase, "midway through life" (Hart Crane was nearly 33) suggests that they cannot duplicate in their work the lower half of the mother's body, the part that *takes* as well as giving with the upper part. A poet who survives may find himself like Yeats writing poetry which is more sexually oriented in his later years. I find it significant here that one's breaking into syntax, an advance which makes poetry possible, comes about rather suddenly as another acquaintance of mine has found,[5] in connection with attempts to deal with the separation from the mother before the age of one. Separated from the breast, the poet begins to rebuild that portion of the mother's body with the mouthing of his poetry, having already as a child rebuilt her face in another way into that of his dolls or his toy animals. But oftentimes the poet would rather die than face the sexuality of the mother (and hence, of the parents together), which keeps him separated from her in the tragic fashion. He chooses death over the tragic encounter, remain-

---

4. In my opinion the poets who most show this in my time are James Wright, Galway Kinnell, and Robert Bly.
5. David Bleich

ing a lyric poet, holding onto his melancholy for dear life, as it were, and falling far short of the true comic moment, the moment of wedding free of ambivalence [the wedding which on the other hand is so often also the wake (as in Shakespeare, Joyce, and Faulkner)].

This concern of the poet with the mother's body, as I see it, helps me to understand why the poetry of the New York School is so unfeeling. Whether Kenneth Koch writes about "The Pleasures of Peace" or whether he writes about "Sleeping with Women," all feeling is leveled, and one is left with brilliant ratiocination and with a bastard comedy which has somehow short-circuited the moment of the truly comic, the moment, I repeat, of wedding. Perhaps we laugh at this poetry for the same reason we laugh at jokes, because we are spared the expenditure of energy necessary to deal with anxieties roused by feelings, and this excess of energy can emerge in the smile. It is easy to see why Koch is such a great teacher of children. There is no body of the mother and no scene of the parents in New York School poetry and so this poetry shows its kinship with abstract painting, which it grew up with. Abstract painting has got rid of the human figure and thus got rid of erotic feeling, for Kenneth Clark has pointed out that there is erotic feeling present at the base of the use of the nude in painting. All figures painted (once undressed in the eyes of the beholder) lead to the nude and hence to the primal scene. The audience as voyeur is spared sexual anxiety in abstract painting. However, it is a self-defeating movement for, as Plato pointed out in the *Meno,* where there is color there shape goes also, and wherever there is shape, I add, there lurks finally (to "rorshock" us) the figure of the parent and its display in the primal scene. The figure finds its way back into pop art and pop poetry only through the elaboration of the child's comic strip (I now see "comic strip" as an unconscious pun) with its curious pointillist composition which visualizes the minute bullets the TV gun shoots us with to form its images. Or again pop art (should I call it mom art also?) elevates to totem status the baked goods and the cans of the kitchen or tubes of the bathroom and so uses figures which hide again the parents and their scene together.

As painting shows erotic concern at its root (a painter paints with the brush of his penis said D. H. Lawrence) so does poetry both at the fantasy level of the body of the work and also at the level of immediate presence, for in poetry there is always breath, the breath of the mouth, and behind it of moist, hidden organs, with their enactment of expulsions. To use an earlier myth, one might say that every breathing of a poem is an expulsion from the garden of Eden, which by the poem's content and by its ritual rhythms, its yearnings, tries to dramatize our return to that Garden. Here, however, I am more directly concerned with genital expulsion out of the mouth—I am more concerned with the displacement upwards from that "other mouth" which the man and woman know, and with the expelling itself, which, looked at from the masculine point of view, is ejaculation, while looked at from the feminine it is giving birth.[6]

The aggressive poetry of hatred, of warmongering or anti-warmongering, of racism or antiracism tries to hide behind the skirts of the poet's mouth to say that the poet is only masculine (and this whether the mouth speaks feminist content or not). I am not saying there is no place in poetry for militancy, the politically persuasive, the feminist or the masculinist. I am saying that what makes something *poetry* in the first place is its musical quarrel with the self, its lyricism. Without that there *is* no poetry though there may well be something else. David Ray once asked me to write a poem about the Hungarian Revolution and I told him all my poetry was about the Hungarian Revolution. "Out of our quarrels with others we make rhetoric," Yeats said. "And out of our quarrels with ourselves we make Poetry." "The spiritual combat," Rimbaud told us, "is more bloody than any human battle." And he should know for he died a slow death of it. Some poets brandish their swords to make us forget they are using words and that words are of the mouth, of the mother, and to make us forget that poetry is

---

6. As an image common to male and female, it might be seen as displaced anal activity.

learned first as a way of separating from the mother's breast, as a way of realizing, through the pain of weaning, the radical separateness, the identity indeed, of the self. So Robert Bly in his "Deep Image" poetry, as it is sometimes called, writes brilliant, strong poetry of the war (against it to be sure) as in "The Teeth Mother Naked at Last" but reminds us in discussion that the true job of the poet is to lead the masculine, aggressive function back a certain way toward the wings of the feminine function. (I may say here that I am mildly suspicious of how successful Bly's aesthetic is at exorcizing the aggressive element, for in an essay he speaks of "dipping down into the unconscious" when this active procedure can in fact scarcely work. One does not dip down into the unconscious, one finds a method of allowing it to well up into one's poem.)

To return, when I spoke of the poet's leading "the masculine aggressive function back a certain way toward the wings of the feminine function," I was not basically using a theatrical image, but I might do that: The poet comes out on the stage in the masculine light of day, under the sun, sometimes too much "I, the sun," indeed having emerged from the dark belly of Jonah's whale onto the shore or, in my present image, having just emerged from the wings. But he must return there, to the belly or the wings, in order to recoup and nourish himself so that he can nourish us, feed us bread, not stones.

Returning from the wings onto the stage, the poet may well lead his brothers, the members of his school, and one thinks first here of the school coming out of the shadow of Black Mountain. I may say that this celebration of brothers, too, is a way of short-circuiting the tragic encounter with the parents, with their primal scene and their judgmental function. One needn't deal with the parents if one keeps in touch primarily with the brothers. In so far as paternal figures are relevant for the Black Mountain group, they indeed seem more maternal or matriarchal than patriarchal, even though they be sexually male (Olson and Williams); for there is more concern in this group with its members being of the same earth than with a judgmental hierarchy of first and second sons or daughters. But I am particularly concerned here with the following fact:

In showing us what good brothers and sisters they are the Black Mountain poets deny the *fight* with the brothers. Now Melanie Klein in her analysis of youngsters has found that sibling battles dramatize the primal scene. The Black Mountain poets thus deny their involvement in that. I know that fraternity is more important, for instance, to Duncan than hierarchy, for when I wrote him in 1961 or 1962 at the time of the beginning of my poetry magazine *Choice* and asked him for poems (having stated that I did not believe in schools because schools tended to elevate lesser talents in the same swim and to ignore greater talents not in the same swim), Robert replied that he did not agree with the policy of printing the best wherever you could find it and thought it much more important to print members of a group. I also know that fraternity is very important not only to the Black Mountain poets as such but to the San Francisco beat poets as well, who constantly talk about one another in their poems and have their pictures taken and published together. The two schools often overlap and give readings or workshops together. I remember a wonderful quotation from Ginsberg who was being interviewed in San Francisco after he, Creeley, Levertov, and Duncan had given a workshop together in Vancouver. "Mr. Ginsberg," asked the interviewer, "I understand you and Miss Levertov and Mr. Duncan taught the craft of verse up at UBC in Vancouver." "No," said Ginsberg, "Denise and Robert and I did not teach the craft of verse. We were all emotionally bankrupt and went around weeping and asking our students for love."

He is right about that. We must love one another or die, said Auden, and before him a character in *Brothers Karamazov*. Poets say they want everybody to love everybody but they (we) mainly want you the audience to care about us, and so we do what we can to make you feel that we care about you. The poet is an anonymous lover, I believe, and his poetry is an anonymous reaching out, which occasionally becomes personal—when there are those present who care to listen. At the personal moment a mysterious thing happens which reminds us of magic, and hence of the power of Orpheus: the loneliness each of us feels locked inside his own skin, and the anonymous reaching each of us does, therefore, becomes a *bond* and hence we are neither alone nor anonymous in the same sense as we were before.

I for my part am a loner, not a member of a school. I want to help others discover their own voices in workshops and I want others upon hearing my work to hear their own voices echoing inside themselves.

Does this allow me to say I have escaped the flight from the primal scene somehow? That I have faced it and stood alone, having earned the right to wear a necklace of "the bad mother's" teeth, having come away from them unbidden and unbitten? Or that I have watched the primal scene untraumatized and have been enabled to move on without the support of sisters and brothers? I might wish it did, but in fact it does not, for in some ways I am jealous of the brotherhoods of poets, which do not number me among them. And as a loner reaching out to you the audience with the long penis of my tongue of poems, showering the sperm of my syllables (like the asperges of water of the priest or the rice thrown at weddings) and breathing on you with the passion of my warm breath, I have only recently learned to look at you as you are looking at me. (It is easier for me to imagine that I am an exhibitionist in the spotlight than that I am a voyeur, which is probably closer to the truth, wanting to peer into the curtained windows of your inmost heart to see what I may be fertilizing there.) In other words I too displace the battle of the primal scene and in still another way: for it takes place between you and me which is (in my terms) more tragic than lyric, for it is the displacement of relationships from my own parents and siblings, with whom I am not at ease. Why do we so much fear that primal scene? Why do poets go to such great lengths (my phrase) to displace, dramatize and (right word) *embody* it? Perhaps because otherwise we would have to see that we are gods: that we have the power and thus the responsibility to give life or to withhold it, to love or to murder, engender or destroy. Though this be true for poet and nonpoet alike, the poet feels it especially: for, unable to account for the gift he possesses, he has already begun to suspect for this other reason that he may be a god.

Such anointment, such mixed blessing brings special, powerful guilt. As I have said in another place and still deeply believe and repeat: "It's not the skeleton in the closet we are afraid of, it's the god."

Foreword to
Hart Crane's *White Buildings*

(1972)

In October 1925 Hart Crane wrote to one of his closest friends, the Cleveland painter William Sommer:

> I know you'll be glad to know that there is a good chance of my first book of poems, *White Buildings,* being published by next spring. In fact Boni and Liveright (at Waldo Frank's persuasion) have practically agreed to bring it out if Eugene O'Neill will consent to write a short foreword. They have lost so much money on the better kind of poetry (which simply doesn't sell these days) that they want to hook the book up with an illustrious name and catch the public that way as much as possible.

Publishing has not changed since that time as far as sales of "the better kind of poetry" are concerned. But the size of Hart Crane's audience has changed dramatically for the better and so has the magnitude of critical attention paid to him—there are some sixty pages of references to critical articles on Crane in David C. Clark's unpublished "Checklist of Hart Crane." How good and useful, then, to have Crane's beautiful first book available in a separate paperback edition. It is a book which he himself was to say contained perhaps his soundest work.

In fact, though O'Neill agreed to do the foreword (and at one time Crane was under the impression that he had finished it), he did not do it. The playwright was enthusiastic about the poetry, but he could not say why, not being "a critic of poetry."

Crane wrote his mother in late July of the following year that the book had indeed been accepted and that "None other than Allen Tate it seems is to write the foreword." He added that—through what seems to me an extraordinary act of generosity—deferring to the greater reputation of the playwright, Tate offered *his* foreword under the name of O'Neill. But Crane himself would not hear of this and ended his letter by saying that "my umbrage toward Allen is erased by the fidelity of his action, and I'm glad to have so discriminating an estimate as he will write of me." That "umbrage" had grown from the strain of the attempts of Crane and the Tates to share a house together, a strain which is perhaps caught most clearly in Tate's later statement that Crane "turned to his friends for the totally committed love, the disinterested *caritas,* that only one's family can sustain."

The first edition of *White Buildings* (the title was taken from a line of one of its poems, "Recitative") appeared in December 1926 with Tate's signed foreword, an apocalyptic epigraph from Rimbaud, whose work and aesthetics Crane so much admired, and a dedication to Waldo Frank, who not only had been his dear friend and correspondent for a long time but who had also done so much to help get these poems published.

It is an astonishing fact that in the *New York Times* obituary of Waldo Frank in the issue of January 10, 1967, there was not a single mention of the name of Hart Crane. Is it possible that the writer of the obituary found the name of Crane unsavoury and was being protective of Frank? There is no doubt that many teachers and readers of poetry found it so earlier—and even recently, as is indicated, for example, by the absurdly bad review of John Unterecker's superb ten year labor of love, *Voyager: A Life of Hart Crane* (1969), in *Poetry,* ironically one of Crane's earliest and most faithful publishers. The reviewer there wrote that moving through the story of Crane's life he felt "soiled by dark secrets which I'd rather not possess at all." This is a feeling that many have apparently shared. One of the reasons for this reaction is surely the fact that Crane was bisexual. Commonly thought to be a "straight" homosexual, Crane twice asked women to marry him, first Lorna Dietz and then Peggy Baird Cowley (formerly Mrs. Malcolm Cowley). At the time of his death Crane was engaged to the latter, deeply in love with her, as he wrote various friends, and had been living intimately with her in Mexico. Except for his relationship with Emil Opfer, the sailor Crane is in part writing about in "Voyages," his closest associations were not homosexual—in fact his dearest friends were for the most part married couples. He delighted in the company of women. Opfer himself was bisexual rather than homosexual and later married and raised a family. Crane tended to dislike the "gay" scene and wrote once after having left such a scene in California, "I never could stand too much falsetto, you know."

I dwell on this motif of *bi*sexuality in Crane's life and work, first, because the biographical fact of it in his case helps to account for the difficulty his poetry had in being accepted by an earlier generation, a difficulty which was compounded by an obscurity sometimes present in the language. This obscurity is due in part to the fact that Crane felt compelled to hide and/or to transform his sexuality in his language, and in part due to a then avant garde symbolist or surrealist mode of expression.

Second, I dwell on this motif because in *White Buildings*, more than in any other first-rate American poetry (the possible exception would be Whitman), there is so much to be learned—beneath, or through, the extraordinary beauty of the work—about the dynamics of human sexuality, particularly about the balancing of feminine and masculine aspects of the personality. This balancing is now increasingly recognized as part of a universal human need. Poets have always shown their awareness of bisexual feeling through creation myths like that of Plato's Aristophanes in the *Symposium,* through the embodiment of mythological figures such as the androgynous Tiresias, or indeed directly, as in Whitman's "self." Recent biology and depth psychology (most notably Jung) have tried to make clearer this implicit discovery of poetry.

I do not wish to suggest that either the biological or the psychological grounds of bisexual disposition have been discovered *since* Hart Crane wrote. They were of course known before (it's not clear, incidentally, whether Crane ever read either Freud or Jung). The general acceptance of them was slow because of the anxieties the knowledge of them rouses and because of the antisocial actions the conflicts generated by these anxieties sometimes lead to. We are now more open to the universal ground of bisexuality, and therefore to Hart Crane's work, and we can be more grateful for his expression, in some of the most moving poetry ever written in English, of the bisexual aspect of the interior life, particularly of its integration there. Not that this is the only or even the principal matter of Crane's work, but it is a too long neglected aspect.

Since there *is* a problem of balancing the masculine and the feminine elements in order to discover and develop one's own identity, there is usually a conflict. It is one which Crane felt painfully. Through his poetry, then, in Lionel Trilling's words, he "expresses the pain we all feel."

It is a conflict Crane finally felt tragically, for he committed suicide on his return from Mexico to be married in April 1932, at the end of a long period of vacillation. During a drunken night Crane apparently sought out men aboard the returning ship, and perhaps did so (the facts are unclear) when he missed (through her going to the wrong place) a meeting with his fiancée in Havana the previous day. He continually and drunkenly sought her out that afternoon and evening after their separate reboarding. Peggy Cowley, upset at his not meeting her and at Crane's drinking, and having suffered on her return to the ship a painful injury from exploding matches, had little patience with Crane. After finishing a huge breakfast on his final morning, Crane went to Peggy's cabin still in his pajamas, unshaven, dejected from his experiences of the night before, during which he had been beaten and robbed, and sat beside her on her berth. When she insisted that he get shaved and dressed (it was nearly noon), he left. He went to the stern deck rail of the ship, which he had been wrestled away from once the night before, already in despair. He carefully folded and placed on the deck the raincoat he had been wearing as a robe over his pajamas, balanced on the rail, leaped, and went to bed in the sea, waving once goodnight before he sank.

In 1926, as though praying that he might fight off the desire to end the pain of his conflict until he had finished more work, he wrote in the magnificent "Atlantis" section of what was to be *The Bridge:* "Hold thy floating singer late." The singer was held "floating" for a few years more; then, just three months short of age thirty-three, he sank.

Hart Crane balanced on the deck rail as he had tried to balance in his life and work. Unhappily, he failed in life. The poetry, however, is controlled by words as the medium of balance; and words, put together by the gift of the poet to make the architecture of poetry, find a higher realization beyond the drives and ambivalent feelings of the poet's unbalanced sexuality. It is this transcendence which we feel as beauty, and one of its characteristics, one of the gifts of art, is the momentary freedom from the kind of acute anxiety that eventually killed Hart Crane.

Looking for the masculine-feminine balance in the imagery of poems in *White Buildings,* we find two early works (1920) of special interest: "My Grandmother's Love Letters" and "Garden Abstract." The former was the first poem Crane was paid for (ten dollars), and he said this made him feel "literary." He also felt that it was a poem "in an entirely new vein," and he wrote of it, "I don't want to make the dear old lady too sweet or too naughty and balancing on the fine line between these two qualities is going to be fun." I think he means the problem of balancing an over-feminine quality, "sweetness," with an over-masculine one (because over-aggressive), "naughtiness." More to the point, it is clear that he identified the poem itself and his own personality with that of the grandmother figure.

Crane was living with his grandmother when he began his poem. To show the identification of the poem with his grandmother, there is his remark in a reply to Gorham Munson, "I enjoyed your letter with its encouragement to Grandma and am sending you a record of her behavior to date. She would get very fretful and peevish at times, and at other times hysterical and sentimental." He is speaking of the poem, not the woman. As for his identification with the person of the poem, it is made in the lovely finished version (italics mine):

> And I ask myself
> Are your fingers long enough to play
> Old keys that are but echoes:
> Is the silence strong enough
> To carry back the music to its source
> *And back to you again*
> *As though to her?*

The italicized phrase identifies the grandmother and the writer. I would add that the line "Are your fingers long enough to play" is a questioning about potency in the double sense of sexuality and poetry. Crane's beautiful poem answers affirmatively its own question.

There is a displacement, in Crane's poetry, of the language of the body to the language of the landscape (as in the phrase, "the loose girdle of soft rain"). Although such displacement (one kind of metaphor) is general in poetry, one might find a hint in the particular appearance of it in this "grandmother" poem that Hart Crane's overt homosexuality is in part a defense against admitting the physical feeling for the grandmother or surrogate mother. Certainly the male poet is concerned here with close feeling for the feminine, and perhaps personally with the homosexual aspect of his own bisexual feeling. He appears to believe he might want to share this feeling but that he should in fact hide it from his grandmother, or from the mother if the one can be taken as a figure for the other, for the poem concludes with the stanza,

> Yet I would lead my grandmother by the hand
> Through much of what she would not understand;
> And so I stumble. And the rain continues on the roof
> With such a sound of gently pitying laughter.

(It is worth remembering that Crane did later, rather disastrously, reveal his homosexual feelings to his mother.) In the concluding passage the word "stumble" (lose power) relates to the question "Are your fingers long enough?" (powerful enough). When one remembers the poet's identification with the grandmother one sees that he is carrying on a dialogue with himself about masculine-feminine polarity. The last line avoids self-pity and succeeds in achieving self-compassion. The poem itself does attain balance and thus allays anxiety—provides "catharsis" or what Dylan Thomas called "temporary peace."

"Garden Abstract," which Crane was working on at the same time, is directly pertinent to the theme of bisexual balance, because in it Crane changes the central figure of the poem from a masculine to a feminine one. The first line, "The apple on its bough is her desire," originally read "my desire." Of course it would be possible to argue that "my" represents the persona of a girl from the first. We would then be dealing with a feminine role assumed by the male poet. In earlier poems Crane more than once shifted from "my" to the feminine third person. At any rate Crane reworked the poem considerably, as he tells us in a letter to a friend who had criticized the earlier version as "phallic." The poem begins with a balance in the first two lines of a feminine image ("apple") against a masculine one ("sun") and speaks of the act of balancing ("suspension"). "The apple on its bough is her desire,—/Shining suspension, mimic of the sun." The word "mimic" therefore has the fascinating suggestion, which we will want to follow up, that the feminine is a metaphor for the masculine.

In the course of the poem the girl is transformed into a tree—in Crane's words, "She comes to dream herself the tree"—and therefore, having lost the sense of herself, "She has no memory, nor fear, nor hope/Beyond the grass and shadows at her feet." The loss of sense of self is ecstatic ("The wind possessing her"), and we discover ourselves in the presence of an archetypal masculine-feminine transformation which many poets have written about—Petrarch, Rilke, Yeats, Pound, and James Wright, among others—and which the poet Ovid speaks of in his story about the metamorphosis of Daphne. The tree is a sexual symbol that is ambiguous, depending on its context either masculine or feminine, for the trunk and bole of the tree together appear phallic, but its wood, material for making, and its fruitfulness suggest the feminine.

I believe that behind the impulse to write lies the attempt, for the male writer, to feel his way into the world of women, and very likely the reverse is true for the female writer. In his poetry, generally, Hart Crane has much to tell us about this. "Garden Abstract" is a poem about poetry itself, for the girl's (the poet's) voice becomes "dumbly articulate in the slant and rise/Of branch on branch above her . . ." The branches seen above form, as it were, figures for the alphabet, the writer's tool. Also behind the impulse to write is the wish to feel one's identification with nature, to end one's exile from it. That impulse is satisfied by this poem, with the girl's identification with the tree. There is no doubt that these two impulses (feeling one's way into the world of woman and feeling one's way into the world of nature) are connected in the unconscious/consciousness of the male writer, for after all woman, besides being person, is a part of nature.

Another poem in *White Buildings,* written two years later than "Grandmother" and "Garden Abstract," where apples appear again as feminine and in which feminine imagery is balanced again with masculine is "Sunday Morning Apples." The poem is dedicated to William Sommer and describes a painting of his. It was written, Crane says in a letter to Munson, "out of sheer joy," and it is possible that the last line, "The apples, Bill, the apples!" associates the masculine figure of the friend with that which is sexually attractive to the poet, and thus the feminine aspect also appears, for the word "Bill" can be either nominative of address or a word in apposition to "apples." The poem twice uses orgasmic adjectives, "bursting" and "explosion," the latter occurring just before the final line, and it is filled with balanced sexual imagery.

In the poem the female nude Sommers had drawn is first described with an adjective reminiscent of apples ("ripe"). "In that ripe nude with head reared/Into a realm of swords, her purple shadow/Bursting in the winter of the world." The feminine figure is associated with the masculine sword while "the purple shadow," which suggests pubic hair, is prefigured by the word "fleece" in the second line. The imagery is balanced too in the final stanza, where it is suggested that the apples be put "beside a pitcher [feminine] with a knife [masculine]."

This is also a poem about poetry, for it speaks of the sexual mystery together with the attempt to inquire into it as being at the source of art: "I have seen the apples that *toss you secrets /* Beloved apples of seasonable madness / That *feed your inquiries* with aerial wine." (Italics mine.) Furthermore, it identifies the painter's strength with that of the poet through the phrase "your rich and faithful strength of line." Finally, the poem speaks in simple diction and moves eloquently, dealing as well as any poem in *White Buildings* with the bisexual balancing I speak of, and it images this balancing itself in the phrase "straddling / Spontaneities that form their independent orbits." Incidentally, the imagery of whiteness is echoed in this poem as in two other poems I write of here, "Grandmother's Love Letters" and "Voyages."

The most ambitious poems in *White Buildings* are "For the Marriage of Faustus and Helen" and "Voyages." I consider the Voyage sequence the greatest achievement in the book and one of the transcendent glories of American literature, and I wish to conclude this foreword by speaking of it in connection with the motif of bisexual imagery.

Crane wrote his mother in late 1924, "I'm engaged in writing a series of six sea poems called 'Voyages' (they are also love poems)." We know that the primary figure of Crane's love in the poem was the Norwegian sailor Emil Opfer, of whom he wrote to Waldo Frank in a very moving letter:

> For many days, now, I have gone about quite dumb with something for which "happiness" must be too mild a term. At any rate, my aptitude for communication, such as it ever is!, has been limited to one person alone, and perhaps for the first time in my life (and I can only think that it is for the last, so far is my imagination from the conception of anything more profound and lovely than this love). I have wanted to write you more than once, but it will take many letters to let you know what I mean (for myself, at least) when I say that I have seen the Word made Flesh. I mean nothing less, and I know now that there is such a thing as indestructibility. In the deepest sense, where flesh became transformed through intensity of response to counter-response, where sex was beaten out, where a purity of joy was reached that included tears.

Yet it is essential to notice that although the concept of the "incarnate Word" is echoed twice in those six poems, once in "Voyages IV" (in those very terms) and once in "Voyages VI" ("the imaged Word"), Crane is *not* writing simply of homosexual love or of one person. This is not only because great poetry is *always* written out of deeper, more interior, and more universalized generalized feelings than those addressed to a given human being. (I am far from wanting to put down human relationships in comparison with art—on the contrary I hold them above art.) The gifted poet connects with the feelings of his anonymous audience because he is *not* primarily writing to one person exclusively in a limited, epistolary fashion—a form of writing which in fact produces *bad* poetry. What may be true is that the person in question serves to activate the muse in some way, though not in a *direct* way. For the muse is also interior and somehow always present as an aspect of the poet, whereas the figure who stirs the muse and begins the poem varies—may in fact be either masculine, as Emil Opfer, or feminine, as Crane's grandmother.

In the case of "Voyages" we can be sure that the poem is not simply addressed to Opfer, not only because it *is* great but also because of its chronology and imagery. I say chronology, since the original version of "Voyages I" was called "Poster" and was written and published before Crane met Opfer. Also, though there is no evidence that Opfer rejected Crane in fact, the final poem suggests, in the classical mode of great love poems, a rejection by the beloved, with a resignation and a turning to the solace of poetry and beauty: "the imaged word . . . It is the unbetrayable reply/Whose accent no farewell can know."

I refer to the poem's imagery, because although there is what might be taken as a strong strain of homosexual metaphor in "Voyages I" (for example, "Fondle your shells and sticks," which suggest the masculine genitalia) and in other poems of the sequence as well, still by the time of the meeting of the lovers in "Voyages V" we already know that the love referred to is not simply homosexual. "Voyages II" introduces clear feminine images: "Her vast undinal belly moonward bends," etc.; and "Voyages IV" ends with the line, "The secret oar and petals of *all* love" (italics mine), bisexual or both homosexual and heterosexual love. If one compares the image "oar and petals" of "Voyages V" to "shells and sticks" of "Voyages I" he may see the former also as an image of male genitalia, but it would be difficult to deny that "petals" is a word with strong feminine associations, balanced against the word "oar," and the sense of "all" is undeniable.

"Voyages VI" closes with feminine images such as "the petalled word," "the lounged goddess" and the line "Belle Isle, white echo of the oar!" If "oar" is masculine, its "echo" is feminine, as are the connotations of "Belle." Thus Crane's poem ends in the mood of "the eternal feminine" like some other great works of western literature such as "Faust," "Ulysses," and "The Sound and the Fury," but this "eternal feminine" mood gives what may be called "a generative, upward movement" (suggestive of the presence of its opposite) at the end of such works because it is integrated beautifully with "the eternal masculine."

The movement from the sexually masculine through the sexually feminine culminates in "Voyages" in something which, containing both, is higher than either. In Crane's words, "sex is beaten out." The achievement of balance between masculine and feminine imagery inside the poems of Crane is symbolic of the integration of masculine with feminine elements in the human personality and of the transcendence of sexuality. There is in such poetry a transformation of what is grounded in sexuality into something else which is perhaps best called spirituality, or in Rudolf Otto's term, used so effectively by Erik Erikson, "the numinous." Adult human experience thus realizes in a deeply fulfilling way, and at a higher level, the primal peace of the infant, who does not distinguish the sexually opposite father and mother.

Ezra Pound
An Appreciation

(1953/1972)

Except for the remarkably beautiful translation work of Paul Blackburn and the work of one or two other less well known poets and except for a few figures already coming to be of a generation no longer young, such as Basil Bunting, Kenneth Rexroth, Charles Olson, where direct influence is heavy and is honored, I suppose, by mutual acknowledgement between master and disciple, I would judge the feel of recent Poundian poetry to come more indirectly through Cummings, Moore, Williams, Eliot. And I would guess the reason for this to be that the later work of these four poets is more assimilated by the new poems than is the later work of Pound. (I am thinking of the *Cantos*.)

I think the new poets may fear for their sense of themselves, witnessing as they do the "Pound Phenomenon" which grows so huge, so ramified, so debilitatingly detailed—what with "The Pound Newsletter" and the university associated (Northwestern University) running analyses of the *Cantos*. And what with the Pound bookstore (actually called Make-it-New) in New York and the associated Pound publishings (The Square Dollar Series, etc.). What with the Pound cults in America and England (the latter around Peter Russell) where everything Pound ever wrote, whether on Confucius, Federal Reserve, Frobenius, or Cavalcanti, tries to sit (diatribe, study, or poem) side by side in the publishing lists. I do not deny the service of keeping in print the whole of Pound, but to tell the truth his greatest gifts lie only in certain directions. And finally, what with the disconcerting Pound orthodoxy, which so much adheres to the sacred canon of Poundian text in its criticism that it will not be interested for instance in a translation of *The Metamorphoses* beyond that of Golding (though it itself requires translation for modern readers) or a translation of the *Oedipus Rex* beyond that of Yeats (though that one is a severely cut adaptation for a particular production done without benefit of Greek) or a translation of *Divine Comedy* beyond Binyon or an *Iliad* beyond Rouse.

But when the Pound Phenomenon (is it a guilty conscience over his incarceration?) abates and tempers, when the Pound reputation is less prodigious and the Pound literature less encyclopedic, when there is a lull in the mining, monstering, and ballooning of the *Cantos,* when the Ph. Dentists have done cleaning, separating, and polishing the teeth of the *Cantos* with their burrs and their floss, then the new poets will no doubt assimilate these poems as they took to their hearts and guts and verses the earlier work in the days when Cummings, Eliot, Moore, and Williams were new.

For myself, the touchstone of occasional lines such as "If the hoar frost grip thy tent / Thou wilt give thanks when night is spent," or the Usura and Paquin passages of the *Cantos* have been of great importance to my sensibility, though it is difficult to say just how. Among the Pound practices, the use of alliteration and consonance as counterpoint techniques (masterful in the "Seafarer") and the double aspect of his diction—the occasional archaism and the more usual beauties of natural utterance—have moved me to try imitation. Among doctrines I have been helped (as who has not) by the Imagist manifesto and particularly by the Fenollosa-backed teaching on the verbalized language of poetry (as distinguished from the noun language of science), though I have been more directly instructed here by the practice of Cummings and Moore, who show one how to gain the effect of the active verb in other elements of the language, e.g., through enjambment technique. And it seems to me that the Pound doctrine of packing the maximum motion into the line has somehow missed the usefullness of inscapes (kinds of motion posited by Hopkins) built with adjectives. Thomas has been more helpful to us in this.

By way of noting a special kind of "influence," let me say that Pound has still a tremendous personal sway on the many people who visited him in Washington. I shall never forget the power of the man, the character of him as focus, in the couple of visits I paid to him at St. Elizabeth's in 1951. These visits are, as a friend of mine suggested, themselves like *Cantos*—where everything goes together: the particular St. Victor Pound loves, the particular Brooks Adams and the particular William James, the method of Agassiz, strawberries brought by friends to dip in sour cream, economics, Mrs. Pound amicable and reticent in her big hat coming each day from her room nearby and not yet liking poetry, Pound himself willing and centering and singing in his impossible voice some French arias from his unpublished opera on Villon.*

---

*This brief appreciation was originally written in 1953 (which explains some of the anachronism) in response to a request from an Italian magazine asking young American poets for their views on Ezra Pound's influence and reprinted in the U.S. on the occasion of Pound's death in 1972.—A. P., Jr.

On My Early Poems

(1976)

I

I'd like to tell the story of my early poetry and shall make references to my later work only where they fall naturally. When I was a senior premedical student (1943) at Coe College in Cedar Rapids, Iowa, I wrote two poems because I wanted to see my name in the student paper and because, honestly, I had some strong feelings I wanted to share—first, the sense of celebration and peace at having been accepted into the Navy and, second, rejection and solitude after having been sent home as a bad risk.[1] The poems were incredibly poor. I am punished for them by being condemned to remember how the first one began: "To travel out in winter time / When all is cleansed with white / While fade the brilliant hues of day / To solemn grays of night. . . ." The poem rhymed and metered.

A few years later (1947) when I was teaching at St. John's College in Annapolis, Maryland, I wrote a sonnet (the only one I ever worked on) which is blessedly lost, but of which I can remember that it took as epigraph some lines from the open-

---

1. I had been accepted at the induction center in Des Moines where I had gone to enlist but was sent home from Great Lakes Naval Training Station because of a slight colorblindness and a heart murmur. (Unless otherwise noted, all notes in this essay are by John Logan.)

ing of the Third Book of *The Iliad* where the noise of the losing Trojans as they prepare for battle is compared to the clamour of cranes and contrasted with the quiet gathering together of the Achaians. The sense of the destructiveness of noise I have carried with me along with the necessity of solitude for creative endeavor and for love. I remember reading in Schopenhauer that the noise of the crack of a whip in the street can abort the birth of a great thought. I translated a poem of Rilke's that spoke of noise inhibiting love, and I took to heart and memorized Dylan Thomas's lines on art, love, and solitude:

> In my craft or sullen art
> Exercised in the still night
> When only the moon rages
> And the lovers lie abed
> With all their griefs in their arms,
> I labor by singing light. . . .

Here is the Rilke poem which I translated and published as part of my "Homage to Rainer Maria Rilke" (in *The Zigzag Walk*):

> If it were quiet once—
> if the casual and the probable
> for once would cease their noise—
> and the neighbors' laughter!
> If the clamor of my senses
> did not so much
> disturb my long watch:
> then in a thousandfold thought
> I could think through to the very brink of you,
> possess you for at least
> the season of a smile,
> and as one gives thanks
> give you back again

The importance of Thomas came much later, but earlier both Homer and Rilke were very important to me, and I read them (haltingly) in their own languages—and, more relevantly for my development as a poet, I translated them into English. It was for my second book, *Ghosts of the Heart,* that I went to Homer and (with some cribbing from the Loeb classics edition) did a very free translation of the opening encounter between Agamemnon and Achilles, Book I, lines 1–351, for a poem I called "Achilles and the King: A Verse Re-telling."

Virgil was also important to me, both for theory of prosody and for subject matter. I was excited to discover in his poetry (through reading the research of W. F. Jackson Knight) that there was a functional counterpointing of the artificial rhythm set up by the verse ictus and the natural rhythm emanating from the flow of prose stress.[2] In my first book, *Cycle for Mother Cabrini,* I published a poem called "Lament for Misenus" based on my translation (this time with some "help" from C. Day Lewis) of an incident in Book VI of the *Aeneid* which, as it happened, provided perfect imagery for the elegy I wanted to write: Fred Miller, son of the head of the Miller Brewing Corporation, was my student at Notre Dame, and we were studying the *Aeneid* at the time he went home for Christmas (1954) leaving a paper on my desk. A few hours later he and his father were both killed in the crash of a small plane which they had boarded to go hunting together. I was very fond of Fred and was very upset by the death. I wanted to write something. As it happened, the assignment Fred's class had been given for their return to school was the section of *Aeneid* Book VI relating the death of the gifted warrior (a trumpeter) Misenus. Young Fred was in the ROTC, and he was gifted at his studies, so I thought

---

2. I got very interested in the complexity of language achieved by such counterpointing, and I wrote to Ezra Pound (whom I had visited at St. Elizabeth's Hospital) for help in finding such technique in English poetry, but he did not reply. (He *had* written me earlier to condemn a poem I had sent him—"Protest after a Dream.") Later I discovered on my own two examples of counterpointing in English, one, the practice of Shakespeare of using four prose accents in an iambic pentameter line and, two, the practice of Auden (imitating the Anglo-Saxon) of using three alliterated words in a four-stress line.

of him as a Misenus figure. Furthermore, the most anguishing things to me about his death—the fire in the plane and the burial beneath a snow-covered grave-stone—for me were given a beautiful transformation in the Misenus story, for Misenus is anointed by his friends and then laid tenderly upon a funeral bier set to flame by them, and he is buried at the foot of a snow-covered mountain.[3] Hence the poem:

Lament for Misenus

> . . . atque illi Misenum in litore sicco,
> ut venere, vident indigna morte peremptum,
> Misenum Aeoliden, quo non praestantior alter
> aere ciere viros Martemque accendere cantu.
>
> P. Vergili Maronis *Aeneid VI*

By the cold shore we came on
Aeolus' son who lay
Young *ai* who lay
Ruined by his smashed
And slivering horn and spear.
He was Hector's friend and fought
By him; we loved him first
As one to move and fire us
On this bended horn.

It may be he was young
And mad and sounded gods
To combat over the sea;
It may be Triton heard
His echoing horn in caves
Of stone or tombs and pale abandoned
Shells, and challenged him.
But Triton's is a rounder
Horn of the howling sea:

Ai here lies Aeolus' son
Come bury him in the wood;

---

3. Actually a promontory north of the Bay of Naples which would no doubt seldom see snow—but so it seemed to my poet's eye.

How use this rock for sorrow
These dried stars' arms this
Rigid face of the fish?
Axe now strike the ilex! Pitch
Trees fall quivering
Ashes cleave and the giant
Rowan trees roll from the hill!

We build his pyre with resined
Wood and the long firing
Oak that's interwove
With mourning boughs, and place
The funeral cypress. And last
Arrange on top the towering altar
His radiant arms,
That catch the glint of flames
Underneath the brazen kettles.

These limbs are cold to wash
With water from the fire. This oil
Anoints more durably than tears
This oil anoints more
Durably than tears.
Now lay him on the bier with purple
Cloths beside his coat;
And now this last melancholy
Office tops his pyre.

We turn our eyes aside to
Fix the funeral torch;
The incense burns, the gifts
And meats and chalices of olive oil.
At last the altar ashes
Fall and flames burn out; we pour
Much wine on the red embers.
And here the priest collects
The bones in a bronzed cask,

And walking round us thrice
Sprinkles us with white
Water as with dew he shook

From a branch of the lucky olive;
And says our farewell word.
We bury him, his spear his
Oar and his remembered horn
Beneath a snowy peak,
A massed a blue and airy

Tomb for Aeolus' son.

in memoriam F. C. M.
killed with his father
in a plane crash
17 December 1954

Other Latin authors I translated or (in the first case) used in translation were St. Athanasius, St. Augustine, Lucretius, and Pliny. Athanasius's *Life of St. Anthony of the Desert* was my source for my "A Short Life of the Hermit"; Augustine (mainly *Confessionum*), for "Prologue and Questions for St. Augustine" (which also uses Botticelli's portrait of him[4]); Lucretius, as I will describe in detail below, gave me the idea for "A Dialogue with La Mettrie"; and Pliny's *Naturalis Historia* for "A Pathological Case in Pliny."

I had been reading in Pliny in connection with my work as a tutor in biology (and Greek and Geometry and so-called Great Books) at St. John's College, and I came on the amazing story of a man who had killed three hundred enemies but could not be captured himself despite many forthright attempts. When at last his enemies did succeed in capturing him, they immediately threw him to the ground and opened his chest to examine his brave heart.

They found the heart covered with hair! The story engaged my feeling strongly and I translated it (again, with some help

---

4. The portrait of Augustine bears the remarkable inscription (in Latin): "St. Augustine so lived that he does not know he is dead." I was fascinated by the presence in the portrait (of Augustine in ecstasy) of various scientific instruments and mathematical books in the background and puzzled in the poem about their significance.

from the Loeb edition) and published it as one of the two first poems to appear in print since I had begun to take myself seriously as a poet—in *Partisan Review* for January–February 1953, when I had just turned thirty.

Two motifs have developed here, one, the influence of writers of other languages (classical and modern) on my work, and, another, the influence of my studies, particularly of biology, on my poetry. Let me first follow out the latter theme: That tale of Pliny's I actually used in a biology class, for we were studying Virchow's *Cellular Pathology,* and I found there a possible explanation for the astonishing phenomenon (true or legendary) reported by Pliny—the pathological growth, in the inner part of the body for which they were not intended, of cells of a certain type which do function normally in other parts. This visceral juxtaposition of substances foreign to each other is a recurring theme in my poetry. I remember being very moved in college by a passage from Thomas Mann's *Magic Mountain*[5] where, in an operation on one lung (to deflate it in connection with the treatment of tuberculosis) the meeting of the metal of the scalpel and the living flesh of the lung is described. This kind of juxtaposition I believe becomes generalized in my poetry into a feeling for a clash of textures, a kind of *collage* of things and also of types of language. An early poem where this clash or collage occurs in a specifically biological context (it describes the preparation of a frog for a laboratory) is this one, published in *Saturday Review* but not yet collected in a book:

The Preparation

While the class waited
I prepared the frog:

I had to hurry the needle
Through the handy opening
Just at the back of the head;

---

5. This consideration is also relevant to the question of the influence of modern writers on my work.

It slipped upon the skin
As on a plastic bag
For iceboxes, as on

A rind of ripe melon,
Then under urging
Entered to touch parts

Never meant for metal—
Causing one eye slightly
To drop from its accustomed

Plane, a cold nearly
Unmuscled leg to draw
Too far up the belly,

An almost imperceptible
Darkening of green
Along the back, in whose

Depression a small amount
Of blood collected, like ours
Red, and causing the mouth

White and inside moist
To stretch (but it was a rabbit
In his cage who

Screamed)
As the hour began.

I am also aware of the heavy influence of readings in biology on some other poems. I have been proud of my use of the anatomical (and musically beautiful) word "hyaline" in this passage from "Mother Cabrini Crosses the Andes:"[6]

_____

6. As a literary source for the events in Mother Cabrini's life I used two biographies, one by Theodore Maynard and another by Lucille Borden. Both books were bad and I got my impulse to write rather from reading *between* these other lines.

But there is nowhere mountain air
So cold or keen or bright or
Thin as is Francesca's wrist
Humming hyaline
Along the risen limb.

Two poems which use material from *The Source Book of Animal Biology*[7] are "The Experiment that Failed" in my book *Spring of the Thief* (where I use a description of an early blood transfusion experiment involving Pope Innocent VIII) and "A Dialogue with La Mettrie" in *Cycle for Mother Cabrini*. (Concerning this latter poem, it made me very proud as a thirty-three-year-old poet who had just published his first book [1955] to have so eminent a critic as Stanley Kunitz remark in his review in *Poetry* that the poem should be in any anthology hoping to represent current writing.) Beyond the sharing of feeling—or perhaps *through* the sharing of feeling, my object in this poem was to take some phrases of the eighteenth-century mechanist La Mettrie and to refute his philosophical position by repeating his own words from inside the framework of a poem.

The influence of classical languages and of science, especially biology, come together at this point, for in my close reading of passages of Lucretius's *De Rerum Natura* in Latin I became convinced there was a strong emotional undertone working in counterpoint against the intellectual statements of the poem, which gives an account of Empedocles' materialism. Surely it is meaningful, I thought, that one of the most horrifying accounts of death and dying in the history of Western literature is the last chapter of Lucretius, which is a description of the plague; yet Lucretius had "explained" why we need not fear death. Lucretius tells us he uses poetry to sugarcoat philosophy and make it palatable. This statement is made *in* the poem, so that it is subject to the feeling-tone of the whole work, and I would say, considering this, that in fact he uses poetry to *refute* Empedocles' atomic philosophy of materialism. If poetry is "mightier than the sword" it is also mightier than the prose

---

7. Edited by T. S. Hall.

statements it embodies. Poetry (and the creative expression of feeling) is a most difficult phenomenon to account for in atomic terms and, thus, Lucretius chose the least likely literary form to teach materialism. It is necessary to conclude that he was either a bad philosopher or a good poet. Reading him, one is overwhelmed by the truth of the second alternative. *The very presence of poetry is both a refutation of materialism and also a witness to some form of human transcendence.* I would never have realized this, a conclusion so important to my own stance as a poet, had I not discovered the dynamics of Lucretius's poetry: I applied it directly in my writing of the poem on La Mettrie (whose mechanism is a variant of Lucretius's, i.e., the materialism of Empedocles). My poem on La Mettrie ends thus:

> For to what do we look
> To purify his remarks, or purge
> His animal images? What
> Piece in us may be cut free
> Of the grievéd matter of La Mettrie,
> That underneath a temporal reeling
> *Took on this arch of feeling?*

The passage I wrote for the book jacket of this first book is relevant to my discussion, and (whatever else has changed) I would still repeat it. The last sentence is most to the point, but I will give the context:

> These poems are concerned with the Saints as heroes of the will and lovers, as incredibles. They treat myth, rememberings of childhood and anticipations of death as acts of spirit, good, bad, or trimming.[8] They reintroduce the superstition of ghosts and the lonely fallacy[9] of the lack of a natural place for man. These

---

8. This word is a coinage (I believe) from Dante's use of the word "trimmer" (meaning timeserver) to describe persons made to wander in Limbo because they followed changing winds of fashion in thought and act and were not worth condemning to Hell.

9. I.e., according to Aristotelian and Thomistic philosophy—Pico Mirandola (whom I much admire) to the contrary.

poems try to disprove materialism by coming into existence; and that is the extent of their apostolate.[10]

One can see that the influences on my early poetry came not from my contemporaries but from the living language of such long dead writers as Homer, Virgil, Augustine (and other devotional writers as St. Thomas, Athanasius, the translators of the King James Version and the Vulgate "Apocrypha," the Catholic novelist and essayist Sigrid Undset[11]), Dante and Shakespeare, who, I will acknowledge, took me out of biology into literature.[12] The recent poets who influenced me were not American but European and South American—Rilke, Rimbaud, Lorca, and Cavafy. Rilke gave me the original, strongest impulse toward writing; Rimbaud, Lorca, and Cavafy expanded irrevocably the horizons of what poetry could be and what it could say.

II

Let me go back to the story of how the poems started at St. John's College. I wrote that sonnet in 1947, the year I arrived there with my wife and my oldest son, and then shortly I began

---

10. I added this because I feared that, as a Catholic, I would be branded a "Catholic Poet," and thought of as using poetry to proselytize for the Church.

11. I should note here that somewhat later the Catholic philosophers Jacques Maritain and Gabriel Marcel and the Catholic novelist George Bernanos became important.

12. Shakespeare was the only literary course I took as an undergraduate. He worked in me, and I read further in English literature. When I graduated, deciding against medicine for financial and emotional reasons (I was afraid of the body!), I became a graduate student in zoology at Berkeley. Haunted by the new world of literature which had been opened to me, along about November (1943) I took my expensive scientific textbooks to a store on Telegraph Ave. and exchanged them for two leather bound volumes of verse—Keats and Shelley. I dropped out. In the fall of 1944 I began an M.A. in English at Iowa and read my first contemporary poetry with Austin Warren there.

to keep a kind of journal, two entries in which were prose poems I wrote sitting on the steps of Great Hall on the campus. These pieces were based as directly as I could make them (the "biologist" writing) on observation. One was about two trees at the back of the college. Their branches intertwined, and the leaves had fallen, and I was struck with the question of how difficult it was to tell whether those entangled limbs were alive or dead. I later published it in an issue of *Beloit Poetry Journal* dedicated to Robert Frost[13] because Frost had used a similar image in a poem (which, however, I had not seen before I wrote my own). Here it is:

Two Trees

> *"The tree has no leaves and may never have them again.*
> *We must wait til some months hence in the spring to know."*
>
> —Robert Frost

Two trees lose clothes of leaves
And light, uncovering their nice embrace:
Distinct trunks with one crown which moulds
Itself like a brain inside a skull
Of sky. The trees' rapture starts the breeze

And whips the talking wind. I joined the quiet,
Anxious men, who cannot comprehend
This age-long intercourse of trees
And who dread that secret spring when two
Trees' bones make the reach of limbs.

This was, so to speak, my "first" poem, because it was based on that earliest journal. But it was revised over a period of some ten years, and it was not my earliest publication of serious poetry. I have not collected it in a book. The second prose poem I spoke of was based on an observation of the changed relationship between trees, grass, and light after rain. I rewrote this one several times and published it twenty-five years

---

13. Chapbook 5 (1957).

later first in a magazine[14] and then in my book, *The Anonymous Lover,* under the title "Abstract Love Poem."

About 1950 (still at St. John's) I began to write poetry in earnest. So far as I can see there were four factors which came together to make this beginning possible. The first was the fact that students had learned I was interested in poetry and began to bring me their work to comment on. This intimidated me—I thought what the hell is the matter with me that I am not writing. I think particularly of the poetry of Robert Hazo (brother of the poet Samuel Hazo) who was my student and who later gave up poetry to become an associate of Mortimer Adler's Institute for Philosophical Research. Thus students have been involved with my work from the beginning, and in fact I have never felt the conflict between teaching and the writing of poetry which some speak of.

Secondly, I had begun work on a Ph.D. in philosophy,[15] taking night courses at Georgetown University, and I began to work up my German in connection with this. If one can see why I chose to pursue German by reading Rainer Maria Rilke rather than by reading Kant or Hegel, he may understand how it happened I became a poet instead of a philosopher. I chose to work at Rilke's early poems, because I could find no cribs for them. These are written in iambic pentameter, and thus I got a feel for this venerable line in English, and my own early line was written in it.[16] Rilke primed my pump to do my own work. I think (apart from the fact that translation got me actually writing lines of verse) this is because I found the translations

14. *Rapport* 1 (1971), edited by Tony Petrosky and Tim Burke.
15. I had finished an M.A. in English Literature at State University of Iowa in 1949. Although the Creative Writing Program was already in existence, I did no work with them, not yet being interested much in writing.
16. My own early work, including the first published poems, was in this metric, but I quickly abandoned it and wrote the whole of my first book in three stress lines, rewriting some pieces in order to accomplish this. I lost most of my first big fee (from *Poetry*) because I rewrote "Mother Cabrini Crosses the Andes" after acceptance.

deeply satisfying—partly because the labor was really hard for an unaccomplished student, partly because it is the nature of the German language to delay essential meaning, since the verb comes last, and partly because it is the nature of Rilke's poems to delay their own secrets because in the latter part of his poems he often changes key and expands the meaning of the whole poem beautifully.

Thirdly, there is the fact that I became a confirmed Catholic in 1950 and was rendered more sensitive to (and more self-conscious of) religious experience which I was moved to express and share. I read deeply in the writings of the church fathers and in the lives of the saints, and although I came to see later that some of this reading (and some of that writing) was defensive in character (against anxiety), there is no question that the Sacrament of Confirmation[17] was indispensable to the beginning of my writing and, indeed, to the production of my first three books, all written at Notre Dame where I taught from 1951–1963. Here is an example of a poem on a religious theme written first at St. John's in 1950 and then revised for inclusion in a longer poem ("Epilogue, Songs of the Spouses, Complaint of Love") in my second volume *Ghosts of the Heart:*[18]

> And others cry for you
> Melancholy
> Unicorn though your bright pen
> Keep you splendid in a field
> Of color where ev'ry flower
> Bends to you. Over-
> Whelmed by violence of scent,
> Struck with color, one fails almost

---

17. I had been baptized a Catholic in Hawaii in 1946.
18. The poem, based on a contemplation of no. 7 of the unicorn tapestries at The Cloisters in New York, was written at the same time as "A Chance Visit to Her Bones," part of *Cycle for Mother Cabrini,* for I had gone out to The Cloisters but by chance got off the A train a stop too early and found myself at Mother Cabrini High School, which houses the remains of the saint at her shrine.

To see where your white
Fur bleeds
Lanced with a formal strength
Strange to such a gentle one,
Such eyes! There is another
Hunt and another gentler
Hunter. There is another
Love and another holier lover.

The final factor involved in my beginning to write seriously
(and, by the way, I have found no way to place these four
factors in an order of importance) was that I was encountering
experiences in the summers of 1949 and 1950 that I could not
handle emotionally: I was working summers in a Maryland
State Hospital for insane blacks (we said "negroes" then). My
work and most of my colleagues' was largely custodial and was
totally inadequate to the suffering with which we were faced. I
turned to poetry as a kind of incantatory prayer for these
unfortunate people, feeling, as it were, unable to do anything
else for them. Of the first two poems I published (with Horace
Gregory's generous help) in *Partisan Review* in 1953, one was
the poem of literary allusion and heroism referred to above,
"A Pathological Case in Pliny" and the other was a poem of
direct experience about feeding an aged, blind, insane, tuber-
cular black. The poem was called "Contagious Ward." I wrote
about eight of these hospital poems in all and published some
of them in magazines but did not feel they fit in any of my
books. Here is one I was fairly well satisfied with:[19]

At Sundown a Slow Procession

At sundown a slow procession
Lurches up to bed. Some grin.
Some frown and form contortions,
Child-like. The faces of most
Are blank. None talk. They slump or

---

19. I cannot remember for sure if I published this in a magazine but it
may have been in Russell Kirk's *The Modern Age*.

Shuffle while others mince arth-
Ritic with age and inching
Painfully. One runs pell mell.

There are stragglers loathe to leave one
Vacant place for another.
Or wishing to breathe and bask
In the twilight air. One night
I saw a gnome move slowly
Through the gray half-light. He car-
Ried upon his back I thought
A lute, as the troubador

Goes sadly from beside his love.

 I wanted to speak of these very early poems because it needs to be noticed that I began writing poems out of direct experience (the unicorn poem is perhaps more removed because based on a work of art), but these I excluded from my early book because I didn't think them good enough or somehow they didn't seem to fit. There is one exception: I included "A Chance Visit to Her Bones," which was based on a *religious* experience. Other than this one, which is perhaps somewhat qualified by the description "religious," I did not use contemporary, adult experience for the poems in that first book, but instead wrote about saints and heroes (who, however, were very real to me) and about childhood. I returned to writing out of adult observation part way through *Ghosts of the Heart* after making an astonishing discovery through paying attention to my own writing. The discovery was that I was drawing smaller circles around myself, that I was getting closer to home. The saints and heroes and children of my first book had given way in the final poem of the book, I realized, to a (more human?) *near* saint and martyr, who happened also to be a *poet*, namely Blessed Robert Southwell. I can tell you that when I first read about Southwell, in a brief biography by Sigrid Undset, I knew I would ultimately have to write a poem about him—which happened months later.[20]

---

20. I was particularly suited to write about a martyr at the time for I was suffering from pleurisy and finding it difficult to breathe (live).

Now, in *Ghosts of the Heart* I noticed I was not only writing about *poets* such as Byron and Shelley, but I was also unmistakably writing poems about poets who had problems with their mothers: Rimbaud, Heine, Hart Crane; and I had even written a poem about a classical hero who had a problem with his mother, namely, Achilles. (My poem ends with his moaning for his mother's aid at the edge of the sea.) How much such a self-discovery was due to the fact that I had gone into analysis a few months before (late 1955) I can't say, but I can say it was such a startling revelation it stopped me completely for a while and I wrote fiction—about fifteen stories, twelve of them published—which concerned my adult, personal experience. However, I first wrote a poem in which I faced as clearly as I was able, my adult feeling about my mother's death ("On the Death of the Artist's Mother Thirty-Three Years Later"), for I had decided, after my recognition, that one could use poetry in one of two ways: either to *avoid* encountering the truth about oneself or to *seek* encounter with it, and I had decided on the latter move. It seemed to me that otherwise poetry would finally become boring. Here is the last stanza of that poem:

> She suffers there [in the grave] the natural turns;
> Her nests on nests of flesh
> Are spelt to that irrational end,
> The surd and faithful Change. And stays
> to gain the faultless stuff reversed
> From the numbers' trace at the Lasting Trump.
> So here my mother lies. I do not
> Resurrect again her restless
> Ghost out of my grievous memory:
> She waits the quiet hunt of saints.
> Or the ignorance of citizens of hell.
> *And here is laid her ophan child with his*
> *Imperfect poems and ardors, slim as sparklers.*[21]

---

21. This poem was written in February 1956. I made this further discovery years later looking back at the poem: I thought I had, so to speak, laid my mother's ghost, but instead I found, rereading the final line, that I had buried myself beside her. The fact that I was still to write more poems about her (and about my guilt, for she had died a

Then the stories intervened, and when I returned to poetry
my style was changed. It was more directly observational and
used the simple discipline of a ten-syllable line (altered from
the stress writing of my first book and of the earlier part of
Ghosts of the Heart). Here is an example of the changed style
written upon the occasion (never explained to me) of seeing
some old ladies at twilight in New York move down East Tenth
Street in a kind of parade carrying lighted lamps. The poem is
called:

New York Scene: May 1958

It is just getting dark as the rain stops.
He walks slow and looks, though he's late. It's all
Muted. It's like a stage. A tender light
In the street, a freshness. He wonders, a
Funeral?: at uncertain intervals,
Up the block, the corner, small, old women
Walk home with soft lamps, holding them with love
Like children before them in the May night.
A few people move down East 10th Street. They
Do not look at these ladies with their lights
Blowing in the rain-wet airs by the stores
Their ancient hands guarding their ancient flames.
Three boys race out of the YMCA
At the corner, carrying the brief god-
like gear of the runner. Two jackets hunch
Over two kids. There is high, choked laughter.
The third wears a sweater, black as his head
Lit with the wet. They sprint across the street,
And are gone into a tiny candy shop
Half underneath the walk. A dialogue
As the jackets and sweater cross leaves him
One clean phrase, "tomorrow again." He grins.
He turns, pauses by a store with small tools
Held in half spool boxes in the window,
With beads, clocks, one hand-turned coffee grinder

---

month after I was born) was confirmed by the first "Monologue of the
Son of Saul" and "Poem on his Birthday," both from *Spring of the Thief*.

And way in the back, a wooden Indian.
Now he stops a girl he feels he knows. He
Asks her where he's going, gives an address.
She teaches him, lifting her arm up, rais-
ing a breast inside her poplin raincoat.
He listens carelessly. He wants to see
The long, full hair that gives form to her scarf
Of a wine and golden colored woolen,
Some turns of it loose about her forehead
Like a child, some lengths of it falling at
Her back as she walks away, having smiled.

After my discovery and my decision to use poetry to en-
counter and explore immediate experience, and to share this, I
did not use reading and allusion and personae nearly as fre-
quently or fully as I had before—with one, large exception,
"Monologues of the Son of Saul" from my third book, *Spring of
the Thief*.[22] They were the earliest poems in the book,[23] and I
will conclude this discussion of my earlier work with some
notes about those sometimes difficult poems.

These poems are written in a thirteen-syllable line, which I
believe I invented, and which I came to partly from a desire to
experience more commitment to the line, so to speak, and
partly because I wanted to break up the somewhat cliché
rhythms set up by the ten-syllable line I had been using and
which a longer line, say, of fifteen syllables would tend to fall
back into.

Except for the first one, the five "Monologues of the Son of
Saul" are heavily allusive, dealing as they do both with the Saul
figure of the Old Testament and that of the New (later "Paul")
and with Odysseus as well, who in my treatment is identified
with the latter Saul through his wanderings in the same gener-
al area. As father to Odysseus and grandfather to Bellerophon

---

22. And of course the translations and the Melville poem from *The
Zigzag Walk*.
23. Joseph Bennett writing in the *Hudson Review* thought them the
best!

the poet, Sisyphus comes into view, and the final Monologue is conceived of as being voiced by him.

The death of King Saul and his sons together at the hands of the Philistines recalls Pyrrhus's murder of Priam and his son, which enables one to find another bridge to the Greek myths, and the fourth Monologue is virtually a retelling of the story of the death of Priam from *Aeneid* II. The starvation of Ugolino and his sons in the tower, as told by Dante in *The Inferno,* also comes to mind, and with it the ambivalent themes of the attack of the father on the son (or vice versa), which further recalls the story of David, Jonathan, and Saul ("Monologue II"). The counterpointed motif of the *salvation* of father by son or daughter brings with it the story of the young Roman girl Pero, who nursed her father when he was condemned to die of hunger, as told by Valerius Maximus and as painted by Peter Paul Rubens in his "Piété Filiale d'une Romaine." "Monologue III" deals with this and with related material taken from a modern tale of the saving of a dying father by his son and a compassionate girl: I mean the final scene of Steinbeck's *The Grapes of Wrath.* The first line of this monologue is quoted from that.

Some other examples in the Monologues of the blending of materials from several sources include the analogizing of the slaying of Goliath by David to the wounding of Polyphemus by Odysseus and the comparing of the accusation against Joseph (by the wife of Potiphar) to that against Bellerophon (by women of Greece).

The stories of Saul, David, and Jonathan, of David and the son of Jonathan, of Joseph and the Wife of Potiphar and that of Moses and Aaron of course come from the Old Testament, and I have made use also of modern commentators on these stories like Joseph Campbell. The story of Saul's conversion obviously is from the New Testament, while the stories of Polyphemus, Penelope, and Odysseus are in Homer. I used Robert Graves's version of the Greek myths dealing with Odysseus, Orpheus, Bellerophon, and Sisyphus as well as Camus's commentary on the latter.

The themes probed by the Monologues as a group as well as by the companion poem in part 1 of the book, "To a Young

Poet Who Fled," are the tragic ones of guilt within the family—or within a family surrogate relationship as that of teacher and student—and the creative ones of the metamorphosis or amelioration of guilt into art.

The movement from the usual contemporary voice of the speaker of these poems (as in "Monologue I") to that of an ancient Hebrew figure ("Monologue II") or that of a Greek ("Monologue V"), or the mixing of similar voices, seems justified by the universality of that community which is determined in the first place by the presence of family and in the second (perhaps consequent) place by human feeling. Without such a community there would be no impetus to the structuring and sharing of serious art. There would also be no need to mask or amplify one's own feeling under the names and situations of others nor, hence, to account for the fact in a note of this length.

Let me quote the poem following the Monologues because it is allied to them in theme and structure (it uses the thirteen-syllable line) and because it leaves us with an immediate, shared, adult experience, which is the place I had hoped my poetry would take us. The occasion of the poem was the fact that an unusually good student (his name is Tom O'Donnell) had gone home at the end of a term, having left on my desk a paper explaining why he was unable to write a paper on tragedy as he was supposed to do. The piece he left was so beautifully written that I took part of it out and published it as a prose poem in the first issue of my magazine *Choice*. Here is the poem:

To a Young Poet Who Fled

> *Your cries make us afraid, but we love your delicious music!*
> —Kierkegaard

So you said you'd go home to work on your father's farm.
We've talked of how it is the poet alone can touch
with words, but I would touch you with my hand, my lost son,
to say good-bye again. You left some work, and have gone.

You don't know what you mean. Oh, not to me as a son,
for I have others. Perhaps too many. I cannot
answer all the letters. If I seem to brag, I add
I know how to shatter an image of the father
(twice have tried to end the yearning of an orphan son,
but opened up in him, and in me, another wound).
No—I say this: you don't know the reason of your gift.
It's not the suffering. Others have that. The gift of tears
is the hope of saints, Monica again and Austin.
I mean the gift of the structure of a poet's jaw,
which makes the mask that's cut out of the flesh of his face
a megaphone—as with the goat clad Greeks—to ampli-
fy the light gestures of his soul toward the high stone seats.
The magic of the mouth that can melt to tears the rock
of hearts. I mean the wand of tongues that charms the exile
of listeners into a bond of brothers, breaking
down the lines of lead that separate a man from a
man, and the husbands from their wives, in these old, burned
    glass
panels of our lives. The poet's jaw has its tongue ripped
as Philomel, its lips split (and kissed beside the grave),
the jawbone patched and cracked with fists and then with the
    salve
of his fellows. If they make him bellow, like a slave
cooked inside the ancient, brass bull, still that small machine
inside its throat makes music for an emperor's guests
out of his cries. Thus his curse: the poet cannot weep
but with a public and musical grief, and he laughs
with the joys of others. Yet, when the lean blessings come,
they are sweet, and great. My son, I could not make
    your choice.
Let me take your hand. I am too old or young to say,
"I'd rather be a farmer in the hut, understood
by swine, than be a poet misunderstood by men."[24]

Buffalo, 30 October, 1974

---

24. When this poem appeared in *Spring of the Thief*, the word "guests"
(8 lines from the end) was singular and "farmer" (2 lines from the
end) was "swineherd." Mr. Logan has since made these changes.
(Noted by William Heyen, editor of *American Poets in 1976*, in which
this essay first appeared.) —A. P., Jr.

Going After Godot

(1962/1982)*

Some of the first suggestions that occur to one, while puzzling about the meaning of "Godot" as a figure, bring out ambiguities in the name as such which are relevant to my understanding of what is meant by *Waiting for Godot*—as idea and as drama. It is impossible to avoid a connotation of "God" in the name, since Samuel Beckett's primal language is English and the first three letters give us that word. Furthermore, the slightest knowledge of French, the original language of the play, gives *godet,* one of the variants on the name employed in the course of the play, as meaning "cup," "socket," or "gather, pucker" in the dressmaking sense, while *dot,* spelled by the last half of the word, means "dowry" in French. To wait for Godot is thus to wait for power (God) and to wait for a woman, preferably well-endowed. I wish to show that these two things waited for, i.e., these two hopes, are related to each other in the play and that the waiting in question is of a fundamental human and tragic kind. The speculation about the name "Godot" is, of course, only important if it relates to what goes on in the play.

Estragon is introduced pulling at his boot, panting. He tries and tries again, but cannot get it off. The boot, by its associa-

---

*Originally written in 1962, this essay was recently revised by John Logan and is being published here for the first time. —A. P., Jr.

tion with the foot and toes, is a phallic figure. The identification of boot with foot is made explicit by Vladimir when he says, "There's a man all over for you, blaming on his boots the faults of his feet." Furthermore, once Estragon gets the boot off he is then seen "pulling at his toes."

The phallic figure associated with Vladimir is the hat, in association with the head. Thus, there is sexual meaning to thought activity for the character of Vladimir and, characteristically when Estragon is seen "pulling at his toes," Vladimir is seen "deep in thought." Also the infirmity in Estragon, soreness in the feet and legs, is paralleled by intellectual defect in Vladimir, and Estragon is interested in, for instance, seeing Lucky dance while Vladimir wants to hear him think. When Estragon crosses the stage, he has a halting step, while at the same time Vladimir's head is bowed.

The specific identification of the boot-foot-toe of Estragon with the phallus is made in an important way which I wish to quote at some length. Vladimir says early in the play that the two of them should have jumped from the top of the Eiffel Tower when they were younger, but that now "they wouldn't even let us up." (A phallic expression I will return to.) Estragon is here given the stage direction, "tears at his boot." Vladimir next asks what Estragon is doing. "Taking off my boot," says Estragon, and he adds in language rather strange unless one sees the sexual meaning of the business, "Did that never happen to you?" (I would paraphrase, "Don't you ever get that way.") Vladimir affirms, "Boots must be taken off every day" (a reference to the recurring need for sexual activity). Estragon now says "(Feebly)", i.e., impotently, "Help me!" Vladimir: "It hurts?" Estragon: "Hurts, he wants to know if it hurts!" Vladimir then refers to his own "suffering," and the precise exchange just given between Vladimir and Estragon takes place in the opposite direction, Estragon being given the question and Vladimir the answer, both in the same words, "Hurts! He wants to know if it hurts!" Just here the specific turn is given to Vladimir's complaint, and through identity of language to Estragon's discomfort also: Estragon points to Vladimir's trouser fly and says, "You might button it all the same," i.e., "even if it hurts and although (I conjecture) it might find some kind of relief if exhibited." This passage should also be read in connection with the fact that Vladimir later admits to a urinary difficulty of long standing. Careful reading thus makes it clear that it is the phallus which is bothering Vladimir and his tragicomic difficulties are based in this.

The "help, it hurts" exclamation, uttered feebly, in context of burlesque patter is too obvious to need comment. The significant thing here is the presence of the identical complaint in Estragon and Vladimir, as well as the specific sexualizing of it by Estragon's pointing and his suggestion.

If we wish to know why Estragon's foot hurts, we are given an answer which enforces the phallic identification and at the same time puts the tragic theme into the traditional context of the problem of Oedipus: in response to Vladimir's question "How's your foot?" Estragon answers, "Visibly swelling." The association between Estragon's difficulty and that of Swellfoot the Tyrant is also emphasized by the following stage instructions: as Estragon plays with his boot, he is to stare "sightlessly before him." Furthermore, the wound on Estragon's leg is later described as festering. There are a number of exchanges where Vladimir directs Estragon to "show" his leg, a request which always requires stage business, and comment, having to do with Estragon's pants. The burlesquelike quality of the "help it hurts" dialogue and of this action, when it occurs, is united expertly to the tragic theme I see in the play, which is therefore aptly called a tragicomedy, ending as it does with Estragon uncertain whether his pants are down or up. I may say at this point that what is necessary, to see the inner meaning of the play, is to take the language as double entendre—as one would do in a burlesque show or in a dream—and to see what is built thematically at the second (double) level.

After this gloss on the nature of Estragon's complaint, his "panting, pulling off" business in the beginning action is seen as onanistic—i.e., as substitute for adult sexuality (which requires a certain power and also a cup or female, to return to connotations of "Godot"; these are being hoped for). Estragon's stage business with the boot throughout the play retains this hidden meaning: "peers inside it, feels about inside it, turns it upside down, shakes it," etc. The specific identification of Estragon's playing with his boot and Valdimir's playing with his hat is perfectly rendered through assigning to Vladimir precisely the same stage business with his hat, in the same terms and *in the same passage.* In addition, Vladimir is given the direction "puts it on again." A few lines later Vladimir tells Estragon to try to put his boot on again. There follows the passage already quoted about "blaming on the boots the faults of the feet."

Estragon, like Oedipus, limps. He has undergone some kind of figured castration from which he suffers as an impotent throughout the play and from which he hopes to be "saved" by Godot, suicide—by relevant means, to which I will return—serving as alternate expectation. The figured castration shows not only in his onanistic play and in the suggestion of homosexuality (Estragon to Vladimir: "You want me to pull off my trousers?", with similar patter common in burlesque, embracings between the two of them, etc.), but in its psychic character it is apparent also through the whole theme of inability to move, which lies at the heart of the play, and in the stifling laughter—risibility being one of the classic marks of the man as man. When he begins to laugh heartily, Estragon stops immediately, "his hand pressed to his pubis," his face contorted. Vladimir says, "One daren't even laugh anymore." Estragon replies in a phrase literally relevant to the understanding of this conflict which I am presenting, "Dreadful Privation." As will be seen, it is meaningful that only Pozzo laughs easily and openly.

As for the cause given in the play for this psychic impotence (the onanism-homosexuality theme is important in establishing that it is psychic and not physical) the expression "daren't" in "one daren't laugh" is a key, i.e., manly behavior rouses fear. There is a classic turn given to this anxiety on the opening page where Vladimir asks Estragon if "they" beat Estragon the previous night. "Certainly they did," Estragon answered. If we ask what Estragon was beaten for, it was because "His Highness spent the night . . . in a ditch." Thus the psychic castration from which Vladimir hopes to be delivered by Godot is related to fear of punishment for action seen as symbolically sexual. The vague "they" are also responsible, according to Vladimir, for him and Estragon not being "let up" anymore (into the Eiffel Tower). Who are "they?" In response to Vladimir's question about the beating, Estragon says he doesn't know if it was "the same lot" as before or not. The only clear clue we have in the play as to who "they" are comes from the discussion of what is expected of Godot. Some kind of supplication has been made to him, "A kind of prayer" as Estragon calls it (one thinks of the ultimate prayer "to rise again") about which Godot has indicated he has to consult others, namely, as Estragon and Vladimir say, "family, friends, agents, correspondents, books, bank account." It is the normal thing to consult these before "making a decision" the two of them decide (significantly one of the few things decided in this play, which like *Hamlet* is about inaction.) These things: family, authorities, moneyholders are the "they" whose reprisal is feared by Vladimir and Estragon and who paralyze them into impotence: eternal boyishness. At the conclusion of the dialogue in which they elaborate the list of things that must be consulted before their "favor" can be granted, Estragon says, "Where do we come in?" (i.e., where do we come). "Come in?" says Vladimir, "On our hands and knees," (i.e., we come only as babies do). "We've no rights any more?" asks Estragon. Valdimir now stifles a laugh as Estragon did (showing this mark of impotence is shared between them). "We got rid of them," he says. This is an indication (which I develop later) of the recognition of their own responsibility in their impotence, something which lifts the burlesque to the tragic. After this exchange the two of them are seen "motionless, arms dangling, heads sunk, sagging at the knees." The "heads sunk" business is properly Vladimir's and the "sagging at the knees" is Estragon's. But the two are given many identifying directions of this kind, meaningfully. In what follows they are described as "grotesquely rigid" (i.e., ineffectually or bizzarely erect). They "listen, huddled together" and they "relax and separate," part of the homosexual imagery.

There is an identification made, therefore, between "waiting for Godot" and receiving permission for some adult action, as though Vladimir and Estragon were boys. (Vladimir's pockets are filled with rubbish. Estragon has been a poet. They long for the happy days of childhood.) Presumably this permission would, among other things, free them to laugh, allow them to "get up" (into the tower), and let Vladimir spend "the night in a ditch" without reprisal. If they do any of these things (virtually one thing) when they "haven't the right," they will be criminals, thieves, as in fact Vladimir suggests they are.

Thus we find ourselves in the presence of the traditional, powerful themes of tragic literature, from *Prometheus* on, Prometheus having undergone symbolic castration (plucking out of liver while crucified on rock) for having stolen his father-brother's tool (fire)—having stolen his father's thunder as it were—which may be interpreted either as having castrated the father or as having cuckolded him through stealing his most precious possession (symbolic incest): it comes to the same crime, and for it he himself suffers castration according to the *lex talonis* with its demand of eye-for-an-eye or tooth-for-a-tooth—one castration for another.

I dwell on this because the *Prometheus Tied* ("Bound") and the *Oedipus Rex* (which dramatizes eye-for-an-eye as castration reprisal) are directly relevant to the glossing of *Waiting for Godot.* The Biblical thieves, like Prometheus, are crucified for their stealing activities. The theme of thievery is introduced early in "Godot" and in the context of the foot symbolism. It first appears after the stage direction "Estragon pulling at his toes," when Vladimir says "One of the thieves was saved." It is returned to on the following page when Vladimir, trying to remember what he was saying about the redeemed thief asks Estragon *instead,* "How's your foot?" When Estragon gives his reply already quoted, "swelling visibly," Vladimir remembers: "Ah yes, the two thieves." Estragon and Vladimir like Prometheus and the Biblical thieves are "tied," which has its own connotations of sterility as well as impotence. The discussion of being tied, in so far as Estragon and Vladimir concern themselves with the fact, follows directly on their speculation about the permission they hope to get from Godot.

It is the thieves theme, or the Prometheus theme as I would

call it, which introduces the theme of salvation in the play. Through Godot, Estragon and Vladimir hope to go to heaven rather than to hell, or to death, i.e., they hope to rise rather than to fall. For them Godot possesses this power or potency and thus the connotation "God" grows from the play, not merely from thinking about the name. It is Christ who is flanked by the two thieves in the image which the play refers to and it is Christ who, so to speak, in the context of the play, "lets one of the thieves up" with Him.

The sign of Godot, as of Christ, is a tree at whose base the vigil takes place. But in this play the tree of Godot, the foot of Estragon and the hat of Vladimir are to be read as phallic figures, being indeed among the commonest mentioned by Freud in his *Die Traumdeutung,* and here salvation means deliverance from impotence, the ability to have one's "bone" rise again and to remain risen (be in heaven), i.e., the ability to have and to maintain effectually the power of the man as man, without fear of reprisal.

Thus it is consistent that for Vladimir and Estragon the alternative to the hoped for appearance of the messiah Godot is hanging, which they say will bring about an erection (one thinks of Joyce's powerful use of this theme in *Ulysses*). This is the new method of suicide they anticipate, access to the phallic Eiffel Tower being blocked. The suggestion of an erection causes excitement in Estragon, but the real interest is not simply in that state itself—no true sign of potency (after all Estragon has had a swollen foot, etc.)—but rather in "all that follows," i.e., in the ejaculation of fruitful semen: "where it falls mandrakes grow," says Vladimir. The mandrake is a complex symbol of fertility, not only through being anciently used to promote conception, but (the use as drug is no doubt derived from this) through having a forked, or man-shaped, root, which is said to shriek like a baby when *pulled*. The mandrake is thus in the play a wishfully-fertile transformation of the onanistic symbolism and is related also to the vegetable phallus of the healthy carrot, which Estragon chooses over turnips or similar things, when he can get them. He (and Vladimir) are carrotless by the end of the first act.

What is desired by Vladimir and Estragon, thus, is sexual

potency. They look to Godot for this or will obtain it grotesquely by hanging themselves. Now what precisely is it they are waiting for Godot to do? Obscurely, to give them a certain permission. But more directly, they are simply waiting for Godot to *come,* a word with a meaning of its own in burlesque which is not to be missed here. Thus there is verbal play with the word "calm" as part of the burlesque patter: Estragon says "voluptuously)": "Calm . . . calm . . . the English say *cawm* (pause). You know the story of the Englishman in the brothel?" etc. Vladimir turns out to be made very uncomfortable by the joke, which has to do with, so to speak, the catholic offerings of the brothel (fair, dark, red-haired) and interrupts the banter in extreme distress. There is a complex relationship relevant to the theme of the play between the notion of "calm" or i.e., free of anxiety, peace, in heaven, and the implication of "cawm," come, sexual release. It is Vladimir whose repression is too insufficient to allow him to enjoy the wit of the joke and it is he who recognizes (and consequently, one is tempted to say, is aware of the connections between lessened repression and self-knowledge) his own responsibility for his impotence.

What do Estragon and Vladimir do while waiting? They do their exercises for the "coming": "movements . . . elevations . . . relaxations . . . elongations . . . to warm us up . . . to calm us down . . . off we go." Ironically, the "off we go" involves a kind of dance in which the two of them hop from one foot to the other—a hopscotch with complex implications of infantile game (possibly more girlish than boyish even), sexual longing (hopping), being crippled (Estragon), and with implied denial of the nature of man similar to the absence of risibility, for man is a biped.

Now it is not clear how Godot's "coming" would give Vladimir and Estragon what they want, unless the redemptive activity of Godot implied some sort of identification between them and him. I think this is the case. Short of seeing an actual identification between Godot and the two heroes, one has to settle for Godot's coming as simply implying permissiveness, but that is not very satisfactory as it is not strictly *permission* that the two want (with implication of being "tied"); they want to be like Godot himself. *They want to come too.*

I see in the play an identification first between Estragon and Vladimir, the two heroes made into one, and I see an identification of that composite hero with Godot, who thus appears as an aspect of the one hero. These equations come about in the following way in the play: First, Estragon and Vladimir are related intimately through being assigned a number of identical stage directions and a number of identical lines, including key ones such as "I'm going." "There's nothing to be done." "Help. It hurts!" They also embrace and are unable to exist separately. However, Valdimir can get along better without Estragon than vice versa. This suggests a qualitative difference between them, which is born out when we notice that Estragon, whose sign is the lower part (foot), is always hungry (relevantly he likes carrots but especially craves "a bone") and at the same time he is dependent on Vladimir, whose sign is the higher part (head) and who is, so to speak, the part that shows some self-knowledge. We have already noted that Vladimir's impairment takes on primarily, but not exclusively, a mental form, while in Estragon it is physical; and Estragon is hard put to do the thinking when Vladimir fails at it, as in the decision about which one shall hang himself first. Estragon becomes angry, "Use your head, can't you?" he says to Vladimir and is himself described as thinking "with effort." These differences suggest a dichotomy between Estragon and Vladimir, like body and mind, or better, like id and ego. Estragon has been the poet. That is, he is characterized, so to speak, by primary process or infantile thinking, whereas Vladimir shows the "intelligence" of secondary process or ego-thinking. At the same time, Estragon's insatiable "hunger" signifies the id. Vladimir is more responsible and more the leader of the two. Without him, as ego might say to id, Vladimir says to Estragon, "you'd be nothing more than a little heap of bones at the present minute, no doubt about it." "Bones" again ambiguous—he might as well have said "a mass of swollen toes." This identification places the apparently homosexual business between them and their talk of honeymooning on the Dead Sea (a "low" romance to be sure in more ways than one) in a different light, while it retains the significance I have already assigned to it at another level. A straightforward allegory is fortunately avoided in a number of ways, including an artistic bumsteer, so to speak, in the names: "*Didi*" suggests id and "*Gogo*" suggests ego, the reverse of the true relation. Also there is a relevant confusion over the weight of the two of them, Vladimir claiming to be heavier. This would be very difficult to square with the body/mind reading, seeing Vladimir as mind, except in the classical sense of "more substantial"; it is less difficult to square it with the id/ego reading, the ego seen as possibly "throwing more weight." But there is still a problem here, which is consistent with the development of the argument between Vladimir and Estragon where the matter of which is the heavier turns out to be a moot point. "There's an even chance. Or nearly." It is as though there were but a conventional difference involved. There is a puzzling distinction, relevant to the qualitative difference whether seen as body/mind or id/ego, drawn by Estragon when he speaks of the results of hanging. He (Gogo) will be "dead," but Didi will simply be "alone." The curious information that Vladimir has less difficulty with urination when Estragon is not around is perhaps relevant here. The realistic distinctions the ego can make about the functioning of the penis are blurred by the id which retains the infantile sense of urination as a sexual activity bringing the individual into competition with his fellows and his fathers on these grounds and raising again questions of "right" or permission, so that because of the id the ego may be subject to anxiety on the occasion of urination. On the other hand, Estragon himself has no such difficulty and Vladimir has none when Estragon is not around.

Being fragments of a single hero in the play, Vladimir and Estragon consequently will stand or fall together, to use a relevant expression, and it is from Godot that they hope to find out, as Vladimir says, "how they stand," i.e., how much of a man they are, so to speak. But there is the same uncertainty about whether Godot has been "there" before as there is about whether Vladimir and Estragon have been, and the name Godot (as becomes clear from the number of variants or trials, "Godin," "Godet," etc., referred to in the course of the play) is compounded from the nick names of Estragon and Vladimir—Gogo and Didi. Godid, i.e., Godot is another facet of the play's hero. There is in one sense, then, no real need to "wait for Godot." He's been there all along—but as an impotent.

Godot has not "come." When and if he does come, he'll be a new man, justifiably signified by a new name. If Gogo and Didi can be seen as id and ego of the tripartite hero, it requires no further insight to see Godot, permissive, authoritative, as superego and the hero's problem can be expressed in terms of getting these three parts together, a problem analogous to that of the reader in seeing the identity between them. The waiting is a tragic waiting; the hero hopes for himself; the hope is frustrated because of himself. "Nothing can be done" only because nothing *is* done. If something were done, something would happen, and movement would be possible again, the waiting ended. "Don't let's do anything. It's safer," says Estragon. To paraphrase Vladimir (and Cassius), the fault is not in their boots but in themselves.

As Vladimir and Estragon together figure the impotent man, so Pozzo (In Italian "posso" means "I can"; "Pozzo" is a well where people come for daily water.) and Lucky together at their first appearance figure the potent man and are thus more like the Godot who is awaited. Thus Pozzo and Lucky are also figures for ego and id, but these two parts seen in closer rapport, like Godot and his horse. Pozzo is perhaps a more realistic form of the ego-ideal Godot, a slightly "fallen" form, his name showing its relation to Godot through the intermediary form "Gozzo" whose "mother had the clap," perhaps a parody of the ideal mother of ideal (God)ot who could not possibly have caught any such disease, never having been in the "position" to do so.

To wait for Godot to be here (be "come") is to wait to become Godot. Go/Did with his pockets full of boyish rubbish waits to be Godot, his manly pockets full of manly stuff, the nearest approximation being Pozzo—pipe-smoking, whip-holding, chicken-eating, his baggage (pockets) under control and well-ordered, rising, falling, performing at will under the name of "Lucky," talisman of potency, rabbit foot and fortunate bean, the beast-man who comes to attention whenever the rope that unites him to Pozzo tautens, but who sleeps otherwise. One of the pieces of wisdom of this wise, loveable play is the representation of "Lucky," when his power is harnessed, as able also to "dance, sing, recite, think." There is an implied theory of art that, like so many elements of the play, calls Joyce to mind; in this case it is the mature view of the artist one finds in *Finnegans Wake* as opposed to that in *A Portrait of the Artist as a Young Man* which comes to mind, and in the context of a long, amazing, burlesqued *Finnegans Wake* passage in the mouth of Lucky.

Godot's horse, like Pozzo's Lucky, is the sign of his power and to detect it (they listen for it) is to detect him.

Vladimir and Estragon remain hopeful in the play, but they grow ill. "Hope deferred makes the something sick," Vladimir muses. The waiting is the form the illness takes, as it does for Hamlet. At the beginning of the play Vladimir is uncertain even that he wants what he hopes for (waits for). "Sometimes I feel it coming all the same," he says just following the "Hope deferred" speech, and continues, "Then I go all queer. (He takes off his hat, peers inside it, feels about inside it, shakes it, puts it on again.) How shall I say? Relieved and at the same time . . . appalled." There is hardly a clearer way to express that the real reason why "the coming" doesn't happen is that Vladimir is not sure he wants it. Godot is a part of himself he imperfectly (with a flaw) desires. Thus there is nothing to be done as both he and Estragon repeat. The surest sign of illness, as Pozzo says of Lucky, is to "refuse a bone," that is to reject potency. The flawed hero Vladimir/Estragon is split, one part against one part, and his inability to move, though he says he's going, dramatizes the conflict of will, as is familiar to one from dreams where paralysis has a similar meaning. Vladimir and Estragon are both crippled—Vladimir walking with "short stiff" strides, Estragon limping. Only Pozzo, early in the play, is able luxuriously to "stretch his legs." The flaw is in the man as man: in his resolve toward manhood. Gogo can't be himself. He can't "get up and go" because he doesn't want to "come." It is an achievement of the play to have related perennial tragic themes to burlesque ones; to have achieved a genuine middle genre of tragicomedy of a profound kind, the tragic, powerful paralysis at the end coming in the burlesque context of being uncertain whether one is being caught with one's pants down or with them up! This is a very nearly perfect figure of the modern man's anxiety. Here is a hero of the "lost generation," the generation whose name diagnoses its illness, a name suitable to serve as epigraph, as it does for a novel (Hemingway's) whose hero is a castrate and which bears the yearning title, *The Sun Also Rises*.

Toward the close of this play, Vladimir and Estragon are looking at the sun. They don't know whether it's going up or not: "It's rising," says Estragon. "Impossible," says the knowledgeable Vladimir. And in another of the flashes of wisdom that comes through the patter of the play we see how uncertainty in this fundamental matter of human potency relates to every larger uncertainty—were they there yesterday? Are they here now? "So there you are again," Vladimir says to Estragon at the beginning of the play. "Am I," says Estragon. Vladimir himself grows weaker in his hold on reality as his illness grows: "Time has stopped," he says. "Don't you believe it, sir, don't you believe it," says Pozzo, the potent so-and-so. "Whatever you like, but not that." The sense of time is one of the hard-won victories of the ego over the id. But Vladimir is getting tired. He is renewing his interest in the timeless or in what preceded the sense of time.

This is an exploratory essay, far from embracing this wise play. If it begins to solve any of the problems of the play and to plumb the secret of its power, it leaves many things untouched. For example, I'm not sure I see at all why Pozzo suffers reduction in the course of the play unless, having shown himself potent, he must inevitably, by the ancient tragic *anangke*, "fall," tumescence being "tied" as it is to detumescence, potency participating in impotence.

Bartleby and Captain Vere as Nay-Sayers to Love

Reflections on the Nature of the Melville Hero

(1962/1982)*

There is a sense in the Melville hero of the inability to accept either the love of women or the deeply felt friendship of men. This terrible isolation has come to be a hallmark of the existential hero in modern fiction, and it makes Melville both esoteric and contemporary in the ways he plays God to his creatures, what gifts and graces he will allow for them. Ahab's dreadful loneliness comes to mind—his rejection of his wife and family, his repulsion of the pleas and overtures of Starbuck (whom he almost permits to warm him), his pathetic, late response to the ineffectual, naive Pip, who can do nothing for him, really.

The image of Pierre also looks out of this context—fatherless, cut off from the relationships that might be expected to sustain him, from his friend Glen, from his fiancée, from his sister ultimately (through the confusion of the role into which he casts her), from his pastor, from his intellectual colleagues, from his publisher. The history of Pierre is a history of rejections which, for the most part, originate primarily from within

---

*Originally written in 1962, this essay was recently revised by John Logan and is being published here for the first time.—A. P., Jr.

him and which culminate in his rejection finally of himself through suicide.

Bartleby is par excellence the Melville hero as rejector: his vocabulary contains only negative elements. He is the nay-sayer, adding to his speech the apparent courtesy but the felt arrogance of the word "prefer": "I prefer not to." And finally Bartleby, like Pierre, prefers not to remain alive.

Bartleby is without family or history, and all we know of him is that he had served as long as he was able at a sorting job in the Dead Letter Office. The image we have of him in this earlier job, one at which he apparently was comfortable and where he *did* prefer to do what was required, is of someone continually receiving tokens of feeling *which are really intended for someone else*. Again there emerges the really heartrending isolation of the Melville hero, seen here on the obverse side of its image: we have in this figure not the man who rejects the love offered to him, but the man who can only accept the love which is really offered to others. Bartleby is the *anonymous* beloved upon whom is heaped (or who takes unto himself) a whole graveyard of human feeling. It is worth noticing the difference from the active *intercepter* of personal feeling on the one hand (the letter stealer or the love thief) and, on the other hand, the hero who receives knowingly the heaped affection of an audience partly anonymous—the recipient of fan mail, say. Bartleby is comfortable with love or with human feeling generally only when it is completely impersonal. The acute poignance of such a figure is seen when we put Bartleby beside the Dostoevskian hero who is incapable of love and so—in the language of *Brothers Karamazov*—finds himself in hell or, when we juxtapose it to the desperate figure of Faust, who has no belief in his own ability to be loved and so is willing to wager all on this: that he will not discover a human delight he wishes to continue.

Moved from his job, where Bartleby finds the minimum investiture of *eros*, he is willing to risk (not to be the beloved but to be the anonymous substitute for the beloved) and so willing to stay alive, he embarks as a scrivener, in the action of the story, on a course of rejection which leads to his death.

For in fact, what is offered Bartleby by his employer is something very much like love. His employer singles him out for tasks demanding special care, the tasks he would do himself if he had no trusted assistant, and offers him the really monumental (one is tempted to say Griselda-like) patience and concern of one who loves. Rejecting the special tasks which would make explicit the employer's feeling for him and so tempt him to grow into a comfortable, sustaining human delight at his work, Bartleby next rejects the corporate tasks which would put him in touch with his colleagues in the office. He keeps to himself, ultimately runs them all out (this is a hint of the hidden, aggressive character of his response), is imprisoned, finds he has no rapport even with the other exiles there (reminding one so much of the Raskolnikov of the epilogue to *Crime and Punishment*), lapses into a state much like catatonia, motionless and irresponsive, and finally dies, falling into the peaceful pose of the curled infant or fetus (the last situation of love he could tolerate?) on the new grass which grows so improbably in a "soft imprisoned turf" amid gloomy "Egyptian" stone in the yard—as though amid relics from the mute Sphinx itself.

Indeed, before the symbolic situation of his dying, one has already become aware of a childlike sense to Bartleby, and one wonders whether the rejection he plays out so thoroughly is not ultimately a childlike rejection of the responsibility associated with human feeling. Certainly it is clear that had he responded to his employer, Bartleby would have found himself invested with responsibility, and he will have none of this. At the same time, his willing acceptance of the feeling intended for others in the Dead Letter Office is perhaps made possible by the fact that it entails no responsibility to the lovers. (I continue to use the word "love" here as an archetypal word for human feeling generally.) So often it is a quality of the modern hero that he is able to admit only hatred or grief into his canon of feeling, but Bartleby seems not even to admit to these. He is nearly mute, like Billy Budd or Faulkner's Benjy, but in these other two there is clearly a sense of great, pent-up feeling. In Bartleby the muteness at first appears to reflect a genuine inner dryness, and this appearance is enforced by the fact that he is not really incapable of speech as they are but he simply "prefers not to" speak, we may say. He will not risk it. Is it because he cannot tolerate the possibility of response and the risk of human relationship which follows? For these relationships are built up so far out of the material of talk.

I shall have to say that finally I am less impressed either by the hypothesis of Bartleby as a rebellious, rejecting child, or by the hypothesis of him as a dried human being genuinely devoid of feeling than I am with the notion of him as a man who has conceived a towering rage and has then buried it in himself so deeply that it can grow only inside—and against himself therefore—finally killing him. That is, in Bartleby's reiterated "I prefer not to," I have a feeling of terrific aggression, but an aggression shown only passively—a fact which at one point as one contemplates it, takes on a feminine cast, so that Bartleby appears grotesquely (but not inconsistently in Melville) as the coy beloved. Bartleby continually says "I prefer not to" to the solicitations of the lover, but he continually stays around to provoke him anew and ultimately usurps what has been his employer's, moving him out of his office, endangering his career and reputation, without a jot of return. Now the usurpation continues to the point where Bartleby breaks his own sad, rock heart and the grass of green feeling is let to grow up again through the shard of it.

In *Billy Budd* there emerges a comparable figure of the hero who refuses to involve himself in positive, sustaining human relationships, when we consider two facts: first, Claggart admits to himself that he could have loved Billy, but instead we see him giving in to what is described as envy or jealousy, a "cynic disdain" of the innocence of Billy (as a lost part of himself) and plots to destroy him. Second, Captain Vere discerns in himself strong paternal feelings for Billy, but does not allow himself to consider them as he determines to carry out what he takes to be the just execution of his "son." It is possible to see as a powerful, effectual rationalization against his own tender feeling his statement that the heart is as "some tender kinswoman" whose consideration the upright judge must rule out of the bench. Vere dies with Billy's name on his lips.

Both Captain Vere and Claggart are figures of painful loneliness aboard ship. Billy himself has rapport with his fellows, but it is worth noting that Melville, as it were, makes him pay for this with his life. The value of Billy as a scapegoat is a direct function of his erstwhile strong rapport. Furthermore, Billy himself, we tend to forget, precipitates the action against himself by an act (albeit involuntary) of homicide. The homicide is rationalized and the filiocide (for here no lamb turns up to stay the knife of Abraham) is rationalized, but the fact is that Billy, the pleasant, inspiring friend to many, is dead and at the same time the possibility of a rewarding relationship between Vere and Billy is abrogated (like the possibility Claggart has rejected).

What I mean to point out is that the Melville hero, lonely, isolated, incapable of receiving the love of men or women, himself guilty of crimes against love, is here seen in a context where, as it were, the crime and the loneliness are both seen as something like virtues, and a certain compromise is affected. There are three violent actions in *Billy Budd:* Claggart's against Billy, Billy's against Claggart and Vere's against Billy. We accept rather easily the sense that Claggart's violence is an alternative to loving, we scarcely consider that Billy's violence is allied to hatred and to impotence, and we find ourselves seeing Vere's action as executioner as though it itself were an action of love!

"Melville has not solved the problem, but has solved the problem of his attitude toward it." By dramatizing a compromise and a paradox of feeling, we may say. But I do not think it is the problem of good and evil (which are abstract); it is the problem of love and hate (which are not). "If I had never loved anybody and nobody had ever loved me, none of this would have happened." Thus spoke Raskolnikov. He could have been speaking of Melville's nay-sayers as well as of himself.

III
Reviews and Forewords

Birthdays from the Ocean by Isabella Gardner

(1956)

In one of her poems Isabella Gardner calls herself "an apprentice witch, a mere familiar of familiars." But with this appearance of her first book she shows herself the real thing, a conjurer, a soothsayer, in connivance with the good- or evil-musing angels—an alternation which could become a confusion and which in an earlier time, among her New England ancestors, might have made another poem of hers her epitaph:

> I saw where a manna of flame had unfallowed the starving
>   field
> where a witch charred
> where her bones roared

She would have taken the chance. It is merely a question, as the witches and the poets know, of the integrity of one's vocation. In fact, Isabella Gardner is one of the new poets who allows us to hope that poetry may once again be *noticed* at least; though one hardly dares aspire to worry over a poet being burned (a fate only scientists seem to be thought to deserve in our time) or banned (this takes a novelist or a theologian) or exiled as of old when it was the poet who "named the gods."

Yet it was a short apprenticeship, and hardly any time went for journeywork. Miss Gardner was first published only five years or so ago, though she admits to having written a good deal as a girl; but she grew tired of her own "facile mewling and mawking," as she once said at a reading, and grew unwillingly aware of "the courage and energy that an effort to really write would entail."

She turned to the stage and played character roles in England and America, wearing wigs and speaking the lines of others. The return to writing was at the same time the assumption of a challenge and the abandonment of masks. It was, as realization of one's vocation always is, the discovery of self; and it demanded the humility specific to a vocation for poetry, i.e., the terrible disavowal of experiences and knowledges for which one does not yet have the words.

It was a hard and honest motion within a family tradition as well, for Isabella Gardner is of the Lowell stock (she is Robert's cousin).

There are few flawed poems in *Birthdays from the Ocean*. More to the point, nine or ten of the thirty-one poems she collects here are extraordinarily good brews, in itself a remarkable achievement even for established witches.

Let me name some of the best: "That Craning of the Neck," "To Thoreau on Rereading Walden," "When in Rome," "Cock A Hoop," "Lines to a Sea-green Lover," "Southwest of True North," and "When a Warlock Dies."

The last poem named is a kind of inverted elegy for Dylan Thomas; it takes its origin in the careful perception that the quantitatively and qualitatively shocking rash of poems marking Thomas's death was due more to a kind of fear than to grief and amounted to the elegizing of oneself in him. Elegies are always primarily consolatory, meant to let us bear our griefs by formulating them, but the plethora, the imitative character, and the despair of the Thomas elegies (they continue to appear) means that in his loss the poets grieve for their own life as poets. A kind of occupational pathology is involved here and it is tied to the fact that in Thomas, more than in anyone, the hope of poetry's being *cared about* (by others than poets) seemed to lie. But that is due more to other poet's weakness than to his greatness, which however I do not question.

But I have already said we have reason to "care about" Miss

Gardner's poems: and her elegy, besides having the guts of honest irony, and in its Thomasonian language a functional integrity denied to others (for here the language is *saying* that Thomas can handle his own elegizing), has a positive strength—the inexplicable reality of this poem helps heal the disease of poetic inferiority out of which the whole elegy-symptom developed. The witch is also witch-doctor. Listen to her good incantations:

> . . . Surely the deft-dirged, over-o-
> ded, buzzard-hungry, heron-lonely, phoenix hearted, gull-
>   lunged
> hummingbird-pulsed, falcon-winged and lark-tongued
> Chanticleer has crowed his own Farewells and Hails.
> . . . .
> The roaring riming of his most mourned Merlin canticles his
>   praise, and His, and ours,
> And Jerichos the walls of heaven with a surfing shout of love,
>   and blasts of flowers.

The first passage quoted is surely one of the finest crescendos anyplace in modern verse. The second passage concludes the poem and stands at the end of this exciting book as a proper coda and summary barrage of perfume, color, and love: the delight and agony of sense are all through these poems and they are, nearly every one of them, about love. More exactly, they are about the modern failure of love, a concern which places Miss Gardner thematically in the mainstream of poetry since *The Waste Land*—where "poetry" does not exclude the drama (consider Tennessee Williams) or the novel (consider Mauriac). The depressing character of such a theme is exorcized or transfigured through the perfection of form in good artists; Miss Gardner is a good artist.

These days, when there is in poetry so much fakery, so much embarassment, so much of the attitude that verse is filler or bauble, the alternate of jokes or decor, it is a delight to come on a book which shows a quite uncommon mastery of the ways of verse and which at the same time restores to verse the concern of Poetry: the inviolable beauty of the truth.

Things of This World by Richard Wilbur

(1956)

It is a commonplace of contemporary criticism that Richard Wilbur is one of our few important talents under forty. Indeed, he shares with Robert Lowell alone the palm of T. S. Eliot who, in language which is perhaps genial—even warm— for the British publisher, "admits to continuing respect" for Wilbur.

I share this respect, and Wilbur's third book, *Things of This World,* will certainly advance his reputation, for it contains ten or a dozen fine poems; but I am not warm to many of these pieces and I think the reason is simply that they do not require any such response as love or hate. I don't refer to their self-sufficiency, for that is a condition of any good art as it is of a blessed life. What I mean is this: few of the poems speak for me as the saint speaks for the sinner and the major poet for the needy fool.

More generally, there is a night side of a man which civilization cows but which is itself indispensable to the progress and building of civilizations and to all the other arts of men as well. "In the realm of mind," wrote Freud, "the primitive type is . . . commonly preserved alongside the transformations which have developed out of it." Believe me, there is little evidence of this "primitive type" and consequently little transfiguring of it in these poems by Wilbur. To that extent they are false to the power of his famous "The Death of a Toad" and to the profundity of his earlier "Ceremony." Still, it may be that every one of the new pieces is true to the sentence of the latter poem: "But ceremony never did conceal/ Save to the silly eye, which all allows,/ How much we are the woods we wander in." If so, I prove to have one of those "silly eyes," or fool's eyes— something I already admitted to in a way.

One surprising exception—there are others—to Wilbur's ignoring of the dark is his handling of images drawn from cast-off clothing, dry, and washwater—fleshy things which he subjects to the most amazing and spiritualizing transformations in several beautiful poems, at least one earlier one, "The Terrace," and at least three in the present book—"Love Calls Us to the Things of This World," "Sonnet," and "A Plain Song for Comadre." It is gratifying to relate one of the themes of the young "kitchen artists" in contemporary Britain and Europe, a group I admire for their willingness to find in the less spiritual parts of the house human things in need of art. I don't know, however, that any of them has followed the style of treatment analogous to the famed elegance of Wilbur's.

I find Wilbur at his best in poems where he employs stanzaic forms of widely varied line lengths, a practice he follows more generously in this book: the advantage of this is that it heightens the rhythm and action, through allowing more opportunity for enjambment, and it breaks up the monotony of his decasyllabic lines. These precious stanzas are a happy product of Wilbur's "genie in the bottle" theory of poetry.[1] But once in a while one wishes for more evidence of the alternate theory of "the bottle in the genie."

---

1. Addressing himself to the matter of form in poetry in an essay entitled "The Genie in the Bottle" for *Mid-Century American Poets* edited by John Ciardi (N.Y.: Twayne Publishers, 1950), Richard Wilbur wrote: "In general, I would say that limitation makes for power; the strength of the genie comes of his being confined in a bottle."—A. P., Jr.

Green with Beasts by W. S. Merwin

(1956)

Exclusive of the appearance of neurosis, W. S. Merwin gives the impression one expects of poets: he is under thirty as poets are always supposed to be; he has long hair and a suffused quality about the eyes; he has tutored the children of a princess in Portugal; he has lived in the household of a master (Robert Graves); his first book won a prize (the Yale Younger Poet's competition); he has the benefit of a wealthy patron (a *Kenyon Review* Fellowship); he spends his energy writing poems rather than in, say, selling insurance, playing publisher or stunning undergraduates in university classrooms.

Merwin has had the courage to publish three books in six years, even though not all the poems are terribly good: there is in the present book a jejeune piece called "Tobacco," a number that are plain dull and at least one really ambitious piece, "The Annunciation," that doesn't come off. It tries for a kind of phenomenology determined by the reverie of a young married virgin and it suffers from the general diffuseness of the technique (which makes the poem "and"-ridden, etc.), from the noticeable failure of its opening image, ("darkness . . . blacker than any night"), from the fact that its "whirring wings" and "no-name-for-it" themes are repeated in a number of other poems in this volume, and from the incontrovertible mastery of Rilke in his poems on the life of the Virgin. Rilke relied on his selfknowledge of the creative act for his understanding of the Virgin's conceiving (and on the artist's painful exhaustion and terrible anxiety over future production for his empathy into the situation of the Pietà). The power and economy of Rilke's Marian pieces should give any poet pause who is not certain of a new success.

To my mind Merwin's beautiful "Burning the Cat" and his "White Goat, White Ram," the latter a fantasy of infant memory, show his religious sensibility to better advantage than the more specifically religious poems—but "Prodigal Son" is a good one.

My biggest objection to Merwin is that he pays insufficient attention to the life of individual lines. These suffer from an excess of harmony, which finally jars, and overconsideration of pause with underconsideration of measure, which results in a dragged gait. He misses many enjambment opportunities and, while writing lines of comparable length, frustrates the search for regular patterns of stress. The overall result is a slackness of line which often destroys the shape of a poem, for a poem is best thought of as first a shape (incarnation) of breath (word) in the ear guyed by the tension of verse lines, themselves breaths. A poem is a kind of breathed ballet for the ear. If these shapes in the ear are slack, then the presentation which the poem should finally be, the vision generated by the dance of sense, just doesn't happen. Such failures give us the distinction between literary noise and poetic art. Merwin is still young and the amount of the former in his work will doubtless decrease in the future. Anyhow the present book is one of the most important of the year.*

_____

*Mr. Logan has asked me to note that he has come to disagree with his old opinions considerably and that he admires the work of W. S. Merwin more than this early review might indicate.—A. P., Jr.

John Gruen's Settings for Wallace Stevens[1]

(1956)

How many ways of looking at a blackbird are there? Thirteen archetypal ways: innumerable other ways that make up the silence of numbers after thirteen. Consider that among all the possible silences, the settings for the remaining Ways after thirteen are bounded by a parallel silence, as sure as the silence of the remaining Ways themselves. We know that whatever Way lies hidden and implied in Stevens's poem, there exists a hidden and implied setting in Gruen's music. The one is a function of the other, in the mathematical sense. I mean that the inevitability of Gruen's settings is the inevitability of the number for the point.

And sometimes, if we are not careful, we confuse the set of numbers with the set of points; we find ourselves from time to time thinking of the music as the poem and of the poem as the music. This is natural enough when we realize, say, that the blackbird's eye *moves* in Stevens's first Way and also moves in Gruen's music. Indeed in this particular case one wonders briefly if the blackbird does not learn more from the composer about how to move his eye here, and then again here, than he

---

1. Song Cycle, "Thirteen Ways of Looking at a Blackbird," by John Gruen. Recorded on *Contemporary Records.* Patricia Neway, soprano, accompanied by the composer.

learns from the poet. For Stevens assumes the movement and shows it abstractly among the mountains:

> Among twenty snowy mountains,
> The only moving thing
> Was the eye of the blackbird.

The eye of the blackbird changes over the surfaces of the snowed peaks as the figures in Ramuz's novel do. But the movement is not abstract in the music: in the first three bars the blackbird's eye shifts, again shifts, and blinks twice.

But in the second Way it is the poem which is concrete and the music which is abstract! So you will see what I mean by the listener's occasionally having to be excused for confusing poem and setting. For here the attenuated spirituality of the trio of minds is in the sparse music, confined largely to a pair of notes in unison (that scarcely even change interval), while the discreteness of the minds, their materiality, is shockingly concrete in the poem's image of three blackbirds in a tree:

> I was of three minds,
> Like a tree
> In which there are three blackbirds.

Yet the setting is right not only as a balance to the poetry but as an interpretation: for the point is not that the blackbirds are distinct from the tree, or, finally, that they are even distinct from each other, but that they are like "I" who "was of three minds"—and mind is attenuated, spiritual, sparse—thus we are back to the music again. You see what I mean about the overlappings of poem and music? Who is to say whether the music interprets the poem or the poem interprets the music here? The answer is neither, except as two lovers may be thought of, one as an interpretation of the other.

In the third Way the whirling of the bird "in the autumn winds" is unmistakable in the music, and the immense suggestiveness of Stevens's "pantomime" ("It was a small part of the pantomime") is spelled out excruciatingly in the final bars of the music. Is the wind a mime of the bird or the bird a mime of the wind or both a pantomime of the autumn or the autumn a pantomime of bird and wind?

The eerie wonder of the union of man and woman, in the fourth Way, is hauntingly brought to us by another spare setting, whose tone takes us back to the intellectuality of the setting for the second Way. The music prepares us well for what would be otherwise a great shock: the awareness that the blackbird belongs in this union, as he belongs in every common or miraculous place (it is this realization which gives us the full range of "Ways of looking at a blackbird"). The voice line catches the union of the three in a disarmingly simple way, by never moving over an interval of more than a halfstep and throughout reaching no more than a step and a half on either side of the first note, the highest note coming with the pronunciation of "blackbird."

> A man and a woman
> Are one.
> A man and a woman and a blackbird
> Are one.

If we do not know how to make the fifth Way, i.e., how to take the fifth point of view, which requires the immense subtlety of distinction between "inflection" and "innuendo," we learn from the music, which illustrates both, and musically ties the whistling of the blackbird to "inflection" and the active silence-of-the-blackbird (after whistling) to "innuendo."

The barbaric stains icicles cast on window glass for the sixth Way are painted for us in the percussive piano setting, and the points of ice become points of tone and they dance the one with the other, or perhaps the one *as* the other, in a primitive jerk-step. The blackbird is here too. Or rather as we come more and more to see, he is behind this dance as he is behind every event (a more accurate way of saying, as I did above, that he is in every place). Again the piano registers the shock of our growing knowledge of the bird. For after all, supposing we looked at him in every way we would know all there is to know of him.

And when we have looked at him in thirteen ways (we aren't quite half through them) will he not already be sufficiently known to be in our power. Or we in his. (We are already almost half way through the Ways!) It is too late for us now, if the blackbird is terrible. For we must go on.

In the seventh Way the drawn character of "The thin men of Haddam" is caught through the slender unadorned line with which the piano enters, to set these words. The thinness is heightened by the piercing immateriality, not of the gold, but of the *shine* of the imagined golden birds. Is this austere? But we have not reckoned yet with the dreadful slenderness of the blackbird's legs as they walk about the delicate feet of the women! As this attenuation outdoes the golden birds within the thin imagination of the thin men, so too the walking movement in the piano, a delicate descending figure, already intrudes in the very setting of the words "you imagine golden birds" and recurs throughout the piece. The thin men are returned to their opening theme in the closing bars, but this apparent generosity is a mask: the music line is no longer so unadorned. The men are not so thin after all; the most austere blackbird is, of course, victor. Therefore, why indeed should the "thin men of Haddam . . . imagine golden birds"? Their foolishness has made them fat.

The "noble accents and lucid inescapable rhythms" of the eighth Way are almost too easy for the composer to set, but before we suppose some kind of ease we must, again, remember the bird. Do we "know noble accents"? Do we know "lucid, inescapable rhythms"? Yes, but the bird is here: he is "*involved.*" How? Because he is himself an accent (his eye?) and a rhythm (his body line?), or because he is that by which we know these things? Who is to say? It is enough to realize that he is involved. The shock of this realization is the most inescapable rhythm of all; and the piano begins and ends with it.

In the ninth Way the blackbird flies and draws and marks the expanding circles of our sight, but is not himself contained within any of them. He evokes each greater circle in turn, with the help of the piano, and then as the circles widen, he himself begins to vanish; he is lost first to the piano, and a little later to the voice too. But the circles are here, so he must himself be here—but *in another way!* Perhaps the tenth?

In the tenth Way the blackbirds are seen "flying in a green light." Their wings undulate gorgeously, or terribly, in the piano setting. And even the pimps for the muse find their senses waked as if by a glissando, and they "cry out sharply" at the color, or at the music, or at the poem, or at the blackbirds.

In the eleventh Way we ride out in a coach over the rapid wheels or trots of the piano. Suddenly a fear pierces us as the voice rises a shocking halfstep over the unchanged tone of the piano. The blackbird! Wait, it must have been the shadow of the coach, for it was a *massive* shade. Then, as the voice repeats the word "blackbirds" three more times, we realize to our horror that we ride "in a *glass* coach"! It casts no shadow! The musical setting has trapped us among the blackbirds, whom it has itself multiplied, and the hugeness of "the shadow" is accounted for in a frightful (eleventh) way!

At last the power of the blackbird is unforgettably and awfully clear and we are quite prepared for the simple affirmation of the twelfth Way, which makes it unnecessary for us to see the blackbird at all, or even his shadow, real or imagined, in order to know his immense strength. "The river is moving" and from this we are sure that "the blackbird must be flying!" The implication is as certain as is the existence of the piano, which, however, is silent here in order (generously) to understate the most lucid and most profoundly disturbing revelation which the voice gives. There is furthermore an almost liturgical cast given to this Way through the use of the unaided voice, and that is proper at this point. For when will the presence, or the power, of the blackbird cease?

The thirteenth Way is marked by the composer "largo," and it proceeds in the chords of a kind of oblique hymn. The liturgical suggestion of the twelfth Way is carried out more formally in this final thirteenth Way; it is a kind of solemn celebration for the blackbird, who is, for the moment (an ominous realization), established, or throned officially in the cedar limbs. It has been "evening all afternoon" (his doing). "It was snowing/And it was going to snow" (his doing: his eye is cold). What next show of his power, we wonder uneasily. The piano refuses to finish its line, but it is suspended: the written music is done. The poet and the composer leave the rest, platonically, to our own effort. Nor did we ever suppose before that we were subject to the superstition of thirteen! But the responsibility, the need even, is clear. The next Way is the fourteenth—.

The Sorrows of Priapus by Edward Dahlberg

(1957)

The fine title "Sorrows of Priapus" is a monad mirroring the world of Edward Dahlberg as it shines from this book. It shows the concision, the music, the feeling and the ambivalent vision which we take as the properties of the poet, and this book is a poem in prose. I'm sorry poets can't buy it because of the cost.

> Where is Apollo who rested his foot on the skull of an ox; where are the wild horse, the faun, the roe, the cubs of bears that were brought to the altars of Artemis? Shall we wed, or woo, or tremble?

Like the lines of poems, Ben Shahn's drawings are built into the work, into its themes and rhythms; and the drawings like the book are erotic, delicate, moving. They, like it, show animals with the grace, fury, and melancholy of people and with it have the curious impersonality of myths as compared to dreams, and of dreams as compared to the beloved in bed. There is an odd, believable mixture of the gross and the gentle, as in the wonderful scene of *Ulysses* where Bloom, trying to nose in his own shirt the odor of the male quietly confuses spunk and lemon soap.

The book is filled with gorgeous images, with important false facts about animals and heroes, with richness of language and mythic material, not only of the Old World. In fact the sustained beauty of the chapters concerning pre-Columbian times in America easily rivals any long poem using American material.

Man's central difficulty, his old hell with his prick, is the motif to which this baroque piece always returns. Here is the full statement of theme:

> The penis, despite the fact that it is attached to each person, has its own disposition; it goes where it will, and though the spurious owner wants to think, it wants to urinate, and if its helpless landlord desires to read or to sow grass it wants to lie in bed. . . . A man may want to study Mark or Paracelsus, or go on an errand to do a kindness to an aged woman, but this tyrant wants to discharge itself either because the etesian gales are acerb or a wench has just stooped over to gather her laundry. The whole matter, when one thinks of it reasonably, is bizarre.

The book is itself bizarre and beautiful. It is distracting, stimulating, disenchanting, and it is not conducive to love nor to interest in men and women rather than in the sexes. It has in fact something of the quality of an elegant, unforgettable, erudite whore.

There is much esoteric scandal concerning the doings of the gods, the greeks, and the greats. The names and costs of the courtesans of the philosophers are recorded, as is Montaigne's unhappiness over the reduced number of erections he was able to produce in a week's time after age forty, or something like that. There is a concern with data of potency and impotency which, style aside, made me think of Dahlberg as a Kinsey of the legendary. (If Dahlberg were concerned with contemporary American folk heroes instead of the older ones, he might well have noted some of those Kinsey himself uncovered, such as the marvelous man who achieved four orgasms a day for forty years and, godlike, lived to be interviewed.)

I am trying to say that it is a puzzling book besides being beautiful. The source of the deeper disturbance is the attitude toward love as it comes to me through the mixed glories. There is a cantankerousness about sexuality, a bitterness? The delight in animals, the investing of emotion on griffin and goose—isn't something, tenderness, feeling, displaced from people? They hardly appear at all except as clear artifacts. I know I am talking about the meaning of myth. I would guess the book's data are from Hesiod, Theophrastus, Paracelsus or such places where we find different creatures treated as projected pieces of human emotional life.

Aristotle's *History of Animals* for example:

> Some are good-tempered, sluggish, and little prone to ferocity, as the ox; others are quick-tempered, ferocious and unteachable, as the wild boar; some are intelligent and timid, as the stag and the hare; others are mean and treacherous, as the snake; others are noble and courageous and high-bred, as the lion . . . some are spirited and affectionate and fawning, as the dog; others are cautious and watchful, as the goose; others are jealous and self-conceited, as the peacock. But of all animals man alone is capable of deliberation.

One wants to add to the last sentence "and *in*capable of feeling, which he foists off on other animals." With Dahlberg's book Ovid's *Metamorphoses* also comes to mind. Aesop's *Fables*. Medieval bestiaries with their central unicorn figure, the creature who actually possessed the strength every youth cries for, the power to protect his purity. Albertus Magnus. Bartholomaeus Anglicus. These authors all explore the relations between man's view of the animals and his view of himself. Aesop's book is about man's hope of morality, Ovid's about man's hope of change, which is close to the same thing, though in Ovid it moves in the special direction of the meaning of art, of sublimation. The modern bestiaries come to mind also. Marianne Moore's. Richard Wilbur's. W. S. Merwin, who has marvelously retold in verse the story of Beauty and the Beast (the sexual man), who for his own salvation requires to be loved despite his bestiality (sexuality) and despite his ability to arouse what sleeps in Beauty.

You can't speak of Moore and Wilbur without going to the beasts of other, older poets and scientists. De La Fontaine. Linnaeus. One moves backwards and forwards to biologists from poets, to poets from biologists. Their interests meet in feeling. The anatomy and physiology (working) of feeling is the business of the poet. *The Anatomy of Melancholy.* The anatomy of love. Here is the unicorn again. Here are the animals that roam the margins of medieval manuscripts. Creatures of marvelous ugliness and of transcendent beauty, without flesh.

The use of animal imagery to render the life of feeling has got a new twist to it in the last seventy-five years from two things—our knowledge that somehow our ancestors were animals and our knowledge that "animality" has reference to our own unconscious life, so that the beast we want chained is in us.

What has always been a deep basis of literature has now become "scientific." What does this do to literature? There is a great deal to puzzle about here. One thing, it seems to make Dahlberg for all his brilliance and beauty curiously old-fashioned at the root of his art, though not at the height of it. If the meaning of the dream begins to be known to them don't the poets, public dreamers, have to have new ones? Perhaps not. I feel unsure as I write.

I am surer of what I mean when I say there are no people in this amazing book, though there are a number of the members of both sexes. I mean there are no wives, no sons, no daughters. No persons sexually loved and no new persons produced by sexual love and so participating in it irrevocably, realistically, spiritually.

The book is wise with the poet's wisdom, who has named the gods, and rich with his full color. It is sad with the melancholy of the young who yearn for freedom from the curse of snakes—of Hippolytus turned by the thought of Phaedra from his beloved horse and bow. And sad with the other sadness of the old who have failed to save their sons, the awful agony of Laocoön seeing the ruin of his sons. Wise, rich, sad. Much academic bravado. But nowhere the tenderness of the father whose serpent is the instrument of his love, and his sons the arrows of his quiver, his daughter the apple of his eye.

The Strange Islands by Thomas Merton

(1957)

Thomas Merton's new book of poems is dull, daunted and reminiscent of Eliot. These three qualities can be illustrated from the first poem, "How to Enter a Big City," which introduces the central, old cliché of the book—namely that Babylon, The Tower of Babel and the Augustinian City of Man are all figures for the contemporary city.

The dullness of the opening poem shows this: "Here,/ Have a little of my blood,/ Rich people! . . . Wheat in towers. Mean on ice./ Cattle cars. Miles of wide open walls/. . . Miles of it. Still the same city." And still the same sad song.

There is a good deal of daunted clucking about the state of the race in the city: "Then people come out into the light of afternoon,/ Covered all over with black powder,/ And begin to attack one another . . ./ Young men full of coffee and/ Old women with medicine under their skin/ Are all approaching death . . ." There's temptation of course, if you can stay alive until evening, "Until the lights come on with a swagger of frauds."

Through the book the Eliotisms are endless and wearying in them, verse form and idiom. For example, in the first poem: "People hurrying along the wall./ Here you are, buy my dead bones.////Those are radios that were his eyes./. . . Do you know where you are going?/ Do you know whom you must meet?" Eliotic images of cataclysmic wind, falling towers, twilight of civilization, the emptied city, etc., continue throughout the enormously long and boring verse drama (one half the entire book) *The Tower of Babel:* "Suddenly the burly dark filled the whole sky. Can you still hear me in this wind?" One longs to be able to answer, No.

The solution to the whole civic anthropological problem, spared us in Eliot but offered to us by Thomas Merton, comes out to be this in *The Tower of Babel:* somehow, with grace, get to the country and be quiet, except at weddings, discarding the machines that man's intelligence and agony have yielded him, tromping on the grapes together, achieving a massive single-mindedness, everybody thinking alike—which is supposed to be peace. The City of God is seen as an outmoded farm, with a vineyard: a kind of quiet, early-Kentucky institution.

Some passages from the drama elaborate this thought: "Men were free because they thought the same thing . . . Because they do not live by the machine, they fear no insecurity (!) . . . Since they live mostly in silence they know . . . life . . . Before the sun was up / We had already milked the cows, / Watered the horses, hitched up the . . . / gutters / . . . And now we all unite / To celebrate a wedding . . . We have heard / The same songs before, at other weddings. / That is why we play them now."

The easy simplification of all this is regrettable in itself (and it goes with a parochialism which is painful: atheism is judged as a comforting illusion on the ground that if God does not exist, then men "do not have to be troubled with the problem of their own existence either.") But more relevantly it means death to poetic art, as the quotation about the wedding music implies, as the Babel-theory of art itself implies, and as this book shows, it having nearly all "been played before." The forms of the poems and their diction, except for "Sports Without Blood," and their rhythms are stock ones or are derived from somebody else's invention, as one of the longest poems in the book, "Elias," follows Eliot's quartet form.

The Tower of Babel says that man's new city shall be built without human wisdom, human invention or human power, and "without hands, without labor, without money and without plans." Natural man is seen here as quite incapable of building, except badly. Man is an incompetent animal. In the Babel-theory of art, I take it the same thing applies, not just to cities and towers, but to products of human making generally, such as these poems: as the work of a man they can only be bad. Then why continue to prove that they can be bad?

Poems of a Jew by Karl Shapiro

(1958)

Karl Shapiro's poems are inspirational in the simple sense that after reading him one goes back to the work of his own life freshened and reflective, stirred with an example of human achievement, an example of what a man can come to. I think in this sense all art is moral, bringing about in the reader, viewer, or hearer a thirst for whatever responsibility it is necessary for him to assume in order to function excellently. Of course this can only happen honestly and in actuality when the art work is indeed excellent. Otherwise there is present always some element of the lie. I dwell on this because I have a strong sense that this thing of human excellence is what Shapiro's book is about.

"The object of poetry is to make man unashamed," Shapiro said in a lecture I heard him give a couple of years ago. His poems effect this, quietly, with exquisite craft, and without genius—which is a luxury the person who is in need of art (and who is not?) cannot depend on.

There are an introduction and notes, also by Shapiro. The introduction has to do with the sense in which the word "Jew" is to be taken in the title, *Poems of a Jew.* (Shapiro emphasizes that it is not to be taken religiously.) The name of Freud appears five times in the brief two pages of notes.

What Shapiro's introduction says is what the poems themselves say. I distinguish between the two meanings, "*poems* of a

197

Jew" and "poems of a *Jew*" and find that either meaning without the other falsifies. Karl Shapiro is a poet: his sense of what a poet is, is conditioned by his self-knowledge of himself as a Jew. His sense of what the Jew is, if I understand the introduction, is conditioned by his self-knowledge of the poet. I make this judgment admitting my own ignorance of the Jew, but taking heart from Shapiro's statement here that it is Leopold Bloom, Joyce's character, in whom the mien of "the free modern Jew (is) celebrated so perfectly." For Leopold Bloom is the most fully drawn human being whom literature has kept. He has top, bottom, inside, outside, dream feeling, intelligence, heart, genital, conscious, and unconscious; and he undergoes the peculiar human suffering which attends the smallest measure of clear self-vision, the thing that makes any change, and so any human excellence, possible. Bloom is precisely that which Shapiro here describes as the modern Jew: "Man in all his raw potentiality." And here is the true meaning of the concept of exile, in which the Jew as a figure meets the artist: that the potentiality *remains* raw, only somewhat advanced, as man remains separated from his true self and from his true home, unplumbed, mysterious, but capable of love and excellence. The two qualities belong together because both of them build to a higher unity, and preserve.

Most of the new poems continue to employ the normal English line, unobtrusively rhymed and free of special diction, a line which Shapiro has championed theoretically and since the beginning of his practice. All of them show the drive to understand and to be understood which always marks his work and which his new title, together with the presence of introduction and notes, reflects. They include a couple of occasional poems commissioned for Jewish celebrations. I like best of the recent poems in the book "The First Time," but I would not put any of them beside the best of his whole production.

The new poem "The First Time" catches strongly an intermediate step in the sequence of emergence from boyish into adult love, a sequence including in this book the remarkably moving prose poem "The Dirty Word," which is about the child's guilty delight in obscenity, "The Confirmation," a complexly realized poem about self-gratification, "The First Time," and finally "V-Letter," which is the husband's solace in his wife and his plaint at her long absence.

The "Adam and Eve" sequence belongs before and behind all those poems about love and is itself about love—and creation and art and exile and survival and human excellence. It is a suite of six poems of unusual power, understanding and beauty, a triumph in American letters to which attention must be paid, and it is in my opinion the meaning of Karl Shapiro's new work, the plot of his poems, introduction, and notes.

What A Kingdom It Was by Galway Kinnell

(1960)

Galway Kinnell's *What A Kingdom It Was* (what a good title it is) is the best first book of poems since James Wright's *The Green Wall* and, cardinal numbers aside, is one of the finest books of the past decade.

Certainly the discerning, small audience of people who continually care about fine poetry will not pass by Kinnell's work, so I have only to call it to the attention of the suspicious, the unconverted, and the disenchanted—those who are aware perhaps of no middle ground between the bland and the horrendous in our diet of verse and so go hungry, those who have found only something with eloquence and no meat, like an hors d'oeuvre ("better magazine" verse) or something with the blood and hair still bristling on it, untamed, uncooked, having to be washed down with much wine ("beat" poetry).

Well, Galway Kinnell's book is aperitif, soup, steak, potatoes, salad, dessert, coffee, and cognac. Nor do I mean the fare is bourgeois. Choose your dish.

It is a full book and it gets better and better—thirty-three poems, many of them sizeable, plus a remarkable 450-line final poem hard to match in American literature, drawn from contemporary life around Avenue C in New York City: "The Avenue Bearing the Initial of Christ into the New World."

Toward that poem as goal, the poems of the book move

from the charming, naive, almost Elizabethan "First Song" and its fellow pieces in part one, one of them giving account of a child's disappointing "First Communion," and another a young man's strength and growth and quandary as a hunter, "To Christ Our Lord." The poems in the long part two include the candid, devoted "For William Carlos Williams" and the beautiful trio "Leaping Falls," "Alewives Pool," and "Promontory Moon," which conjure a kind of intense, romanticized Robert Frost. Elsewhere one feels more of Father Whitman. Part three is made up of six unusually ambitious poems, as the nostalgic and touching "Freedom, New Hampshire" and the extraordinary "Seven Streams of Nevis" where Mr. Kinnell, more than any other place in the book, shows himself in the role of the Irish Bard.

The concluding poem is an unforgettable experience of reading which recreates the sounds, textures, odors, melodrama, and pathos of Manhattan's Avenue C. There are fourteen sections, beginning with the early morning music:

> pcheek pcheek pcheek pcheek
> They cry. The motherbirds thieve the air
> To appease them. . . . Ringing in its chains
> The New Star Laundry horse comes down the street
> Like a roofleak whucking in a pail.

On the Avenue in the spring sunshine we meet a dying patriarch ("His beard like a sod-bottom / Hides the place where he wears no tie"); a wonderful boy who "From a roof-top . . . fishes at the sky, / Around him a flock of pigeons fountains"; the news woman, "The oldest living on Avenue C. . , / She lives shadowed, under a feeble bulb / That lights her face, her crab's hands, her small bulk on the crate."

We visit a pushcart market, where "A crate of lemons discharges light like a battery," which reminds of the later "phosphorous flashings in the sea, or the feverish light / Skin is said to give off when the swimmer drowns at night."

There is an important and sustained imagery of fish in the poem, often associated with dying. In the market,

> Fishes do not die exactly . . , there is little pallor.
> Only the cataracted eyes which have not shut ever
> Must look through the mist which crazed Homer.

We watch the naked fire at Gold's junkhouse ("mausoleum of what we were"):

> Perambulator skeletons, bicycles tied in knots—
> . . . Carriages we were babies in,
> Springs that used to resist love, that gave in
> And were thrown out like whores. . . .

and go home as the light fails and

> The figures withdraw into chambers overhead—
> In the city of the mind, chambers built
> Of care and necessity, where, hands lifted to the blinds,
> They glimpse in mirrors backed with the blackness of the
>   world
> Awkward, cherished rooms containing the familiar selves.

Night time on the Avenue is "The nighttime / of the blood," and its people "are laughing and saying, / Our little lane, what a kingdom it was! / oi weih, oi weih." Just so, we laugh and say, and the lament of the street of this poem, chock full as it is with the overwhelming life that strikes the visitor to it, is made bearable—even loveable—by art.

In Defense of Ignorance by Karl Shapiro

(1961)

Allen Tate recently wrote, "I would think that after T. S. Eliot's death . . . there will be a violent rebellion against the whole Eliot influence. There are signs of it right now. It's inevitable and I think Mr. Eliot would approve of it." Karl Shapiro's new book of essays is just about the most articulate "sign of it" one could expect to find, appearing as it does by the hand of one of the most gifted artists of his generation, Pulitzer Prize winner, Consultant in Poetry at the Library of Congress, and former editor of the prestigious *Poetry* magazine, where Eliot's work first appeared.

In Shapiro's book the Eliot-Pound-Yeats axis is struck head-on in separate essays devoted to the re-examination of each, with an added knocking at Auden. As a literary disclaimer it reminds one of Robert Graves's iconoclastic work *The Crowning Privilege,* parts of which were published in the American press separately, eliciting at the time (1956) outrageous response in the form of letters from Shapiro himself and other writers of reputation. In addition to the four giants Shapiro now attacks, Graves also attacked Dylan Thomas, whom Shapiro retains high in the canon.

In Shapiro's view, Yeats comes off by far the best (it is his alliance with the esoteric and the cultured—capitalized—to which Shapiro objects) and Eliot emerges the most battered. Indeed, I could find only one essay in the entire book, whatever its subject, which does not rail at Eliot at some point, and that one denounces Pound. "The criticism of Eliot and Pound has blighted enormous literary areas, as far as we can tell," writes Shapiro.

It is time the graduate student plagued with the problem of making an index to Eliot's erudite, crabbed essays and at the same time puzzled by the shabby scholarship of Pound (whose literary essays Eliot calls the most important body of literary criticism written in our time) should be afforded the catharsis of an intelligent, negative view of these "fathers." Still there is more than a suggestion of animus in such a statement as Shapiro's, "Pound is not worth my time or yours." Or "In general *The Four Quartets* appears to be a deliberately bad book, one written as if to convince the reader that poetry is dead and done with." And I am surprised at the lack of aesthetic perception (which in a man of such extraordinary sensitivity strikes me as a depth blindness) in Shapiro's remark that one can interchange the sections of *The Waste Land* without changing the sense of the poem. Nothing would be easier to refute.

The oddest part of all this to my mind is that Shapiro's notion of *The Waste Land* as bad writing close to canard corresponds exactly with what some readers thought of it when it first appeared—but it is commonplace that a truly original work is hostilely received at the beginning, so that what Shapiro tries to accomplish here is really the undoing of the years of love and labor which have been spent on the poem to secure it a key place in our literature. In feeling, it's a little like having a respected neighbor and former friend of your father tell you that the rumor you once successfully scotched about your dad's having a bastard son is, after all, true. Yet when the neighbor repeats the charge every time he sees you, you begin to wonder whether he is not saying something obscure about himself rather than something lucid about the father.

Besides the patriarchs of twentieth-century poetry there are other things on the negative side of Shapiro's ledger which come in for recurring assault. These include "culture," religion, and modern psychology (with the exception of the doctrine of the renegade Freudian, Wilhelm Reich)—the latter fact at odds with the occasional motive-hunting in depth Shapiro undertakes when trying to account for the failure of writers he disapproves.

The positive side of Shapiro's writing I find much the most attractive. Besides the deeply engaging, brash, insightful opening essay, "The Critic in Spite of Himself," and the haughty, winning, whistle-in-the-dark "Poet and Psychologist" (both of them required reading for American poets in the search for their image among their fellows), there is some really brilliant analysis and celebration in the book, particularly the essays, one each, on W. C. Williams ("The True Contemporary"), Dylan Thomas, Whitman ("The First White Aboriginal") and D. H. Lawrence. The Dylan Thomas essay is a very moving, sober, independent assessment of the whole range of Thomas's work, with due attention given to his flaws. It is the best single study of that poet. The Lawrence essay is really magnificently put together as a dialogue between a younger poet and an oracular figure, half T. S. Eliot and half Freud, on the status of poetry and poets. The thesis that emerges is this, that poets are out of work because they have tried to do the jobs of other professional men—priests, scholars, sociologists, psychologists—forgetting their true vocation in association with the magicians and the witchdoctors who by their art *make things happen* unaccountably in the world of the auditor.

Lawrence, according to Shapiro, remained true to the vocation, and thus allied himself to the few others of the century who (we discover in the course of the book) have done so: Dylan Thomas, W. C. Williams, Whitman, Hart Crane (with qualifications) and the splendid non-American triumverate: Lorca, Rilke, and Cavafy. A scattering of earlier writers who also receive Shapiro's attention and help make up his own canon include Hopkins, Milton, and Blake, who, like Whitman, are deprecated by Eliot. At the same time, Shapiro disapproves of certain writers in the Eliot canon, for example Donne and Baudelaire. I find his approval of the first group a great deal better substantiated than his disavowal of the second group.

If there is a single statement in the book which shows the issue between the goods and the bads, it is this ironical one, "Lawrence has committed the horrible sin of expressing his own feelings in poetry. Instead of following the 'discipline of rational constructed imagination' [Eliot] Lawrence *expresses*." There is certainly great need for the return to feeling in poetry, though when we say a writer "expresses" it, it is perhaps clearer to note, not so much that he expresses himself (which everybody does willy-nilly) but that he expresses *us*, his readers, which only the artist can do.

The title "In Defense of Ignorance" is obviously a reference to such a book as Ivor Winters's *In Defense of Reason* with its excessive, killing rationalism and its invention of critical jargon, terms used as spears to impale even such a gifted artist as E. E. Cummings. The title also calls to mind Nicholas of Cusa's brilliant *De Doctrina Ignorantia* with its platonic cast of *felt* learning, its cant toward mysticism, and its (irrationalist?) citation of the reality of contradiction in this life.

In the final essay Shapiro juxtaposes the epigraph to his book, "Everything we are taught is false," with Rilke's admonition taken from "An Archaic Torso of Apollo": "You must change your life!" It is in this last, most curious essay on Henry Miller, entitled "The Greatest Living Author," that the missionary cast of the book emerges most clearly. Miller is described as "a holy man . . . Gandhi with a penis," who more than Lawrence or Joyce (both of whom Shapiro says were not free of "puritanical salaciousness") deals freely with "the overpowering mysteries and glories of love and copulation." It is also at this point that the extraliterary character of Shapiro's present concern emerges: "It is not art that Miller cares about; it is man . . . as a writer Miller may be second or third rate or of no rating at all; as a spiritual example he stands among the great men of our age."

Now literature, whenever it is important, goes outside itself (despite Shapiro's contention that religion and psychology and sociology, etc., get in the way of the poet) and we cannot quarrel with his celebration of Miller on that score, though we can note the paradox of saying "the greatest living author" is someone who "may not rate at all . . . as a writer." Nor can we deny that the reading of Miller's books is a rewarding experience—particularly for those who admire "beat" novelists like Kerouac but are unaware that Miller is immensely more talented, more intelligent, and wiser, and is a consummate, past master of what Kerouac is simply good at: the challenging achievement of occasional, transcendent, lyric flight out of the earthbound morass of naturalistic material. (Miller's best books of course are nearly all of them still officially banned in America. This means of course that they are available only to those who are really interested and who will go to the trouble to obtain them. Miller, who makes a mystique out of "obscene literature" as an esoteric cult, is well aware of this fact and I am sure would not have it otherwise.)

However, if our attention is really to be directed to Miller as a *figure* rather than as a practitioner of literature—and particularly as a figure who has supposedly understood and revealed the mysteries of love—then how can we fail to note the melancholy fact that the aging Miller is currently rattling around lonely in his Big Sur home besieged (it is not a contradiction) by random visitors and nuts, separated from his wife and children once again. My tendency would be to look for another leader in these matters of life and love. As for Miller's being the new hope and true leader in literary matters, I find it a bit ominous that Shapiro's style disintegrates in the essay where he talks about Miller. . . .

Yet, I believe the Miller essay, despite my problem with it, gives us the clue to many of the seeming contradictions and clashed textures of the book as a whole. For in this essay Shapiro writes: "Those poets who follow Whitman must necessarily follow Miller, even to the extent of giving up poetry for its formal sense and writing that personal apocalyptic prose which Miller does." Perhaps this is just what Shapiro has himself done. His book is not so much a sober "Defense of Ignorance" (which means innocence, uncorruptedness, unsophistication, the championing of the heart, with "its reasons the mind knows not of") though it is that in part, as it is a somewhat dionysiac and apocalyptic, canting work of art in its own right. Exciting and knowing as the book is, still some of Shapiro's readers may be forgiven for saying to themselves from time to time, "Karl, Karl, please be still about criticism, as you are always promising to do, and write some more poems for us." To be sure, that is always the poet's problem.

Twenty Poems of Georg Trakl Translated by James Wright and Robert Bly

(1962)

Twenty poems of Trakl, in a double text with the original German, beautifully designed and printed, a moving Bosch detail on the cover, may be had in a new translation by the poets Robert Bly and James Wright. At $1.00 this is surely one of the extraordinary bargains of our time. The poems are powerful and their power stays, reminding us that the best art changes the very gestures of our souls and moves with us out of our exile into the City of God itself.

Trakl constantly juxtaposes to images of violence a tender or lyrical figure which controls and calms the force the poem has released. This is true even in poems of war (Trakl was a medical aid at the front): "Yet a red cloud, in which a furious god,/the spilled blood itself, has its home, silently/gathers, a moon-like coolness in the willow bottoms." There is a deep and moving religious sense, the sense of human transcendence, of love and of grace at the heart of the work. Some of Trakl's images are specifically religious: "The soft orphan gathers the sparse ears of corn./Her eyes graze, round and golden, in the twilight/And her womb awaits the heavenly bridegroom." There is much use of the imagery of silence, of silent things, which to my mind is also religious, for it is only in their silence that created things betray the loud presence of their God.

For Trakl the gift the artist brings to the world is the gift of tenderness, and he made of himself a kind of marvelous machine for refining the cruelty he found in the world's offering into gentleness and beauty, which was his own offering. In this he was like a Christ. It is not surprising to learn that for an individual of such extraordinary sensitivity the mechanism broke down in his own life—which had to deal with such alarming scenes of hatred as that one where he was left overnight without help in a barn to succor ninety wounded and dying men. Whitman became father or mother or both at such times. Trakl's reaction was much more intimate. To him the barn groaned with dying images of his own soul. He could not save all of them. The metamorphosis into tenderness failed only where it touched himself, and he died a suicide at twenty-seven.

American Poetry in 1962

(1963)

The year was richer than most for American poetry. The best books of 1962 to come to my attention were created by John Ashbery, Charles Bukowski, Robert Bly, David Cohen, Robert Creeley, James Dickey, Clayton Eshelman, Suzanne Gross, Samuel Hazo, George Hitchcock, Richard Hugo, Richmond Lattimore, Anthony Ostroff, Muriel Rukeyser, William Stafford, and Richard Wilbur. Half of these—Bly, Cohen, Eshelman, Gross, Hugo, Hitchcock, Ostroff—are first books, which is fine. If I were to single out one volume as containing the greatest quantity of stunning, original poetry, it would be James Dickey's second book, *Drowning with Others*. This volume must in all justice receive the Pulitzer prize or the National Book Award.

William Stafford and Richard Hugo together surely deserve some sort of award for having produced out of the same earth (that of the Pacific Northwest) two extraordinary and utterly distinct books. These are fine poets. I don't mean that it's unusual for any one area to produce two such good, young poets. I mean that it's unusual for two artists to put down such deep and fruitful roots into a common earth at all and at the same time to keep these substructures so distinct. . . .

The volumes of Dickey, Ashbery, and Bly are all issued in the most distinguished American poetry series, that published by Wesleyan University Press.

Ashbery's book contains free-wheeling, surreal, associative, long poems displaying the kind of fecundity of the creative imagination which so delights and so intimidates one in the presence of great jazz artists (John Coltrane, for instance).

Dickey's poetry is highly controlled, formal, building its richly evocative, transformed, and haunting world out of recognizable, human situations often involving family. In the tightness of its form Bly's poetry lies between Ashbery's and Dickey's. To put this another way, there is less "secondary elaboration" (Freud's term) in Ashbery's work among these three and most in Dickey. Tighter form is not of itself better form. One cannot distinguish between good and bad poetry according to the tightness of the form any more than one can distinguish between good and bad dreams according to the degree of secondary elaboration.

Bly shares with Dickey what I can only call piety, in the ancient sense. I have an idea the poetry in Bly is primarily filial and that in Dickey it is primarily paternal. This is reflected in the greater openness of Bly to natural phenomena and in the noticeable, metamorphosizing yearning of Dickey. Dickey wants to build his own part of the world and to love that. Bly wants his own part of the world, which he loves, to build him into it. Both make superb poetry out of their angles of desire (I almost said angles of vision, but that is not quite what I mean). A crucial and deeply satisfying union of the paternal and filial feeling in the more usual sense is found in Dickey's long "The Owl King," in the climax of which a blind child embraces the huge-eyed owl—much as in the famous detail from Bosch's "Garden of Delight": "The owl's face runs with tears / As I take him in my arms / In the glow of original light / Of heaven," writes Dickey.

Robert Bly writes of silence, shadows, sleep, moonlight, and snow in Minnesota. Among living things he is apt to write of horses or grass or of man in a moment of inaction. This could be pretty dull. But it is not. It is quite lively and beautiful. For what interests Bly in silence is the articulate quality of it, its creative noise; what interests him in sleep is the fact that the inner man is *dreaming* or finding some other, more obscure way to blossom, whereas in some sense the outer man, man awake, sleeps. "The fundamental way of poetry," says Bly, "is the inner world." The epigraph to his book is the German mystic Jacob Boehme's statement: "We are all asleep in the outward man." So that in Bly the sleep of man becomes by a kind of inversion the symbol of man most alive. Horses and grass sleep (they do) on their feet, so to speak, so they image man alive. "I have suffered and survived the night / Bathed in dark water, like any blade of grass," writes Bly.

At the same time, seen at his usual mundane actions—or even at his esoteric ones, such as the writing of verse—man seems not to reveal his truer inner life, except through the invisible daydreams and recollections to which his work prompts him, and for which he is dependent on his daily labor. Here one thinks of Robert Frost: except through the shortcut of another's art, one simply does not get the profound vision of the apple picker or of the mower, for he lacks the specific muscular fatigue and consequently the specific sleep and dream of the mower or apple picker. Thus in Bly only "After Working" (in the poem of that name) is one able to accomplish the extraordinary listening involved in discerning the sound of moonlight—like "the deaf hearing through the bones of their head." Further revelations in other poems come only on the occasion of the feeding of livestock, for instance, or the hunting of pheasants. There is a peculiar quality—close to the active inaction of the inner man—in the passive action of a man driving a car or riding a swift train through the landscape and, moreover, the landscape itself, in its artificial change brought on by motion, begins to image the genuinely dynamic inner topography. So Bly has several poems that take their source from driving or riding.

Snow is strange in Bly. He is the only poet I know who would begin a *happy* poem with the lines: "It is a cold and snowy night. / The main street is deserted." In his work snow is associated primarily neither with death nor with purity as it is so often in poetry. Rather, it is associated with positive change, with achievement. We can see how this comes about if we recall (a) the power of snow to transform surfaces, (b) the intricate craftsmanship of the snowflake. "The white flake of snow/that just has fallen in the horse's mane" shames or chastens a man for having had thoughts of giving up all ambition. Snow "covers the husks of the fallen ears/With flakes infinitely delicate, like jewels of a murdered Gothic prince." It speaks "of virgins/with frail cloths made of gold." Snow weathers oars; it delineates train tracks from the night they are part of or the wheel tracks of a combine from the day. It becomes the object of an insane man's desire—as though it were like sanity, were like humanity, and in Bly so it is. In the skiff that carries one toward death, the poet sings "of feathers and white snow"—as though the two together, the trace of a winged thing and the trace of an element, formed an image of The Divine. And so in Bly they do.

The Looking Glass by Isabella Gardner

(1963)

Convinced of the excellence of Isabella Gardner's poetry, which ranks among the best we have in recent years, I want to speak of the feeling content of her work—and so of the poetic truth of it. The appearance of her new book, *The Looking Glass*, provides occasion for this.

Toward the beginning of *The Looking Glass* there is a group of elegies: "Zei Gesund," "In Memory of Lemuel Ayres," and "And Thou No Breath at All." Now there is a recurring motif in these poems, viz., an assurance that the speaker of the poems will also soon be dead. In the first of the three we read, "Our spirits shall by your quick soul be fed / until our bodies, too, are dead." In the second, "I that indulgently/am still allowed to be / address these lines. . . ." and at the end of the same poem, "The shame is you've few friends who / dared to expect to do / their dying old." Finally, in the third elegy, "Your art . . . will lend us gold beyond our death / . . . when we like you end, as we must, all out of breath."

In each case the poem gives for the space of its own life some life to those who are mourned, and on the other hand assures them that the speaker and her audience will not have life either. Indeed, as the one poem states so explicitly, the speaker does not even expect death to be delayed into age. From this we see that some concept is operating here beyond that expressed in the beautiful Skelton lines Miss Gardner uses as an epigraph

(I almost said "epitaph") to one of these poems: "It is generall / to be mortal," for one may be mortal and still die old. One is reminded of the line from "The Masked Shrew" in Miss Gardner's first book, *Birthdays from the Ocean,* where it is said of this animal that it "lives for a year of hurly-burly / and dies intolerably early."

Also in the earlier book there is an elegy for Dylan Thomas entitled "When a Warlock Dies." There we see the same motif as in the later elegies: "The homage of our elegies whistles against the night / that looms too close for comfort since his death *and our own uncomfortable respite.*" (Italics mine.) The phrase "uncomfortable respite" as a description of the speaker's state is meaningful, of course. It suggests a pain beyond grief, a pain for which the speaker does not anticipate relief before her own death. Perhaps the pain in question is guilt, I do not mean guilt of wrongdoing but that of anointment: guilt for the continued, unearned, gratuitous gift of life, which is so gratuitously denied to those who in each case are grieved for.

It is worth noting that each of the persons mourned is about the same age, still youthful, fortyish at the time of death, as that is about the age of the poet herself at the time of writing. But more profoundly they are deaths which in these poems are capable of moving each of us. "Every tear is for ourselves, for our own loss," writes Miss Gardner. We know John Donne's remark, in one of his sermons, "Everyman's death diminishes me." What is the truth of Donne's statement? Why do we feel ourselves "diminished" by the death of others? It seems to me that it is to protect ourselves against the very guilt of which I have spoken. The guilt is distinct from the grief in the usual sense—the sense of loss we have when deprived of someone *personally* dear to us. Of course, by analogizing we can recall losses of our own and so feel personal grief on the occasion of reading elegies such as these of Miss Gardner's, but I suspect that, though it is more hidden, the guilt of these elegies is more moving than the grief (at least to the readers if not to the writer), for this very reason that we are guilty of the death of anyone whose dying happens simply to have left us alive. And it is more tolerable to us to transform the pain of guilt into a sense of loss, which is here assuaged by the anodyne of art.

I have dwelt on this so long for I believe what we are apt to think of as a *memento mori,* as every man's death serves to be, is often stirring to us really for the reason that it is a *memento vivere.* We find the vision of our death more tolerable than the burden of our life. I do not mean this in the obvious sense because of the frequent sadnesses of our life (*sunt lacrimae rerum*), for death too is sad and may be painful, but rather for the very joy of it, the happiness of it, which the dead can no longer feel and share, at least in the same existential sense, so that we are guilty if they are dead—and not now because we wished them dead or any such thing, but simply because we are decent human beings and know that we deserve perhaps even less than what they now no longer have. This variety of guilt, that which is based on anointment rather than on offense, is painfully familiar to artists if not to others, for they must deal with it in respect to the mixed blessings of their own creative gifts. Perhaps that is one reason why Isabella Gardner's elegies handle this material so well.

"Death is not a problem to be solved," writes Gabriel Marcel. "It is a mystery to be entered into." The problem to be solved is life, and this turns me to another aspect of the content of Miss Gardner's poems, for in her art, as in all good art, we find played out the hope and the hell of our own lives. I refer now particularly to those poems dealing with the failure of communication, the failure of feeling, ultimately the failure of love.

I will show this theme in Miss Gardner's work shortly, but first I wish to remind us how contemporary such a theme is. In the recent Italian film *La Dolce Vita* this motif prevails, for here a father will not stay to speak to a needy son, a girl makes use of an accoustical gimmick in a castle in order to whisper in the ear of a man *around the corner and in another room* that she loves him, and another girl, beautiful, young, innocent, simply cannot make known to this same man (because of the sound of the sea, i.e., the noise of the unconscious) whatever it is she wishes to say to him.

In another contemporary work, Salinger's "Zooey," we see with what immense, sweating effort, and through what obstacles self-interposed, a man must labor to speak to those he loves—talking to them as Zooey does through a shower curtain, or through a handkerchief *and* a telephone (deemed necessary though the young man is in the same apartment as the person he is addressing), or flat on his back, his face hidden this time by his own feet! Maria Jeritza once sang the aria "Vissi D'Arte" from this same position, having fallen to the stage in a violent scene. Understandably the audience was amazed that the sound came out at all well. It is a paradigmal situation to me, for it is as though Maria Jeritza or the fallen young man Zooey were speaking really to the audience of angels rather than to that of persons: this makes it perhaps less surprising that the amount of energy expended is enormous, *yet it is not so great as would be required to speak directly to the beloved,* or to those one has any kind of feeling for, and that is the essential point.

In Isabella Gardner's superb "Mea Culpa" the title ambiguously refers to the feeling of the woman-speaker in the poem, the man about whom the story is told, and finally either the male or female reader. The compassionate woman of the poem is unable to touch with her speech the unhappy physician next to whom she is trapped in a plane—unable to help him feel more at ease about the critical lateness of his flight and the burden of his responsibility for life or death. The man and the woman remain hidden from one another though their bodies are juxtaposed. They avoid one another's eyes. It is noteworthy how often this scene recurs in Miss Gardner's poems, particularly in her most beautiful work. In "The Widow's Yard" the speaker looks at snails instead of at the widow "meaning to spare (her) vulnerable eyes." In "The Searchlight" the supposed lovers look at the sky or the surroundings instead of at each other. Very similarly in the moving "Lines for a Seagreen Lover" from her earlier book the lovers watch the gulls and hold hands, while staying, as it were, miles away from each other. And in "To Thoreau on Rereading Walden" we are told: "Were you, like Lazarus to rise,/you would look everywhere but in my eyes." Most notably, in the best poem of that first book, "That Craning of the Neck," we find that the speaker fails to arrest the attention and feeling of "a great blue heron," surrogate perhaps for a powerful, visionary lover. In none of these poems do the figures nearly approach that nakedness before one another which is characteristic of deep feeling and particularly of love.

The last-named poem, "That Craning of the Neck," has for its epigraph Martin Buber's statement, "The primary word is I-Thou. The primary word I-Thou can only be spoken with the whole being. The primary word I-It can never be spoken with the whole being." In the cases where personal touch, the meeting of person and person, fails to take place, then what Buber calls the primary word quite simply fails to be uttered and the pair are condemned to the language of I-It. The heron of this last poem "has damned itself an It and I shall never fly." Yet in the poem "Southwest of True North" from the earlier book, despite the alien and "indecent territory . . . at this compass point," the speaker manages to "sing, occasionally on the wing." In another poem Miss Gardner writes, "My lover never flew with me." However, the poem itself is a flight, even though the poet remains a mocked albatross, out of element, as in Baudelaire, or a lapwing, as in Joyce.

As a matter of fact, the touch which poetry itself makes possible between people clearly represents a compromise (one would not say "solution") for the problem of the failure of feeling between people, the problem of speaking "I-Thou." For artists, their work objectifies their yearning for love, "thatched" as we all are "in a thicket of loneliness, huddled in onlyhood." That is the situation of figures in "Mathematics of Encounter," a poem from Miss Gardner's recent volume, *The Looking Glass.* One is moved by the wishful naivete of this poem's conclusion: "Love is resolved/to one plus one, dissolved again to those, these two absolved,/and the equation solved." Now a characteristic note of dread or of something like death comes into this love poem through its imagery: "The marrying of marrows . . . /blood shimmers and arrows, bones melt/and meld, loins lock." There is more palpable dread in "The Searchlight"—here the lovers lie down awkwardly in the grass and suddenly their embrace is interrupted by an anti-aircraft searchlight in "A grave/rehearsal for another night. The field/bloomed lovers, dined and blind and target-heeled."

The searchlight of the poem in question becomes curiously complex—it is an eye, a kind of conscience, as well as a masculine weapon. (Its character as a phallus is extraordinary for it guns down the great birds of aircraft, themselves figures for aggressive lovers.) Relevantly it is the machine which is fertile rather than the "lovers" themselves. The frightened lovers are, as it were, the progeny of the searchlight for it causes the dark field to "bloom" men and women, sprung as if from the dragon's teeth in the old myth. It is a dangerous fecundity and so brings to mind comparable images, such as the following from the earlier poem "Fall in Massachusetts": "A manna of flame had unfallowed the starving field." (The fertile flame burned a witch.) In "The Widow's Yard," perhaps the best poem of the new book, there are further images of destructive procreation: "parasites invade/their flesh and alien eggs are laid/inside their skins." The animals referred to are snails, whose "mating . . . is perilous [and turns] their faces blue with bliss." We might say that the line "mating/too is perilous" determines the feeling of several poems. It is the key to the character of the lover as hero or antihero in these poems.

In the beautiful "Letter from Slough Pond," the yearning for the absent lover is expressed in the following line, which with its imagery of wind and bone very subtly suggests death: "The soft wind sighs through my wishbone"; and in "The Compleat Angler" from the earlier book, lovemaking is described in an imagery of fishing which includes the fatal sounding "a ridden hawk screams like a cat/as hook is caught as mouth is reamed."

Thus, in these poems there is frequently a juxtaposition of the themes of sexuality and death. One thinks of Faulkner and of Joyce, or, if death signifies evil, one thinks of Hawthorne. Perhaps the true insight of such a juxtaposition is based on the perception that sexuality apart from personal relationships and personal intimacy (I-Thou) is dissociated really from love and hence is allied to hate and to death. This seems to me more meaningful than that reading which would see the more usual Manichaean or American or adolescent association of sexuality and evil, though the former reading does not so obviously account for the theme of dread.

Returning to the late poem "Letter from Slough Pond," I wish to consider it from a different but related point of view: for the speaker of the poem there is in the absence of her lover something of the feeling of abandonment. Now death itself is the ultimate abandonment, the ultimate experience of absence. It is cruel of those we love to die, leaving us with our loss and with our guilt. At the same time *our own* death implies not so much an abandonment as a kind of meeting perhaps. For the speaker of these poems, generally the meeting with Death is the ultimate *impersonal* encounter. Indeed we may ask whether the word "encounter" may properly be used for a genuine meeting between people (I-Thou). It is the word rather to describe the "I-It" relationship, and as such it recurs in the poems.

Now "It" is the name of "a fatal Irish ghost," a figure of death in the ambitious, moving poem from Miss Gardner's earlier work, "Of Flesh and Bone." The piece ends with the line: "I shall not close my eyes when *its* eyes stare out of mine in every mirror." There is a close relationship between this poem with its mirror imagery which rehearses stages of growth from "child to girl" to womanhood, and the fine title poem in Miss Gardner's new book, "On Looking in the Looking Glass." The latter poem begins in the present with the speaker facing a mirror. "Your small embattled eyes dispute a face / that middle aging sags and creases." It returns "in an instant's blink" to "date the total innocence" of "the *child* you were," moves in another "wink" to the *girl* "I see and fear" (where the note of dread now familiar reappears "in your blistered eyes"), briefly turns "for a tic's lending" to the vision of the *adult* muse "that familiar whom you stint / so prodigally," and finally, closing the "infant, ancient, naked eyes," the speaker sees herself dead "with imagination's eye." It is a powerful poem in which the strength of the willed or imagined closeness to death at the end puts one in mind even of Keats's famous lines in his "Ode to a Nightingale."

I feel the poem "On Looking in the Looking Glass" represents an advance in the attitude toward death over the earlier poem, "Of Flesh and Bone," in two ways. In the earlier poem the vision of death is behind in the mirror with eyes opened and secondly it is resisted violently, whereas in this poem the vision occurs with eyes closed and without vehemence. One is again reminded of Marcel's saying: "Death is a mystery to be entered into rather than a problem to be solved." An acceptance of reality seems to be implied in the change. At any rate, such a sense is more characteristic of the second book and it has affected the style, which seldom verges on the hysteria (artistically controlled to be sure) of poems like "The Milkman" and "The Panic Vine." To savor this changed tone most easily one should look at the two poems, "Part of the Darkness" and "Not at All What One Is Used to," which with three others, "The Widow's Yard," "Mea Culpa," and "On Looking in the Looking Glass" give us the best work in the new book. In "Part of the Darkness" there is a sense of disenchantment about reality (with a perfectly natural resultant "bereavement") and in "Not at All What One is Used to" there is a sure assessment of growth in maturity as it is related to career. As the existence of these poems themselves witnesses, Miss Gardner's own progress in mastering the reality of her situation has come in connection with her acceptance of the vocation of poet, with which she is more at ease in this volume than in the first.

The fact that in both "Of Flesh and Bone" and "On Looking in the Looking Glass" the vision of death is had in connection with a mirror points up the verity of guilt through the association of the motion toward death with the moments of conscience, for it is our conscience we watch in the mirror. At the same time the very intimacy of the vision of death, its failure to be externalized (a mirror is perhaps the least external of all external objects) objectifies how much the struggle with death is a struggle with a part of ourselves and how true it is that the ultimate failure of love is based on another, interior one, the failure to have love for self. We remember that Eliot's *Waste Land,* where the failure of desire and of touch was dramatized so effectively forty years ago, is preceded by a good ten years by "The Love Song of J. Alfred Prufrock" whose mock-hero fights the calamity of self-abandonment, striving for touch between the parts of himself. "Let us go then, you and I" cannot be wished until one succeeds in getting "myself and I" to go together. The true tragedy of I-It as an expression is that so often it is the only word we can speak *to ourselves,* where the internal It (Latin *Id*) is a slovenly, aging, unattractive animal emptied of honey—like the bear in Miss Gardner's "A Part of the Dark."

There are three levels of meeting to be discerned in these poems: self with self, self with another (often an ambivalent lover), and self with Death. Sometimes these three meetings are blurred believably, dynamically, in the poems. One finds oneself associating the "ultimate encounter" with death in "Zei Gesund," the encounter of the love poem "Mathematics of Encounter" (with its very final "and the equation solved"), the "gently expected encounter with a lover" (who did not come) in "When in Rome" and "the engagement some tomorrow" with death seen in one's own mirrored eyes in "Of Flesh and Bone." The latter encounter is described as the "unrefusable embrace."

Lovemaking, the abandonment (that word again) of self, the commitment to another world, the world of the other person, may seem like a dying. It is almost as if our being in love committed us to being abandoned and hence as if commitment to love meant commitment to death.

The "raw widow" of "The Widow's Yard" has lost her husband and is victimized by the pain of this, but she possesses a relic of him—the snails he loved and cared for, which, curiously creative as they are, "litter with silver . . . / the rose and laurel leaves" in her yard. Stronger than Sisyphus struggling with the rock of his heart's grief, these snails are able to haul "a wagon toy loaded with a whole two hundred times their / body's burden."

It seems to me these heroic, silver-leaving, "tender-skinned" creatures are figures of the poet herself (or himself) and that the conclusion of the poem expresses the desire all artists share—that the misery resulting from their extraordinary sensitivity and from the burden of their gift will issue in the beautiful litter of their art, in a kind of song:

> at the first faint chill . . .
> the snails go straight to earth . . . excrete
> the lime with which they then secrete
> the opening in their shells . . . and wait for spring.
> It is those little doors which sing,
> she said, when they are boiled.

The Hazards of Holiness by Brother Antoninus (William Everson)

(1963)

Antoninus, lay brother of the Dominican Order, serving at St. Albert's College, Oakland, presents some formidable problems to the critic who would speak of his new book of poems, *The Hazards of Holiness*. Let me say at the offset that I find him an artist of great, even overwhelming strength. But I have chosen the word "overwhelming" carefully and I do not mean it entirely honorifically.

Many of Brother Antoninus's poems are too long. Their diction is often archaic ("maid's evasive sire," "But hold," "solitary covert," "dulcet song," "Did you not so?"). Their mode is confused with that of rhetoric, a rhetoric curious for its being addressed to the self more than to another. One wearies of Antoninus's using the poems to compare himself to St. John of the Cross (the theme of "The Dark Night") and John Donne (the motif of "Batter my heart, Three-personed God . . ." with its conclusion, "Take mee to you, imprison mee, for I / Except you enthrall mee, never shall be free, / Nor ever chaste, except you ravish me.") and Gerard Manley Hopkins (even the language of "Sleep Tossed I" seems imitative of Hopkins's anguished, quarreling, "terrible sonnets"). One grows tired too of Antoninus's figuring the relationship to God under terms of rape and castration ("annul in me my manhood," from an

225

earlier book and the following, for example, from this one: "Make me! Slake me! Back me! Break me!" "God! Suck me in!").

Reading straight through this new work one shakes with the relentless hatred of self and of sexuality which Brother Antoninus shares with the beat poets, and one is hurt by the relentless succession of poems violently written on violent subjects: the wrestling of Jacob; the encounters with Christ as witch or dog-woman (Sphinx), aggressive or fawning female; the beheading of John the Baptist; Judith and Holofernes; the violent conversion of St. Paul.

Yet after all is said, still for sheer power and for a certain kind of bravery and commitment to art, willing to take risks in language and risks in self-revelation, one can find very little indeed to compare with Brother Antoninus's *Hazards of Holiness*. It is a moving book. And it has the special interest of presenting a group of poems which are prefaced both with biblical quotations (in one case a quote from the *Verba Seniorum*) and also with lengthy, fairly full accounts of dreams. There is an archetypal character to the situations of the quotations which puts one in mind of Jung's doctrine of the racial unconscious, juxtaposed as these samples are to dream material from the personal and individual unconscious. These three modes: myth (I do not use the word pejoratively), dream, and poem are used together in some very interesting pieces here, the best of which seems to me to be "A Frost Lay White on California."

One needs to remember in reading these that a written dream is already an interpretation of a dream and that when it is written in the cadences of an artist, as are these prefacing dreams, they are actually prose poems. The economy and simplicity of language and the richness of image in these dreams of Antoninus is remarkable in its own right, and if left to choice I would say that in some cases I should choose the beauty of the dreams over that of the poems that follow them. I remember seeing some of Antoninus's prose poetry recently in *Ramparts,* and I remember the peculiar strength and brilliance of some letters of his in *Sewanee Review* and the touching tribute to

Robinson Jeffers he published recently in *The Critic*. I wonder whether the more centrifugal movement of prose poetry might not make it a specially happy medium at which to look for new work from Brother Antoninus. Perhaps I'm being obscure. By more centrifugal I mean less self-indulgent, that is, less egocentric. For Antoninus to make another step forward as an artist he needs to take a risk which for all his courage he has not yet taken: the risk of giving himself to an audience. Instead, Antoninus asks an audience to give themselves to him, to join him in his flayings of himself (and ultimately of themselves also). One feels this at his readings as well as in the poems. I can't think of an aesthetic *less* calculated to lead Brother Antoninus forward as an artist than the one he quotes in this book (after T. S. Eliot) in which one uses one's gift (and in Antoninus it's a considerable one) "not to communicate with anyone" but to "obtain relief . . . experience a moment of something very near to annihilation." I have to say that to me this sounds much like an aesthetic of self-abuse. The artist brings a natural grace to his audience, he brings a natural absolution, " a momentary peace" (in Dylan Thomas's phrase) to them. He has no right to expect this for himself except to the extent he is willing to join his audience—and I repeat this is very different from expecting one's audience to join him.

The Branch Will Not Break by James Wright and The Lion's Tail and Eyes by James Wright, Robert Bly, and William Duffy

(1963)

James Wright is one of the two or three finest young poets of the present generation. His third book, *The Branch Will Not Break,* is his best. One of the marks of superb talent is its capacity for change in expression and form as the artist himself grows. The new book shows the fruits of Wright's encounter with the rich contemporary poetry of Latin America. His sensibility has undergone transformation since his first book. He is now more in touch with the depths of his own feeling and has begun to produce not simply metaphors or similes, which have a two-term polarity, both terms identifiable and capable of being named in language, but images where what is imagined is a gesture of the inner life of man, itself nameless apart from these very images themselves which the poet, by his gift, turns up into the light of language ("small antelopes fall asleep in the ashes of the moon"). The book is beautiful and it is important.

A shortcoming derives from a certain aura of romanticism which (contrary to the proper inward movement of Wright's best poetry) is actually tied too much to the outer world, for it is related to echoing, the sounds trapped in the outer ear from one's early reading and the feelings caught at the edge of the heart from one's young experience. There are too many "moons" in his poetry and too many "horses." The horse, so important a figure in, for example, the Spanish poetry of Lorca, must not be allowed to multiply grotesquely like a rabbit in the new American poetry.

My objection to the number of horses in the poems of Wright, Robert Bly, and William Duffy in their fine collection *The Lion's Tail and Eyes* constitutes but a cavil in an unusual, exciting volume which serves ideally to lead readers into the extraordinary, creative world of three Minnesota poets who are familiar with the contemporary poetry of several nations and who together are bringing to American poetry a powerful new direction away from academicism. These three artists are presenting what I would like to call "organic" poetry, poetry which experiments with content rather than with form and whose life does not depend upon its metrics but upon the life of the poet himself. "A poem," Robert Bly says in his introductory note, "grows from a man like an ear or a hand." Bly's "Evolution from the Fish" is a splendid example.

Poet's Choice Edited by Paul Engle and Joseph Langland

(1963)

A good idea of the sad extremities to which the older, academic American poetry can go—so opposed by younger poets like Robert Bly and James Wright—appears in the following comment by J. V. Cunningham. Cunningham is speaking about his own poem "Epitaph" in the new anthology *Poet's Choice,* edited by Paul Engle and Joseph Langland, which contains the personal choices of their own best work by 100 American poets together with a comment on the selection. Thus Cunningham: "I like this poem because it is all denotation and no connotation; because it has only one level of meaning; because it is not ironic, paradoxical, complex or subtle; and because the meter is monotonously regular."

Cunningham, who used to teach at the University of Chicago, is now at Brandeis. Although Cunningham does not, in this statement, share the interest in complexity of an intellectual kind which one finds in academic poetry, he does reveal an interest in the unreality which is the hallmark of such poetry. Richness of connotation is an actual characteristic of language as it is used by people in their attempts to touch each other by talk, whereas such language is also marked by a certain vibrancy and variation of cadence. The poet exults in these true qualities of language when the state of his art is healthy—it is the scientist who tries to exorcize them. The interest in mechanical metrics ("monotonously regular" in Cummingham's phrase) is an attempt to insulate the poem from the feeling of the writer and of the reader, to construct a world in which one is safe as in regular, parallelepipedal box, that is, as in a coffin. Such poems bury a part of the poet instead of resurrecting it with new life or exploring a new mode of living thought. (For this reason Cunningham's "Epitaph" is an apt title. He has several poems similarly named in the body of his work.) This insulation against reality academic poetry shares with two other highly intellectual genre: nonsense verse (or light verse) and mystery fiction. One can read them for relexation and as a removal from life, but they are of no use in helping one to engage the reality of one's own situation, as all great poetry does help one.

At the opposite pole is Karl Shapiro's comment on his prose poem, "The Dirty Word," in this same anthology. He says, "Why must grown people listen to rhymes? Why must meters be tapped out on nursery drums? Why hasn't America won the battle of Iambic Five? When are we going to grow up?. . . I feel ashamed when I write meter and rhyme, or dirty, as if I were wearing a dress." Regularity of form can betray a highly intel-lectualized process, an insulation from reality, as I have com-mented, but Freud reminds us that it can also be very primitive or infantile, springing from our yearning for repetitive ele-ments and from our attachment to what Freud calls primary processes. The monotonous regularity Cunningham pays trib-ute to is one of the unmistakable qualities of neurotic process and of the creatively sterile, energy-draining unconscious. The true creative unconscious (Freud called it the Preconscious System; Maritain beautifully names it the Musical Uncon-scious) is characterized not by monotony but by flexibility, nov-elty and variation; it is lifelike. Shapiro's abandonment of reg-ular, set forms represents a development in his work which has ordinarily been marked by a strong sense of the stanza and by patterned rhyme—though he was always a great master of the unobtrusive end rhyme, a movement toward the elimination of dependency upon rhyme. The prose poem "The Dirty Word," which Shapiro now singles out as his favorite, was an early exception which has now become the rule of his later work.

Louis Simpson in his comment on his poem "Walt Whitman at Bear Mountain" in this anthology speaks of a change from his earlier work in which he showed great skill at "form," but which still he ultimately began to feel as a straight jacket. He found that he was trapped by his "polishing" activities into practices (for example, the rhymed final cadences of his poems) "that some times distorted my real meaning . . . I wanted to write a poem that would be less 'willed,' I would let the images speak for themselves." The results—a more "organic" kind of poetry, as I have described it elsewhere, we should see in good measure in Simpson's new book *At The End of the Open Road* to be issued by Wesleyan University Press this fall.

The Animal Inside by Josephine Jacobsen

(1966)

Josephine Jacobsen's third book is certainly her best, and with it she wins recognition among the most gifted women poets of her generation. Mrs. Jacobsen has a fine ear, which is a *sine qua non* (and still a rarity) for any true master in poetry, and she has a superb command of enjambment technique, which itself seems to be bound up intimately with the sense of line as line— that is, with what it is that separates poetry from prose.

I want to concern myself here with the title of her book, "The Animal Inside," and with three poems which involve it. To begin with, the title phrase may itself mislead one from the actual idea behind it, for one may perhaps think it refers to the notion of the animal element of man in the sense of *lower* element as the classical view would have it. On the contrary, it refers to the life element or, better, the spiritual element, as one learns from the quotation which begins the book. I give it here entirely except for Mrs. Jacobsen's ellipses:

> . . . If an animal lives and moves, it can only be, he (the savage) thinks, because there is a little animal inside which moves it; if a man lives and moves, it can only be because he has a little man or animal inside who moves him. The animal inside the animal, the man inside the man, is the soul . . . to this some of the blacks replied, Yes. yes. We also are two, we also have a little body within the breast. . . .

The quotation is from *The Golden Bough* by J. G. Frazer, and Mrs. Jacobsen prints it under the title "The Animal Inside the Animal."

I remember being with James Wright and Robert Bly when Wright pointed out a similar passage—I believe in C. W. Bowra's *Primitive Song*. We were all excited about it, as Josephine Jacobsen apparently was. If I were to say why such a passage should stir poets deeply, I would suggest it is because for them the "animal inside the animal" is first of all the "muse" itself as the ancients spoke of it, or "the musical unconscious" as Jacques Maritain, following Jung, so beautifully renamed it. The life of the poet is the poet inside the poet. Morris Graves has superbly figured it in a number of paintings: "The Little Known Bird of the Inner Eye," "Fish Reflected Upon Outer and Mental Space," et al.

The first poem in Josephine Jacobsen's book, "The Animal Inside," is a reaching and lyrical piece, which explores the relationship between the idea of an interior figure (the animal inside) and two kinds of exterior ones, the shadow and the reflection. The use of one of these as an analogy for another (a further form of reflection) is quite brilliantly handled. "When his eyes open inward not to see / but for your sight—its glimpsed shadow is beautiful, dangerous / only to this companion whose it is." (part one). "So that the particular body throws / The universal shadow on the sand. . . ." (part two). ". . . the water image then with a light shiver / drew down its lover / letting the foundation-laughter play its gleam over the rooted bloom." (part four). I found the idea of a narcissism which involves a reflected *inner* image to be provocative in its own right. It brings to mind the attitude of Joyce's Stephen Deadalus toward himself. (I did not quote from the third section, for it seemed to me the less successful part of this ambitious poem.)

"Deaf Mutes at the Ball Game" is a superb poem in which the image of the deaf-mute sitting silent but active, fingertalking, amid the noise of baseball fans is developed through the notion of being "in the hurricane's eye" (as though at the heart of the life-struggle itself) forward to the idea again of the animal inside the animal. "While secret secret sits inside / Each, his deaf-mute; fingerless." It is great material for poetry, used greatly. The image of the fingerless mute inside the fingered one was very stirring to me. First, because of the idea of the mutes as "audience" in a curious literary way—they read *everything*, including speech. Second, because of the idea of the mute as a figure of man—which emerges not only because the last line of the poem relates the mute to each of us (the animal inside us all is "fingerless") but also because we all begin as inarticulates and to a certain degree remain that way, struggling constantly to hear ourselves more clearly. "We fog bound people are stammerers," wrote O'Neil. "Wovon Mann nicht sprechen kann daruber muszt Mann schweigen," wrote Wittgenstein at the end of a long book (long speech).* A third reason why Josephine Jacobsen's idea-image is so stirring here is because of the concept of the "Poet as Mute," which is the title of another of her poems, one dedicated to Hans Andersen.

Another piece which uses the title motif (not entirely successfully to my mind) is "My Uncle a Child," where Mrs. Jacobsen writes: "The caged and simple thing inside him watched / the parts' disintegration." I had difficulty with this poem, for it remained obscure to me after several readings. I take it to concern an uncle become like a child again (the "second coming") through the regressive effects of illness, so that his sickroom appears a nursery (or perhaps his sickbed is placed in the nursery?). The theme of the mute appears again in connection with this material: "toothless / and without words among the wicked toys of enamel (sick room utensils?) he teetered. . . ." I take it here the "animal inside" awaits the death of the outer one ("The simple indivisible watcher waited./It peered forth without warning, using my uncle's eyes."), and that this watching is ended for good with the last line ("my total uncle answered.") but I am not sure.

The mute-theme is well developed in the poem: "It . . . expressed itself suddenly in a powerful silence closing his lips."

---

*See footnote number one in Logan's essay "On Poets and Poetry Today" in this book.—A. P., Jr.

But other things don't seem as well integrated as in some of her poems, or at any rate I don't understand them all. Furthermore there is a curious practice of ending line after line with the article "the" plus a noun. For example, four successive run-on lines read this way: ". . . *The moon*/ moved at night, staring, and *the clouds*/ approached in silence and turreted softly away. *The earth*/ spun so unobtrusively that *the children*/ receding like a. . . ." (Italics mine.) The content is fine but, unless there is a mannerism whose function escapes me, the line endings seem unrevised. And there are five or six other similar endings (sometimes with a third word) in the next dozen or so lines, though these are mainly endstopped, which is perhaps less objectionable when such endings are employed in successive lines.

Nevertheless, the truth is that there are a number of fine, thoroughly satisfying poems in the volume. Dylan Thomas has an image of his book as an ark filled with animal poems. So are there here, to take Josephine Jacobsen's related image, several beautiful "animals inside the animal" of her living literature.

Northfield Poems by A. R. Ammons

(1967)

A. R. Ammons is one of the most prolific and, at the same time, most intelligent and gifted poets of recent years. *Northfield Poems* is his third book to appear in two years—with *Corsons Inlet* and *Tape for the Turn of the Year*—and there were two others in the previous ten-year period: *Ommateum* (which was privately printed) and *Expressions of Sea Level.*

Tape for the Turn of the Year, perhaps the most interesting single volume, is a continuing poem, mainly unrevised, which Ammons composed by inserting one end of an adding machine tape in a typewriter and proceeding to the other end. The imposed limitation of form apparently provided a pressure which helped to produce some very beautiful writing, all 200 pages of it in the mode of a journal extending over a period of about a month. The long, thin poem is occasionally ascetic in its effect (as an El Greco figure) and again it is snake-like. There is a passage where the poem shows a striking self-recognition of its phallic character:

> If I had a flute: wdn't
> it be fine
> to see this long thin
> poem
> rise out of the waste
> basket:
> the charmed erection,
> stiffening, uncoiling.

Another passage catches from inside the work, toward its end, the speaker's sense of his own utterance:

> I wrote about these
> days
> the way life gave them.
> I didn't know
> beforehand what I
> wd write, whether I'd meet
> anything new: I
> showed that I'm sometimes
> blank and abstract,
> sometimes blessed with song: sometimes
> silly, vapid, serious,
> angry, despairing.

The free form of the poem (despite its strict limitation on line length) and its willingness to risk "prose" and looser diction, has given it an utterly original tone, a curious blend of confession, lyricism, and observation of two kinds—the strikingly concrete and the near abstract.

All three of these qualities recur in other books, though there is less of the first—indeed less personal portraiture of any direct kind—in *Ommateum*. Confession begins with *Expressions of Sea Level* where, combined with childhood reminiscence as in "Nelly Myers" and "Silver," it has given us some of the most beautiful poems of our time:

> I will not end my grief, earth will
> not end my grief,
> I move on,
> we move on, some scraps of us together,
> my broken soul leaning toward her to be touched,
> listening to be healed.

A number of poems in *Expressions, Corsons Inlet,* and *Northfield,* as the names of the latter two hint, are based on experiences of places in South Jersey, where Mr. Ammons was for many years an executive in a chemical glass factory before turning to teaching.

Ammons's voice is unique and would not fail to be recognized even in the first book:

> So I said I am Ezra
> and the wind whipped my throat
> gaming for the sounds of my voice
> I listened to the wind
> go over my head and up into the night.

There is a return to the oracular, Old Testament–like persona of "Ezra" in the poem "The Wind Coming Down From" in the present volume. The poems of this book reiterate several motifs we are familiar with from the others, and they range from the highly abstract game stance of "The Numbers":

> be confident
> as you turn to the numbers
> veracity
> links segment to segment: a sausage bliss!

through the lecturelike sound of "The Motion" to the Biblical incantation of "Joshua Tree" on the one hand or the very direct, sure, imitative dialect of "First Carolina Said Song" on the other:

> We got there just in time to see her buried
> in an oak grove
> back of the field:
> its growed over with soapbushes and huckleberries now.

"Joshua Tree" is a moving piece in which the speaker is related to the wind who instructs him to

> settle here
> by the Joshua Tree
> and make a well.

The speaker, after lamenting that he is

consigned to
form that will not
let me loose
except to death

so that he "must go on" until then, asks that later the wind—
muselike and yet like a man—

enter angling through
my cage
and let my ribs
sing me out.

The wind is a frequent persona in the poems, as breath itself
becomes fleshed out. Considering wind as breath, one begins
to see the connection between the poems of external landscape
and the elements (which fill the first book and reappear here)
and the poems of internal geography:

When I go back of my head
down the cervical well, roots
branch,
turning, figuring
into flesh.

I don't like the line "meat's indivisible stuff" because its texture
jars with the rest of the *coulage* of diction, but otherwise this
poem, "Landscape with Figures" is one of the strongest in the
collection.

There is a constant playing off of the interior world of mind
and cells against the exterior world of things where self lies
dispersed and in need of the gathering force of a poem. The
rapport of interior and exterior is itself expressed in a perfect
short poem entitled "Reflective,"

I found a
weed
that had a

mirror in it
and that
mirror

looked in at
a mirror
in

me that
had a
weed in it.

The half-solipsistic character of this is projected beautifully to
trees in a fuller sense in the poem "Halfway":

birches stand
in

pools of them
selves, the yellow
fallen

leaves reflecting
those on
the tree that
mirror the ground

From the idea of external-reflected-in-internal, one can
move rather easily to the notion of the cosmos reflected in
small in one of its parts, as in the striking poem, "The Con-
stant," where the galaxylike, moving film of sand in the water
of a clam shell seems to reflect the scope of sky, so that:

a gull's toe would spill the universe
two more hours of sun could drip it up
a higher wind could rock it out. . . .

There is a marvellous imagining of the tentativeness with
which things "live and move and have their being" as the Old

Fellow said. This mood is seconded in "Contingency" where, contemplating all the life and change started by a sprinkler, one reflects that:

> (a) turn of the faucet
> dries every motion up.

And it is brought into a new key in the poem, "Zone," which suggests that a myth of creation is completed only by its parallel myth of uncreation. There is a constant need for recovery, whether for the shadows of trees (in "Recovery") or for time future (in "Passage")—

> tomorrow emerges and
> falls back shaped into today: endlessly

—or for the life of man himself. For poets, this latter kind of recovery is accomplished by the writing of poems, and when the poems are as good as these, it is sometimes accomplished for others by reading them.

Intellectuality is a prime trait of Ammons's work, as is suggested by the abstract character of several titles in the new book: "Height," "Reflective," "Contingency," "Interference," "Saliences." Sometimes, as in the latter poem and in "One-Many"—two of the most ambitious and strongest poems in the book—there is too much cerebration demanded of the reader, I believe, before the poem begins to burgeon. There are some other faults. Occasionally influence obtrudes itself, as that of Marianne Moore in "Uh, Philosophy" or of Dylan Thomas in these punning elegaic lines:

> If bleak through the black night
> we could outrun
> this knowledge into a different morning!

or of T. S. Eliot in this passage: "though the world ends and cannot end" and "To death, the diffuse one going beside me, I said. . . ." (Yet the most pervasive influences—those of William Carlos Williams and Ezra Pound—have been well assimilated to form a highly original body of work.) There are occasionally bad lines: "O ablutions!" Yet, a careful look at the whole body of Ammons's work, particularly *Tape for the Turn of the Year* and this new book, will show that we are dealing with a major talent, one who has the courage and the heuristic power to discover new form, as well as the eye and ear and the mind to hold us and to give us what Thomas called "the momentary peace of the poem."

Body Rags by Galway Kinnell

(1968)

Each generation looks about to see who the great ones are in the arts and in our time we can single out Galway Kinnell as one of the few consummate masters in poetry. His third book, *Body Rags,* is uniformly strong beside *What A Kingdom It Was* (1960) and *Flower Herding on Mount Monadnock* (1964) and it takes some risks those books do not. In two of the three poems in the final section of the new book, "The Porcupine" and "The Bear," there is some of the best poetry to be found any place today, while the long poem about civil rights, "The Last River," which makes up the entire second section, is one of the most pertinent and ambitious poems of the time.

The latter poem turns the situation of a jail in the deep South into a Danteesque drama and reflection of considerable complexity. (One should know that Kinnell was in fact jailed for civil rights activities in Selma, Alabama.) Although I admire it, I do not find the poem entirely successful because the elements of formal repetition and of classical allusion sometime appear too heavy-handed. For example this:

> He comes out of the mist.
> He tells me his name is Henry David.
> He takes my hand and leads me over the plains of crushed
>   asphodel.

However, if one's going to seek an analogue to Vergil as a guide through the hell of Selma, it would be difficult to better the choice of Henry David Thoreau who, in a planned act of civil disobedience during the Mexican War, refused to pay taxes to a government he considered abstract.

"The Last River" repeats many of the images of the nineteen (mainly short) poems which constitute the first section of the book. There is a good deal of specifically religious symbolism ("Let's go, I say, a big salty wafer of spit in my mouth") and there are wings, flowers, and flames employed in connection with a Roethke-like motif of opening and/or being transformed. But the longer poem, understandably in a poem of the South, lacks the snow that frequently falls in the shorter ones—sometimes in a climate a bit like that of Robert Bly:

> Soon it will be spring,
> again the vanishing of the snows,
> and tonight
> I sit up late, mouthing
> the sounds that would be words
> in this flimsy jew's harp of a farmhouse. . . .

The farmhouse, by the way, is a real one near Sheffield, Vermont, red, windy, on top of a beautiful hill at the end of an isolated, unimproved road. And it has for some years been a site of inner and outer lookings and of labors which Galway Kinnell has turned into poetry.

"The River" also contains the title motif:

> a man of noble face
> sits on the iron bunk, wiping
> a pile of knifeblades clean
> in the rags of his body.

This is varied twice in the description of the horrid Charon-figure in the poem: "limbs tied on with knots and rags," and once in "The Porcupine" where the title phrase—"body-rags"—occurs directly. The title is perhaps meant to echo the famous "aged man" passage from Yeats's "Sailing to Byzantium," possibly as prefigured by Pound (Yeats's secretary at the time) in a letter to Viola Baxter, October 24, 1907: "This body-rag thing tattered on my soul."

The two poems, "The Porcupine" and "The Bear," I think are the best in the book. They make up a pair on related subjects having finally to do with the poet and with poetry. There is a strong identification of the poet-speaker with the animal in each case and the animals themselves share certain qualities—ponderousness, voraciousness, and resilient brute strength.

Kinnell details seven highly ironic points in which the porcupine resembles man in general and poets in particular. In his bear poem, the identification of the poet and the bear is made extraordinarily close—in the first place, through the starving speaker's subsistence on the blood-soaked turds of the bear he hunts, so that which has passed through the bear passes also through the poet, and in the second place through the fact that the poet cuts open the warm carcass of the bear and takes shelter there against the vicious wind and cold:

> . . . lumbering flatfooted
> over the tundra
> stabbed twice from within
> splattering a trail behind me.

He is born out of the body of the bear again, having thought in his dream that he "must rise up and dance"—and he writes his poem. But first he makes an agonized step, infantlike and bearlike as well (it is a "hairy-soled trudge"), and like the ancient mariner he wanders the rest of his days wondering "what anyway . . . was that sticky infusion, that rank flavor of blood, that poetry, by which I lived?" The present poem is to be seen as the fruit of that wandering, and it is a remarkable one in its reenactment of the existential loneliness, the sense of abandonment before the elements, and the dual role of hunter and hunted under which we all live out our lives.

The image of poetry itself as a "sticky infusion" of bloody

bear shit must make us reflective when we find it in the work of one of our best poets. The figure of the poet-as-bear is familiar from the work of Theodore Roethke and Delmore Schwartz. Roethke's bear, like Kinnell's, dances: "O watch his body sway!/This animal remembering to be gay." Schwartz, Roethke, and Kinnell are all big men, and they have projected their size into an image whose emotional dynamics all poets share to a certain extent, beginning with their disbelief in the likelihood of a creature such as melancholy, flesh-heavy man bursting into song.

The element of bearlike ponderousness or awkwardness we are familiar with in the image of the poet for it relates to his (no doubt justified!) feeling of being "out of his element" like Baudelaire's albatross on the deck of a ship.

Voraciousness is another element in this image, for the poet gluts himself with reading and experience out of which to write, and it contributes to the concept of ponderousness, particularly in those constipated times when one produces nothing. Kinnell's porcupine is as voracious as the bear—and on a diverse diet as if for making poems:

> Fatted
> on herbs, swollen on crabapples,
> puffed up on bast and phloem, ballooned
> on willow flowers, poplar catkins, first
> leafs of aspen and larch,
> the porcupine
> drags and bounces his last meal through ice,
> mud, roses and goldenrod, into the stubbly high fields.

The last line reminds us of Eliot's line adapted from Mallarmé's description of poetry: "Garlic and sapphires in the mud."

The resilient strength of bear and porcupine is the quality the poet desperately needs in order to counterbalance his (killing) sensitivity and which, like them, he sometimes possesses sufficiently to survive.

But neither the bear nor the porcupine in Kinnell's poems *does* survive. They die slow, terrible deaths, the first from the inner stabbing of a sharpened stick coiled in his food and the other from being shot three times and falling to unwind his guts from a tree limb.

Seeing the poet as imaged by the bear returns one to the image of poetry itself as the excretion of the wounded animal: "that sticky infusion, that rank flow of blood, that poetry by which I lived." The visceral connotation is not of itself arresting, for again it is part of the general image of poetry which, when it is any good, comes certainly from the inner depth—and the sexual ring of "sticky infusion" is predictable and right. But there is an aura of violence (self-destructive dying) to the visceral imagery of the poems and to the phrase "rank flavor of blood" which stops me, and I want to comment on it.

In the porcupine poem the self-pain is quite specific:

> In my time I have
> crouched, quills erected,
> Saint
> Sebastian of the
> scared heart, and been
> beat dead with a locust club
> on the bare snout.

And in the bear poem the figure of the poet's dream (himself) is "stabbed twice from within" (compare the "self-stabbing coil/of bristles reversing" in the porcupine poem) while the trail of generative blood behind the dying bear is related to the umbilical cord or lifeline of the producing poet. This figure of the agonized generative trail is repeated in "The Porcupine" and in the third poem which makes up this final section of the book, "Testament of a Thief." In the latter poem it takes the form of a pewkworm whose path, as it is drawn out of the body, "by winding him up on a matchstick/a quarter turn a day for the rest of your days" creates a "map of my innards," that is, a poem of the interior life. In the former poem, it is figured in the strung-out intestines of the shot porcupine who "paying out gut heaved/and spartled through a hundred feet of goldenrod" before dying.

Poetry is a wandering trail of blood and bear shit. It is a pewkworm wound through a hole in the buttocks or cheeks of a man. It is the tree-hooked entrails of a porcupine. The images are all repulsive and they are all figures of the slow destruction of the self. They remind specifically of George Barker's description of poetry: "I give you the image of the captive of the Gaels whose torture was to . . . unwind his intestines around a tree, for this is the poet . . . whose bowels are wound around the Eden tree in coils at once agonizing and glorious. I mean each turn is a poem." Kinnell writes very similarly. "I have come to myself empty, the rope / strung out behind me in the fall sun / suddenly glorified with all my blood."

The idea of the poet as masochist emerges. Sartre levels the accusation tellingly in *Literature and Existentialism.* But I would insist that poetry is not a record of self-destructive experiences. Rather, it is often a record of recovery from them. It is not the blood-soaked shit of a dying bear. Rather, it is the gold into which that stuff is turned by the magus-gift of the poet. Thus the horse droppings in a poem of James Wright's "blaze into golden stones." But perhaps this is basically what Kinnell means by putting his poetics inside a poem like a hunter inside a bear which shelters and transforms him into something fecund, dreaming.

On the other hand, if the content of Kinnell's bear poem does really have a masochistic bias to it, then this emphasis is (quite brilliantly and purposefully) weakened by the choice of a form in which the material is repeated from a dream inside the poem. For the meaning of the dream-within-the-dream, Freud has said, is often to put down the significance of the content so displayed, to say in effect, "It was only a dream."

These two poems are very rich and mind-seizing and might be seen in other ways. I want finally to mention two other angles of vision. One might look at the images of porcupine gut, pewkworm, and bear trail simply as derivative from or extensions of the figure of the poet into something quite real—the poem. And one might look at the immersion of the hunter in the warm, colorful vitals of the bear as a figure of the contemporary poet who, withdrawn at last from libraries and psychoanalysis (the book of himself), sleeps himself instead in the pied field of human experience, partly revolting, partly serene and beautiful—like the porcupine amid the mud and the goldenrod.

Changing the Windows by Jerome Mazzaro

(1972)

Jerome Mazzaro's first book of poems follows closely two other books of his—a translation of Juvenal and a study of Robert Lowell. His work is that of a man of letters of consistency and integrity, and his books influence each other. Thus one finds the ironic tone of Juvenal in such a poem as "The Poet at Seventeen," one of his surest—a portrait of the speaker's aunt. "The greedy, shrivelled up, hell spouting ass/who gave me first communion, he supports her./ He stuffs her full of Christ and heaven's grace." And one finds the echo of Robert Lowell in choice of subject (religious sensibility in encounter with re- ligious practice on the one hand and with secular reality on the other); choice of form—heavily iambic lines, often pentame- ter, often rhymed in a variation of the envelope quatrain as in the early Lowell; choice of mode (monologue from the point of view of the Catholic woman, which has produced some of the best work of both poets); and finally in the choice of musical cadence itself: "Our target looms into its zero hour. / We roll, and all turns flak and spark and fire."

The influence of Lowell is indeed strong, but it is assimilated well into a fine intelligence and talent. Although the heavy iambs recur even in the very artful syllabic poems, these are on the whole more felicitous rhythmically. Frequently the music of Mazzaro's poems is less dissonant than Lowell's. Even the diction of this line reminds us of Keats: "as if to pipe their final, soft goodbye." Yet a few lines later in the strong poem "Survivors" there is a very striking contemporary image and idiom: "My stare goes onto some vague memory/strung like a wet wash in the inner eye. . . ." This poem, which carries through an archetypal situation of uprooting to move elsewhere—long continuity established only by an ivory statue of a shepherd boy—has some bad lines ("reminds of those days gone by") and it ends with a rather calculated image, "My speed's too slow. I press on faster." But on the whole it is a swift, narrative piece, as is the long concluding poem, perhaps the best in the book, "Committal."

There is a strong Catholic sensibility behind these poems, several of which as Mazzaro has maintained "show the survival of Christian civilization despite all attempts to destroy it." To be sure that which has survived does not always appear in a particularly attractive light here. One is somehow more interested in the intelligent, sensitive *person* who is "Survivor" in the poem of that name.

In the Sleep of Rivers by Joseph Stroud

(1975)

Joe Stroud has always been my friend, even when he was my student, and I have known some of his poems for years—have watched them (even a poem he has dedicated to me) grow like children coming of age. I cannot be expected, therefore, to look at his poems (I should say *listen* to his poems and to the wind in their sails) as if they were ships which just now docked at my shores. Besides the influence (which quotations and titles often acknowledge) of Roethke, Rilke, Keats, Bly, I can even see some echoes of my own work in Stroud's poems, as in the phrase "weep quietly in the wood" or in the lines we both stole from Rilke, "Lord, it is time now" or from Shakespeare, "that poor, bare forked animal [man]," in the ambiguous use of "Christ" in a phrase like "Christ / Bartleby" or, perhaps, in the tone of his poem about two brothers heading home, solicitous for the welfare of each other.

But, for that I can only say, "If a poet is going to have influences (and he *is*), they may as well be good ones." And Stroud's voice is always his own, whatever other song he assimilates. Besides, I am well trained in the reading of poetry and in the editing of it, so that you can depend on me when I tell you there is not a young poet around who can so transport you with his music and his images that you are brought to another level of life which you perhaps did not even know existed and which you surely cannot remember until you experience it again, as if for the first time. In this way Stroud's poems are like acts of love rising to orgasm—for who can say what that is like until it happens again.

No young poet fulfills better the priestly idea of Henry Miller, who said of the job of the poet that he should "take the sour dough of human experience and change the dough into bread and the bread into wine and the wine into song." In fact, the weight and sourness of "the dough" (such as the death of the poet's mother, to whose memory the book is dedicated) are often spared us and we begin at the level of the sensuous, aromatic, well-shaped bread itself. In short, this is a gorgeous book, classically designed by Capra Press and adorned with superb drawings by the gifted Tom Thompson of San Francisco.

I have said that listening is especially important in Stroud's work. This is not simply because of the constant song in his poems but because of the special sounds that he releases from the page. The sounds, for example, of "the stunning electric hum of our world," "the skeletons of insects (crumbling)," or the sounds of cicadas and dragonflies and (most often) of bees as in "the sudden cries of bees," "A morning of bees" with its Thomas-like pun on "mourning." Again, when have you heard this sound:

> I entered the field
> Where the cow lay on its side
> A crater into its stomach.
> And inside, thousands of worms
> Writhed and boiled,
> A sound like the pure whine of generators.

Sometimes the sound is of a unique silence: "The tall grass is quiet," "green music of strawberries in the wood," "The silence of those early, February flowers," "The dead breathing of beautiful horses under the earth," or, finally, the phrase "train wrecked into silence" (an adaptation from Miguel Hernandez) which reminds so much of Lorca's shattering quiet in his image, "the silence of overturned locomotives."

The ability to conjure such sounds and such silences is that of a master. I once heard Carolyn Kizer in a critique of students berate Stroud's poetry because of what she said was too much imitation of Roethke, particularly in its hovering at the edge of madness, but surely Roethke had no corner on that feeling: anyone who emerges from adolescence has skirted that edge, and it is poets like Joseph Stroud whose healing music help us to emerge whole into maturity.

Sailing Too Far by Milton Kessler

(1977)

Milton Kessler is one of the best poets of our time, and so it is a deeply satisfying thing to have *Sailing Too Far*. Some of these extraordinary poems had appeared in limited editions, accompanied by the very beautiful graphics of Robert E. Marx, but they were not generally available. The appetite—the need—for more of Kessler's work was whetted by his fine first book, *A Road Came Once,* which appeared several years ago.

Kessler's voice is unique and his range includes the delicate, melancholy lyricism of "Fingertip," "Song," and "Lost Song," as well as the deep, more violent Jewish *schmerzen* of "A Dream of Weeping," "*Chad Gadya,* One Little Goat," and "The Rant of the Ordinary Life." To these six poems I would add four others to name a small anthology of some of the best work in the book: "Songs for Paul Blackburn" (which contains the title line), "Hospital Poem," "Letter," and "The Inertia."

I have some trouble with the ambitious "Summer's End" because of the elliptical character of the writing, and I had difficulty understanding two poems, "Untitled" and "Coffee Room," although there is power in the writing and I learned much from these poems, too, as I would like to make clear.

The difficulty of "Untitled" and "Coffee Room" comes from a shift of tone in the two poems—from a positive feeling to a negative one—which the reader may find hard to follow. However, looking at these shifts with a certain distance, a second time, one may find them to be an expression of the true complexity of experience. "He laughs and is very happy," Kessler writes in the former poem and then adds immediately, "The girl in the ship's movie said / into the telephone, 'I'm feeling very / bad.'" One notes that there is a locational difference between the first statement, which refers to a game situation between father and son ("He") in a pool on board ship, and the second statement, which quotes an actress in a movie on board. Thus, there is a delicate evocation of the poignant mystery of things.

In "Coffee Room" the line, "What happened, she *smiles*" (italics mine) is followed shortly by "Tomorrow they're going to cut me open—." Here the more literal sequence of statements expresses a genuine paradox given rise by the speaker's awareness that she is being responded to erotically when, in fact, she is unwell and about to be operated on. The slightly playful ironies of the situation of both poems may technically be thought of as forms of "sailing too far," and on reflection one notes that the exploration of the complexities of such juxtapositions of human feelings is part of the very rationale of the book.

Loneliness is not, in these poems—nor in the nature of things—finally mitigated even by the ties with family and friends, though indeed figures of these appear in more than half of the poems, as if one had hoped it might turn out differently. Furthermore, loneliness is intensified by feelings of self-depreciation, as in the lines, "self-pity is awful" or "I'm not much to look at" or "I look up to myself appalled," and it engenders defensive feelings of violence, extending beyond the Yiddish shrug or laughing-at-oneself which it also suggests. Grief becomes rage, so that "tears were smothering his face with blood as if / an ancient wound had hemorraged in his head." Thus the words "broken" and "blood" (or "bloody") recur several times each and appear in one poem together, "*Chad Gadya,* One Little Goat": "My shoes are high and broken,/. . . Each day the men come home/with great bushels of blood paper." The image of paper brings the mind to writing and reminds us that the poet often can handle his negative feelings in a poem. So Kessler writes movingly in "The Inertia," "And here is the same hand,/grown strong then weak again,/a trembling thumb/that will not hold this *paper*,/a false hand stuffed with the blood of sheep." (Italics mine.) If there is a tinge of violence left after the exorcism of the writing, it is handled in the recurring image of a grotesque mouth, scarcely able to speak a poem: "The slaughtered mouth," "the frothing mouth."

Kessler is a great master at exposing the melancholy in the human mystery itself (the *lachrimae rerum*) and of transforming it into something Godly and healing: he is very right to tell us, "Poems be my body of shining." The poet is always "sailing too far" but, thankfully for us, he finds his way back again inside the boat of a poem.

Night Conversations with None Other
by Shreela Ray

"The windows are open/and the sleepy violets of the blood/ stir towards the dark outside." These lines from Shreela Ray's beautiful poem "Night in April" describe the process of her poetry. "The windows are open" there in her work, and the sometimes gently, sometimes violently awakened creative intuitions of her interior life ("violets of the blood") move towards the responding "dark" inside each of us.

Ms. Ray is a native of India who has been living in this country for fifteen years, and her work therefore shows the influence of both lands. Her knowledge of Indian places and of Indian gods gives richness to her diction, while her expatriation gives a special turn to that sense of exile which we all feel to a certain extent. Indeed, Paul Tillich described original sin as that very sense. "It is possible that I have come too far," writes Ms. Ray. "The moor, the gypsy and the saint/ are left behind in mysterious union with cripples and thieves./ I sit stiff and upright in the chair/and drink to them alone./I bless them, I write for them/but the song can't find the way back."

There is a brilliant sense of image and of language in these poems. She writes, "The March snow is with us/between the two stalled maples./Its rude white silence glitters." Another poem, "Quasimodo," must be quoted entire to show this gift:

No longer able to believe in God
I ascend to the angels floating
in all the rooms of my head.

They are princely and opalescent.
Their wings fold and unfold in the slow
motion of an appeal. They thicken

as in its pure arc the spine prepares
to cut, to multiply, to listen
for the red heart's chime, endlessly, endlessly.

Difference of skin color is often a visual sign of difference of race; Ms. Ray uses this very movingly in the imagery of her poems. For example, in one of a strong series of pieces for her "Halfbreed Child," Gawain, the son of her marriage to a Caucasian American, there is a special poignancy which she catches in her reference to Plato's *Symposium:* "If you should meet Aristophanes first/ask him, when a man goes in search/of his sundered female half,/ must she be of the same race?" And in "Two Love Poems of a Concubine," which articulates the pain we all feel at rejection after love, there is an extraordinary twist of the knife in words reflecting the difference of color between the two lovers:

1

Crawling into the black box on the wall
I call myself in the name
of fathers and friends and lovers
and most of all
in the name of one whose face
engraved on a stone turns
away from the me and looks
into its heart.

2

Afterwards
when you turn your white back to me

> I lie awake in the dark remembering your words.
> "I wanted to keep some distance between us."
> Had I no rights? Was something
> wrong with me? I touch
> my Indian body lightly. . . .

Yet every man or woman, trapped inside his own skin, inside his own religion or neurosis, is seemingly of a different "race" from every other—indeed, sometimes we can be so split from our own selves that it is as if each of us were of a different race or color, even from oneself. Poetry, like love, can bridge these great suffering gaps in our experience—that is one of its functions, and Shreela Ray's poems perform this function extremely well.

Eggs in the Lake by Daniela Gioseffi

(1979)

I find Daniela Gioseffi's poems imaginatively rich, startling, intelligent (with a wide range of reading behind them) and eloquent in a manner relevant to one of the most profound issues of our time: the relationship of the masculine and the feminine principles inside the self and society. A feminist writer who celebrates what it is to be a woman, Ms. Gioseffi is also genuinely a poet whose work comes from the part of the personality that gives, shares and creates bonds rather than from the part that is divisive and militant. Fortunately, there is little politics here—something ill-suited to poetry. And there are very few feminist writers of which this can be said.

Ms. Gioseffi is inventive, usually in a surreal mode, and she shares with the lyric poet generally that loneliness which comes from the struggle with the self. "In My Craft or Sullen Art" is the title of a poem by Dylan Thomas, and we remember that the word "sullen" comes from the Latin "solus" which means "alone." Yet when the poetic *gift of sharing* is present, by which I mean making public in a beautiful fashion, as it is in Ms. Gioseffi's work, then that loneliness—which is itself part of the human condition—becomes altered ironically and one is not alone in the same way as before the experience of art. Rather, one is brought, through the poetry, to what Dylan Thomas called "a momentary peace." This "peace" I see as the natural equivalent to grace.

Ms. Gioseffi brings us such moments again and again. "I am a lost and primitive priestess/" she writes, "wandering in a walled city of the wrong century." Still, "I would have been what you were searching for/. . . if you could decide/what sleeper you resemble and which of your dreams/struggles behind your eyelids."

There is also a special kind of loneliness Ms. Gioseffi writes about in a poem titled "The Loneliness of the Pregnant Woman":

> She dreams
> trees push limbs up
> through her belly; her body
> is an oven baking bread, a moon
> presses from between her lips,
> floats, a loaf of sun in winter light.

I want to comment on two further aspects of this passage. One is the image of the tree—Ms. Gioseffi has struck an archetypal note here, for the changing of the woman into a tree (cf. also her poem "My Venus Flytrap is Dying") occurs again and again in the history of literature, from Ovid's story of Daphne through Dante to modern poems of Ezra Pound, Hart Crane, and James Wright. (The title poem of Wright's most recent book, "To a Blossoming Pear Tree," is a beautiful piece about the transformation of a woman into a tree.) Norman O. Brown has an essay in which he sees the metamorphosis of Daphne as being at the very heart of poetry itself. "Undulate the branches of your arms/in the wind, goddess of trees," Ms. Gioseffi writes in another poem.

The other motif in this poem I want to note is the androgynous one which is introduced by the juxtaposition of the feminine moon with the masculine sun. I believe that one of the deepest motives for writing is man's attempt to feel his way into the world of woman and woman's attempt to feel her way into the world of man. This is not opposed to the search for self-identity on the part of man or woman poet for each finds the other at the heart of self. In another poem of Ms. Gioseffi's she uses an epigraph from Rimbaud which combines the theme of self-identity and androgyny: "The poets of the future will come when the infinite servitude of woman will be broken, when she will live for herself and by herself . . . she will also be poet! Woman will find the unknown!. . . The two sexes will then make one . . . the great Androgyne will be created, humanity will be woman and man, love and thought, tenderness and strength, grace and energy."

Ms. Gioseffi's "The Sea Hag in the Cave of Sleep" is one of the most ambitious androgynous poems of our time. Here the lines occur, "He swims into me in clouds of semen," and "Sea and shore mix in one giant sex." The poem ends with the astonishing image of the female assuming the penis at the moment of giving birth: "I come out from between my own legs into this world."

As in all lyric poetry there is a strong search for identity by the speaker in these poems: "I can be anything I will myself to be. I spend all my time . . . willing to be/what always/I am about to become." Again, "a vast lonely conscience strains to give itself a name." Here is a quotation from her work which reflects the eternal yearning of the poet for an audience who will help him assert his identity: "I wake . . . /and think there must be someone there . . .; who listens to me here in the dark."

Yet the poems present a very strong self-identity of the speaker as woman. In "Caves" Ms. Gioseffi writes: "At the hour of sleep a woman enters her own body/through mouths hidden beneath the skirt of night." Though there is compassion for the hardships of a woman's life, as in the elegiac words for her grandmother ("She died, her body wearied/from giving and giving and giving/food and birth.") still the overall tone of the book is the celebration of the status of woman—particularly in the essential creativity of the maternal impulse.

The poem "Caves," from which I quoted, is taken from a section of the book entitled "The Vases of Wombs"—a phrase in which Ms. Gioseffi reveals her unusual intelligence, for it is taken from her long and deep research into the historical and psychological development of the woman (in this case she is echoing Eric Neumann's monumental *The Great Mother,* which sees vases since ancient times as ikons so to speak of the woman's womb).

One of Ms. Gioseffi's poems, "The Belly Dancer," reminds us how far her researches have taken her: from her reading she discovered that what has come to be called "the belly dance" was in reality a *birth* dance given by women to assist at and celebrate the births of children. The dance originally had nothing to do with the market place and the entertainment of men. She has acted on her own research and learned the art of the "birth dance," frequently supplementing her programs with lectures on the dance and readings from her poems. She has written and published a novel called *The Great American Belly Dance.*

On this aspect of Ms. Gioseffi's work one cannot do better than to look at an article on her poems by Harold Schechter entitled "The Return of Demeter: The Poetry of Daniela Gioseffi" (*Psychocultural Review* 1:452–57). Schechter in a Jungian analysis reminds us that behind androgyny lies sysygy, the union and vital exchange from the heart of the feminine to the heart of the masculine and vice versa, and he also reminds us that in promoting the matriarchal over the patriarchal—in particular that aspect of the former which is benevolently maternal (creative) as opposed to the vengeful, terrible "tooth" mother (cf. Robert Bly's poem "The Teeth Mother Naked at Last") one is promoting a healthier, richer society—a society of hope—the newer, higher order which Ms. Gioseffi presents in her poem "Peace Prospect": "A better race will come. I feel/bright animals waiting/for the right genetic moment."

Still it is not in such partly didactic poems as "Peace Prospect" that I feel Ms. Gioseffi's strength so much as in those which dramatize a genuine erotic moment ("We might touch ourselves into peace") or show a deep rapport with other created things—rapport with sun, sea, and salt in "Beyond the East Gate," with plants in "Talking to My Philodendron," or with ancient creatures of the deep as in "Wearing Breasts" and in "For Prince Myshkin."

Because so much of Ms. Gioseffi's work touches the common, deep experiences of mankind (what Jung would call archetypes of the collective unconscious) I believe Jung should have the last word here in our approach to her poetry. "Whenever the collective unconscious becomes a living experience and is brought to bear upon the conscious outlook of an age, this event is a creative act which is of importance to everyone." Need I add this means you and me.

IV

Poems Discussed in
Interviews

From *Cycle for Mother Cabrini*

(1955)

From *Mother Cabrini Crosses the Andes*

IV

Air shivered in the Andes
As full of color as blood
Or bells, or ice the saboteurs
Left on Lytle Street
When angered by her sick and alien

They opened the mansion pipes;
What was this to her
Who dynamites hearts: rivets,
Quarries, shapes bricks, and built
In Chicago two hospitals
Besides the one they chilled awhile

And burned a little bit.
But they kicked the sisters out
Of Nicaragua—the schoolgirls no trash
These, necks blue as Andes
Snow thin as moons: and hair

Black as the bird-live valleys;
The saint was away on business—
New Orleans orphanage or the Villa
Or the novitiate at old Manresa
On the Hudson. (Or was it the hotel
In Seattle?) And there was trouble in France

Since the archbishop was on the Riviera,
And the priests turned her a cold
Parisian shoulder, but she moved in
At a gilt estate where the sisters
Had to put up sheets over the many mirrors.

Whether they went on their continents
Or ours the austere skirts
Were strangest brushing by the summerhouse
In Rio the intemperate flower parts:
Though here the black was closest
To the holy red that flowed her into God.

In Chicago, upon her martyrdom.
She should have died in Lombardy
Safe from a saint's life and the traveler's
Malady that chilled her and brightened
Her gown, like a bell she jangled in her room
Where she rocked and, died, in a wicker chair.

Pagan Saturday

Hiking out to Ratcliff
School we took our shoes off
In the field of stubble
Where the graveyard ends; we ran
Shouting thru the stalks

Of pain that grow tipped
And colorful as grain.
We swarmed the woods and looked
For fun and fuel and packed enough
To pile and build to a roar

A very satisfying fire.
We set our mouths on hopes
Of stolen corn and raided
An easy field behind a barn;
And burst the milky kernels

On our thumbs. Letting
The fire at one side turn
To ash we buried our yellow
Catch inside its wraps of husk
And later, ate in heights

Of joy the cindered ears.
And racing along the rim
Of Indian Gully sudden
As fear light as laughter I felt
A creature flare with beauty

At the back of my eye;
I knew my limbs and body
Sang on me sometimes—
But this was brighter than my arms.
Coming back we played

Some rapid hide-and-seek
Among the graves; I hid
Awhile and searched the stone
Face for mother; and ran on
Into the pointed groves of pine.

Grandfather's Railroad

I think my grandfather knew
I'd never seen a negro
Before I thought I saw

The shallow trough that cut
The field he showed me real
As a railroad, and reached

North for Kemling Store.
I could have seen the bright
And keen two rails where they

Grow so thin I could have
Run, vanishing where they did.
My grandfather told me

The old underground railroad
Wound thru Montgomery
County; he pointed a fine

Haired finger and led
Across the dust-lit land
The believed negroes—gold

Lithe and wild as the wind
Burned wheatfield.
My grandfather didn't see

My pickaninny doll had three
Pigtails she shook like
Ribboned wings on wires

From the train windows, and fires
Shivered in our capturers' eyes
Who cares! the cars of great

Black men roar past
Shadowing the field like clouds
Or giants that seem to slow

And stride as lean as trees
Against the north sky.

A Dialogue with La Mettrie

Since thought visibly develops with our organs, why should not the
matter of which they are composed be susceptible of remorse also,
when once it has acquired, with time, the faculty of feeling?
                    —La Mettrie, *Man a Machine* (Leyden, 1748)

Where does one look
To purify the remark of an ancient
Cynic? I am afraid not
To the Eighteenth Century
And the mechanist La Mettrie;
If he is one, for here
The ambiguity

Begins. Let me explain.
The ancient has us build on
Supposed Plato's supposed
Definition, Man is twolegged
And without any feathers: add,
To tell him from the plucked bird,
His nails are flat.

Now this idea of the dog
Diogenes, shook me. But,
Let me say, no more so
Than the mind of La Mettrie
I think we are not mushrooms
Swollen for a day, nor even
"Flowers Bordering a ditch."

And I want a violent leap
Beyond the dog. Do not
Tell me from him as you mark
The ape by his more intelligent
Face. For once there was
A blurred and giddy light
In my enormous eyes.

A few more wheels a few
More springs than in,
Say your better animal?
And with a closer heart
To fill the brain with blood
And start the delicate moral
Hum in the anxious matter.

Suppose I agree the soul is
An engine, admit Descartes
And the rest never *saw*
Their pair of things—never,
As you say, counted them;
Then here's the ambiguity,
And a further problem:

You say you find an inner
Force in bodies, and watch
The smallest fibre turn
Upon an inner rule.
Now I don't see that this
Is such a clear machine!
In fact I think I wish it were.

For I have weighed
your evidence: I don't forget
Your newly dead
And opened criminal
Whose still hot heart
Beats like the muscles in the face
Of the severed head.

I don't forget you say
The flesh of bats
Palpitates in death,
And even more of snakes,
That never sweat. "Why then
Do men boast moral
Acts, that hang on these?"

Besides injected warm
Water animates the heart;
The hearts of frogs move
If put in the sun or if the heart
Is placed upon a hot
Table or a stone. If it stops,
It may be poked or bathed.

And Harvey noted this
In toads. (The great physician,
I could add, once
Professionally cut a toad
A burnt witch had kept
For her familiar,
And found it puffed with milk.)

A piece of a pigeon's heart,
Lord Boyle has shown, beats
As the whole one did.
It is these same motions
Twist along the eel,
In spiders or in the tiny
Hands sliced from moles.

And last, Bacon of Verulam
Has in his *Book of Spears*
The case of a traitor caught
And opened alive: his heart
In a pan of boiling water
Leaped several times
To a perpendicular

Height of two feet.
Let us then conclude
Boldly! Man is a machine.
And there is no other thing
Underneath. Except I believe
Ambiguity, with its hope
Or its ancient agony;

For to what do we look
To purify his remarks, or purge
His animal images? What
Piece in us may be cut free
Of the grieved matter of La Mettrie,
That underneath a temporal reeling
Took on this arch of feeling.

A Pathological Case in Pliny

Hirto corde gigni quosdam homines proditur, neque
alios fortioris esse industriae, sicut Aristomenen
Messenium qui trecentos occidit Lacedaemonios. . .
—Plinii *Naturalis Historia* 11.1–20

The guards sleep they breathe uneven
Conversation with the
Trees the sharp cicadas
And knots of pine the flames
Have stirred to talk: their light

Shows him rolling in his bonds
As if he dragged his bones
Again beyond a tall
And ghosted mist of blood;
He took three hundred lives

And will not give his own for capture
Even. The smell of searing
Hemp and flesh startles
As the scream of birds—
Should wake the guards of men

Or dead. The fire flares and frames
A running giant his wrists
Caught between his thighs;
A burned and awkward god.
Once he tried the foxes'

Paths out of the shattered quarry.
No way now. One may
Kill his hundreds; still
No way. How can he live
Without his heart. Throw him

To the ground and prepare knives!
Do they by their hate
Or wonder break the breast
He shut to fear? Mock
Or pray as they cut flesh

Crush ribs and lay all open
To the alien chill of air.
No scream tears
From him; the tiny veins
Along his eyelid swell

And pools of sweat gather at its corners.
But they do not see his
Slowly swinging eye
They watch his heart; its brown
Hair is whorled and dry.

The Death of Southwell

A Verse Melodrama with Homilies on Light and Sin

> *I never did take so weighty a man,*
> *if he be rightly used.*
> —Richard Topcliffe, *Letter to the Queen*
> 6 July, 1592

Cold dawn Harrow-On-The-Hill.
The unquiet curtain is too
White this hour, the candles
Too drawn their flames rest-
Less ruddying the cup
Of thin breads with its thin
Hands not yet bodied
In the dawn: the priest's face
Floats like cloth fair
For sacrifice, watch! his vestments
Are gaudy as dawn light grows.

Topcliffe's horses shake
The steam of grey morning; men
Grow sad with cold.
The house is sketched well-marked
Where mass is said. What argument:
The traitor's vested. Take him.
Cloak his colors! These horses
Scream. Now load his books,
His papist images; and this
Damned altar furniture
That burnishes with sun!

Westminster six o'clock
Topcliffe binds him hangs
His hands to pull the gentle
Wrists with weight of flesh.
God its bulk on these thin bones!
Down from the altar to be tall's
A curse. How real these heavy

Limbs! Is death a stretching
That makes flesh more slight;
A thinning of the blooded brain?
And emptying of eyes.

Fainting breaks these days
And nights by the wall. Toes
Touch sometimes. Won't
Say priests or people or place
Of meeting or color of his horse
That might be seen by houses.
Fainting breaks it. Look!
Here's fire! The child flames
In white and wintered places!
The paper lit to his face
He vomits blood, and wakes:

"Your fire is angular as pain and keen
As stone that killed the haunted Stephen.
Still its corners cannot hide
Its numbers or its god. Why look these gentle
Fires gesture to their home. They're tongues
Of doves, are leaves and many-colored prongs
Of bush. How can a Child of Light
Forget His every perfect gift
Of art or ken! Well then! Our Christ
Is our Prometheus: His steep
And formal angle keeps our flame!"

No mass how is a man
A priest, without his folk.
Why, when you come for cauliflower
Take away his blessing from his tower.
A poet and no ink? Let him read,
His Bernard's here; his Bible: the lilies
Business, foxes light
And blood of grapes the seven

Porches on the greying pool.
But he writes with pins only tallies
Of his sins and the pious name of Christ.

This priest that hath a boyish
Look's a man most lewd
And dangerous! Keep him closed
Three years lonely in his cell.
(Perhaps Arundel's dog shall
Visit him to seek the blessing
Lions gain that with
Their paws have digged the graves
Of saints.) And now at sword's
Point drive the traitor
Forward to the bar for trial.

He knew he'd hang, and the rest.
He was always very white of face.
What falconry he had he
Put in poems. Uneasy in disguise.
No champion. In fact quite
Unfavorably compares to Campion.
A slight man, a poet pulled
Into the common prose of crowds
And guts; the comic Cinna screams;
Ignatius offers English wheat
The lion's head shall thrash for bread.

He speaks from his cart at Tyburn:
"When you are free of the whale's
Belly you cannot hope
To sit with Jonas in the shadow,
Except some envious worm
Gnaw apart the ivy's
Root. And should you move
From thorn or briar to the sweet
Odored cedar, your worm,
That cannot breed in you shall gnar
About and snap his teeth.

"Your proper devil all his imps
And instruments shall feed
Like storks upon the venomous
And evil acts of men.
And shall rejoice, if we
Amend, at men's calamity.
The delighted ravens fly
To the smelling corpse, but won't
Hunt the sound body;
So the wicked flock and stick
About us if we stink with sin,

"But if the healing soul
Slough from it this wanted
Flesh, it will abandon too
These hundred melancholy loves.
In winter when the vine is bare
Let the devils lie
They shall be struck in April
When the flowers starts, and at
The wild scent of virtue
Die like snakes
Beneath the blossom of the lime."

HANGMAN SITS IN TYBURN TREE
PREACHER SAYS HIS HOMILY
NOW HIS CART IS PULLED EMPTY
HANGMAN HANGED HIM AWKWARDLY
LOOK THE PREACHER'S HAND IS FREE
BLESSES HANGMAN BLESSES ME
HERE'S A FRIEND TO PULL THE KNEE
GHOST NOW LEAVES HIS YOUNG BODY
THIS POET SAINT WAS THIRTY-THREE
THE HANGMAN MOANS IN TYBURN TREE
NOW UNBLESS HANGMAN, UNBLESS ME.

From *Ghosts of the Heart*

(1960)

On the Death
of the Poet's Mother Thirty-Three Years Later

To Isabella Gardner

> *The tongue fits to the teeth and the palate by Number,*
> *pouring forth letters and words.*
>
> —St. Augustine

> *Years ago I came to the conclusion that poetry too is*
> *nothing but an oral outlet.*
>
> —A. A. Brill, M.D.

I

My mother died because
I lived or so
I always chose to believe.
At any rate I nursed
At a violent teat with the boys
Of the bronzed picture. In my
Memories of taste I find
Bits of the tart hairs
Of an Irish dog that hangs
Its red arch over me; I'm not

So sure of that beast
That it has stole as much from me
As I shall suck from it.

It has an eye of milky
Glass with a very
Reddened spot that sent
Threads or streams of red
About the eye's globe
And this eye moved
Among the long red hairs
At the skull of the dog as it
Leaped in the childhood grass,
As it springs in the childhood
Trace, as it arched and pulled
And arched and pulled the sheath of its livid
Tongue through the wisps of its breath.

July began with the Fourth
And the moon in a box
Like a flaming house in the grass
At the edge of the fair with the frames
Of the fireworks there, but next
It floats, like a carnival balloon
That drops out weights of men,
And turns the festival tips
Of the sparklers hot: fear
Shot up in a kite when it burned
My throat white—like an eye
My friend once cooked in his head, as he mixed
Carnivals of fluids in a shed.

Yet I was not so scared
Or scarred I could not
Scream and climb to find
My aunt to cry for help
High in the mounts of bleachers:
I saw a face and told it

All my needs, but my hot
Throat beat with fright
As a strange mother bent
From the stands—her flanks were blood
In the moon and festive light
As she heard my plea of hurt and
Saw my burnt neck twitch,

Arched over me a God-like Bitch.

II

Don't think I took this dog
Too quick for mother:
I looked for another in the book
Of art where I found the Latin
Kids at the dugs of the wolf,
But most of the stone women
Wore no clothes and some of them
(With help from a borrower's pen)
Showed the genitals of men.
I looked for her in girls
At games and aunts who said
Her face was mine—so I tried to catch
Her in some epicene line.

I guess I looked the most
In father's wife
Whose hair was Welsh and red
Who rocked me once so ten-
Derly on her lap
As I could not lace my boot
Today I remember that—
The boy and his mother and his shoe
His wrists so thin and his hands
Fit so wrong around

The square boot-thong the work
They did or sometimes would not do
Made him weep for them.

I looked in Palgrave's book
She left, and I looked
Through her pearled glass.
But did she read the verse?
And where in that still
Unpretentious town
Did turn the brass wheel
To clear the glass? How many times
I tried the German names!
And felt the foolery of gems:
Pearls like "Braes of Yarrow"
Let new Palgraves gather (and let
Me help my mother, if after

These aids she had no other).

III

I watched at last for her
Among our sacred
Stones, for I was grown
Before I found her tomb.
Today I point to that:
It's there my heavy mother
Rots. Remember!—
Of all the grades the last
Before the next is beautiful,
The lines of ribs, the grace
Of skulls, exquisite levers
Of her limbs; the next is spirit,
Musical with numbers of the flesh:

The formula of eyes'
Ellipse, the thrust
In the gentle eye's lash,
The figures of the listening
Fingers' nerves and of the
Foetal logarithm curves,
Of hidden colors of the guts,
Of buffered tensions of the blood
'Figured in the drift of stars,'
And pale Ameba's gestures.
Self forcing numbers
Enticed into her hyaline tips,
That stop in earth—and smell to Christ.

She suffers there the natural turns;
Her nests on nests of flesh
Are spelt to that irrational end,
The surd and faithful Change. And stays
To gain the faultless stuff reversed
From the numbers' trace at the Lasting Trump.
So here my mother lies. I do not
Resurrect again her restless
Ghost out of my grievous memory:
She waits the quiet hunt of saints.
Or the ignorance of citizens of hell.
And here is laid her orphan child with his
Imperfect poems and ardors, slim as sparklers

February, 1956
After a definition of Xenocrates
and a poem of Richard Eberhart
and after lines of Eliot and
Alejandro Carrion

The Picnic

It is the picnic with Ruth in the spring.
Ruth was third on my list of seven girls
But the first two were gone (Betty) or else
Had someone (Ellen has accepted Doug).
Indian Gully the last day of school;
Girls make the lunches for the boys too.
I wrote a note to Ruth in algebra class
Day before the test. She smiled, and nodded.
We left the cars and walked through the young corn
The shoots green as paint and the leaves like tongues
Trembling. Beyond the fence where we stood
Some wild strawberry flowered by an elm tree
And Jack-in-the-pulpit was olive ripe.
A blackbird fled as I crossed, and showed
A spot of gold or red under its quick wing.
I held the wire for Ruth and watched the whip
Of her long, striped skirt as she followed.
Three freckles blossomed on her thin, white back
Underneath the loop where the blouse buttoned.
We went for our lunch away from the rest,
Stretched in the new grass, our heads close
Over unknown things wrapped up in wax papers.
Ruth tried for the same, I forget what it was,
And our hands were together. She laughed,
And a breeze caught the edge of her little
Collar and the edge of her brown, loose hair
That touched my cheek. I turned my face in-
to the gentle fall. I saw how sweet it smelled.
She didn't move her head or take her hand.
I felt a soft caving in my stomach
As at the top of the highest slide
When I had been a child, but was not afraid,
And did not know why my eyes moved with wet
As I brushed her cheek with my lips and brushed
Her lips with my own lips. She said to me
Jack, Jack, different than I had ever heard,

290

Because she wasn't calling me, I think,
Or telling me. She used my name to
Talk in another way I wanted to know.
She laughed again and then she took her hand;
I gave her what we both had touched—can't
Remember what it was, and we ate the lunch.
Afterward we walked in the small, cool creek
Our shoes off, her skirt hitched, and she smiling,
My pants rolled, and then we climbed up the high
Side of Indian Gully and looked
Where we had been, our hands together again.
It was then some bright thing came in my eyes,
Starting at the back of them and flowing
Suddenly through my head and down my arms
And stomach and my bare legs that seemed not
To stop in feet, not to feel the red earth
Of the Gully, as though we hung in a
Touch of birds. There was a word in my throat
With the feeling and I knew the first time
What it meant and I said, it's beautiful.
Yes, she said, and I felt the sound and word
In my hand join the sound and word in hers
As in one name said, or in one cupped hand.
We put back on our shoes and socks and we
Sat in the grass awhile, crosslegged, under
A blowing tree, not saying anything.
And Ruth played with shells she found in the creek,
As I watched. Her small wrist which was so sweet
To me turned by her breast and the shells dropped
Green, white, blue, easily into her lap,
Passing light through themselves. She gave the pale
Shells to me, and got up and touched her hips
With her light hands, and we walked down slowly
To play the school games with the others.

Shore Scene

There were bees about. From the start I thought
The day was apt to hurt. There is a high
Hill of sand behind the sea and the kids
Were dropping from the top of it like schools
Of fish over falls, cracking skulls on skulls.
I knew the holiday was hot. I saw
The August sun teeming in the bodies
Logged along the beach and felt the yearning
In the brightly covered parts turning each
To each. For lunch I bit the olive meat:
A yellow jacket stung me on the tongue.
I knelt to spoon and suck the healing sea . . .
A little girl was digging up canals
With her toes, her arm hanging in a cast
As white as the belly of a dead fish
Whose dead eye looked at her with me, as she
Opened her grotesque system to the sea . . .
I walked away; now quietly I heard
A child moaning from a low mound of sand,
Abandoned by his friend. The child was tricked,
Trapped upon his knees in a shallow pit.
(The older ones will say you can get out.)
I dug him up. His legs would not unbend.
I lifted him and held him in my arms
As he wept. Oh I was gnarled as a witch
Or warlock by his naked weight, was slowed
In the sand to a thief's gait. When his strength
Flowed, he ran, and I rested by the sea . . .
A girl was there. I saw her drop her hair,
Let it fall from the doffed cap to her breasts
Tanned and swollen over wine red woolen.
A boy, his body blackened by the sun,
Rose out of the sand stripping down his limbs
With graceful hands. He took his gear and walked
Toward the girl in the brown hair and wine
And then past me; he brushed her with the soft,

Brilliant monster he lugged into the sea . . .
By this tide I raised a small cairn of stone
Light and smooth and clean, and cast the shadow
Of a stick in a perfect line along
The sand. My own shadow followed then, until
I felt the cold swirling at the groin.

From *Spring of the Thief*

(1963)

To a Young Poet Who Fled

> *Your cries make us afraid, but we love*
> *your delicious music!*
>
> —Kierkegaard

So you said you'd go home to work on your father's farm.
We've talked of how it is the poet alone can touch
with words, but I would touch you with my hand, my lost
    son,
to say good-bye again. You left some work, and have gone.
You don't know what you mean. Oh, not to me as a son,
for I have others. Perhaps too many. I cannot
answer all the letters. If I seem to brag, I add
I know how to shatter an image of the father
(twice have tried to end the yearning of an orphan son
but opened up in him, and in me, another wound)
No—I say this: you don't know the reason of your gift.
It's not the suffering. Others have that. The gift of tears
is the hope of saints, Monica again and Austin.
I mean the gift of the structure of a poet's jaw,
which makes the mask that's cut out of the flesh of his face
a megaphone—as with the goat clad Greeks—to ampli-
fy the light gestures of his soul toward the high stone seats.

The magic of the mouth that can melt to tears the rock
of hearts. I mean the wand of tongues that charms the exile
of listeners into a bond of brothers, breaking
down the lines of lead that separate a man from a
man, and the husbands from their wives, in these old,
    burned glass
panels of our lives. The poet's jaw has its tongue ripped
as Philomel, its lips split (and kissed beside the grave),
the jawbone patched and cracked with fists and then with
    the salve
of his fellows. If they make him bellow, like a slave
cooked inside the ancient, brass bull, still that small machine
inside its throat makes music for an emperor's guest
out of his cries. Thus his curse: the poet cannot weep
but with a public and musical grief, and he laughs
with the joys of others. Yet, when the lean blessings come,
they are sweet, and great. My son, I could not make your
    choice.
Let me take your hand. I am too old or young to say,
"I'd rather be a swineherd in the hut, understood
by swine, than be a poet misunderstood by men."

Song on the Dread of a Chill Spring

I thought (and before it was too late)
my heart had begun to turn, that was
shut to love, for I was adamant
as saints, and tough as the martyr's heart,
as a wooden statue of a god,
where my father sat in the straight pew,
my mother bowed to the stone, bearing
flowers she had cut out of the earth
of my life. Ah the candles bloom cold
in the earthen air of early Mass,
like the tops of wan hepatica
that lift their light cups in the first time.
So shy we touch at these Ides of March!

Winter was too long and cold. The spring
is brief. These tulips offer up their gold
and the purple plum our grief.

Lines on His Birthday

I was born on a street named Joy
of which I remember nothing,
but since I was a boy
I've looked for its lost turning.
Still I seem to hear my mother's cry
echo in the street of joy.
She was sick as Ruth for home
when I was born. My birth
took away my father's wife
and left me half
my life. Christ will my remorse
be less when my father's dead?
Or more. As Lincoln's minister of war
kept the body of his infant boy
in a silver coffin on his desk,
so I keep
in a small heirloom box of teak
the picture of my living father.
Or perhaps it is an image of myself
dead in this box she held?
I know her milk like ivory blood
still runs in my thick veins
and leaves in me an almost
lickerish taste for ghosts:
my mother's wan face,
full brown hair, the mammoth breast
death cuts off at the bone—
to which she draws her bow
again, brazen Amazon,
and aiming deadly as a saint
shoots her barb
of guilt into my game heart.

From *The Zigzag Walk*

(1969)

Three Moves

Seattle, April 1965

Three moves in six months and I remain
the same.
Two homes made two friends.
The third leaves me with myself again.
(We hardly speak.)
Here I am with tame ducks
and my neighbors' boats,
only this electric heat
against the April damp.
I have a friend named Frank—
The only one who ever dares to call
and ask me, "How's your soul?"
I hadn't thought about it for a while,
and was ashamed to say I didn't know.
I have no priest for now.
Who
will forgive me then. Will you?
Tame birds and my neighbors' boats.
The ducks honk about the floats . . .
They walk dead drunk onto the land and grounds,

iridescent blue and black and green and brown.
They live on swill
our aged houseboats spill.
But still they are beautiful.
Look! The duck with its unlikely beak
has stopped to pick
and pull
at the potted daffodil.
Then again they sway home
to dream
bright gardens of fish in the early night.
Oh these ducks are all right.
They will survive.
But I am sorry I do not often see them climb.
Poor sons-a-bitching ducks.
You're all fucked up.
What do you do that for?
Why don't you hover near the sun anymore?
Afraid you'll melt?
These foolish ducks lack a sense of guilt,
and so all their multi-thousand-mile range
is too short for the hope of change.

Twilight Land

(after Georg Trakl)

1

The moon stepped like a dead thing
Out of a blue cave,
And many flowers
Flutter all along the rocky path.
A sick thing weeps silver
By the pond of evening.
Over there the lovers
Died in a black boat.

Or the footsteps of Elis
Sound through the wood
Hyacinth-colored
And die away again
Under the oak.
Ah, the form of the young boy
Fashioned from crystal tears,
From shadows of the night.
Jagged flashes light up the forehead,
Which is forever cool,
And now on the hill just turning green
The echoing
Of the year's first thunderstorm.

2

So gentle are the green
Woods of our home,
The crystal wave
Dying along the broken wall—
And we wept in our sleep.
Now we stroll and linger
By the thorn hedge,

Singers in the summer night,
In the holy quiet
Of the distant, radiant vineyard.
The shadows of the cool castle
Of night are mourning eagles.
A moonbeam closes gently
The crimson wounds of grief.

3

You great cities of stone
Built on the plain!
Mute, his face, dark,
The man who has no home
Follows the wind
And the barren trees on the hill.
Distant twilight floods!
The mighty, terrifying sunset glow
Is shuddering
In a mass of thunderheads.
Ah, you dying peoples!
A pale wave
Shattering on the night shore,
Falling stars.

On the House of a Friend

(for Robert Sund)

Under the lightly leaved
April trees,
your small red house seems to speak—
mildly. It lets you come down
into it from the easy sloping lawn.
Your house is very clean,
for each room
has been well swept by your young friends.
You gave up your bed to them
because they are in love: the lean,
glad girl with long hands
who shares easily all she has
with her blond, gentle boy.
It is this the house seems to say
at the Dutch, open half-door:
their love and yours.
Look, a hapless slug
suns and glows on the madroña stump
beside the porch. So slow, so
slowly it goes
toward the great, full mushroom
resting there. That home
shall keep him from harm.
Beside the rhododendrons in the yard,
your red, Iceland
daisies make a light sound.
Their music seems to change and go
between the flowers and the glass in the window.
Robert, now this small
red house (as in a child's
book) smiles
with the smile of your own face.

The Search

But for whom do I look?
The whole long night you will see me walk
or maybe during the day
watch me pass by.
But I do not wander—
It is a search. For I stop here,
or here, wherever people gather.
Depot, restaurant, bar.
But whom do I seek?
You will see me coming back
perhaps at dawn. Sometimes
the faces seem like tombs.
I have tried to read the names
so long my eyes darken in their graves
of bone. (The bodies of our eyes
lie side by side
and do not touch.)
But for whom do I look? My search
is not for wife, daughter or for son
for time to time
it has taken me from them.
Or has wrenched me from my friend:
I will abruptly leave him,
and I do not go home.
For whom do I seek? Out of what fear?
It is not for queers,
for my search leads me from their bars.
It is not for whores,
since I reject their wares,
or another time may not.
Then for whom do I look?
When I was young I thought
I wanted (yearned for) older age.
Now I think I hunt with so much rage
that I will risk or lose
family or friends for the ghost of my youth.

Thus I do not know for what I look.
Father? Mother?
The father who will be the mother?
Sister who will be the brother?
Often I hunt in the families of others—
until hope scatters.
I will call up friend or student at night
or I will fly
to see them—will bask and heal in the warm
places of their homes.
And I must not be alone
no matter what needs be done,
for then my search is ended.
So now the panicked thumbs of my poem pick
through the grill. They poke
the lock
and put out a hand and then an arm.
The limbs of my poems
come within your reach.
Perhaps it is you whom I seek.

From *The Anonymous Lover*

Two Poems for Women

I

(for my daughter)

This red
    Italian hand
blown glass
        vase
narrow as the very young
stem
    of your age,
Theresa, has a flame
shaped
      flaw
white
      as the stark
movement in
        my scarlet brain
when
      I think forever
(like a curse deliver-
          ed *to* me)

of the fire screaming in the Christmas tree
New Year's Day night
you fled tall
          with your beautiful
fire
   colored hair
(your face white
even in the heat)
into the flaw-
          ed snow
with its wrong
          red tongues.

II

(for Phyllis)

At my best I'll
                drive
around
      that island
just with you again and
wade
    in the glinting warm
Hawaiian
            waves,
put my hand
around your nicely naked waist
as it shimmers with wet
about the islands of your breasts
and drink champagne
letting it spill
              and surf a little
on my chin
when I'm
startled by your living face
beside me suddenly at the beach cafe.

From *The Bridge of Change*

(1981)

Five Preludes for Buffalo's Own Forest Lawn

1

"I say, instead of the white man
converting us let us watch *him,*
and if there is any difference to be seen, *then*
we will listen for his white God."
Seneca Orator, Chief Red
Jacket's body was converted from its native grave
to the sod of Forest Lawn, where the flag of his brave
tomahawk still waves above the statue of his form
rather far from the folks at home.

2

Ominous, marble-hooded figures lean over bowls
and continually vomit out of their bowels.

3

Pyramided within glass slopes and arcs of marble,
you cannot be dead in The Blocher Memorial,

for you with your rock beard and book
opened across your chest lie life-sized upon your back—
fully clothed even to your coat—
by two mourning and scolding folks, mother and father,
both of them quite full-sized as well,
and, above: a life-sized angel!,
who, the story goes, is the girl
your parents would not let you wed.
She hovers now (forever) above your cold, stone bed.

4

About the spring pond in this elementary town,
flowering trees drop their white and purple petals down
as mallards nest and the baby ducks waddle around.

5

The angel has begun to chip
over the child's grave. To see this,
go in the Delavan-Delaware entrance and turn
left about a block. Someone who cared placed a glass box
about the angel, for it *should* be more durable
at least than the body of the child, whose flesh falls off
so quick inside his own box. His friends are unable
now—or just do not want, perhaps—
to guard his grave: some of the glass about that box is
broken. The angel guardian
dissolves in tears of falling stone,
and those who were so attached to him have all gone home
except for one who makes now this protective poem.

Assateague

Tamar and Royce are in love.
They run up the beach and give
each other a hand. I walk
behind and brood. I'll try my luck:

Grey the beach at Assateague.
Grey the sky and grey the sea.
A white heron whirls off now
and a spider crab comes out

of its hole, scuds swiftly back
having sensed a big mistake.
I find a white plastic bit
I had thought was a devil fish.

The washed-up wood of old ships
breaks the sand, with shells like coins
lost from Spanish galleons
that used to try these awful seas.

One ship torn up on the reef
left a heritage of dwarf
wild ponies from centuries
before, and still two herds of these

roam the shores and live on marsh
grasses. The round-up is harsh
yearly, decimates the herds
driven before the waves and winds:

They swim across the channel
goaded by the boys and men
and up the beach into pens
pattering up over moist sands

and dashing the placid salt
pools into myriad drops.

Roped and with spirits broken,
the ponies are driven inland

and for the rest of their bound
lives they yearn for salt and sedge
they fed on under the ridge
of snow along the island edge

as we yearn for our childhood
or the love we never had
or else had but could not keep
until we came to Assateague.

for Michael and Robin Waters
—1978

Grace

We suffer from the repression of the sublime.
—Roberto Assagioli

This artist's sculptured, open box of mahogany
(ivory white inside) is strung
with vertical and horizontal layers of mus-
ical wires that sing when struck, and bits of bright garnet
rock tremble where they intersect.
These gems flash in the candle light,
and before me all my beloved childhood looms up
in the humming levels, each one deeper than the other.
I tip this sculpted box and my child laughs and moves there
in his own time. You'll hear me moan:
Oh, you will hear me moan with all the old, sure pleasure
of what I'd thought I'd lost come back again.
Why, we have never left our home!
On the leather lace fixed about my neck, blue, yellow,
red and black African trading beads begin to glow:
their colors all weave and newly flow
together like translucent and angelic worms.
And beneath these my neck is as alive with gentle,
white bees as is a woman's breast.
Beside and in the light river
figures come on stage exactly
as they are needed. I tell you, I conduct my own
act! A boy poses so youthfully,
so beautifully, his slim arms a graceful arrow
over his small, brown head, and he dives!
Limbs and body push supple as a whole school of fish.
And then his vacant place is taken by another—
a man dressed in denim and in boots of red rubber.
He is wrenched from the shore and pulled
through the fresh, bright stream by a kid
who tugs on one of his hands and holds a fishing rod.
And, too, this man is dragged in the opposite direction
by a red dog on a leash shaking his wet

great coat into the stippled light.
That man just sashayed: he zigzagged
this way and that. The man is me!

A bluejay does a dance for us!
He hops beside a tree that rises inside of me.
He half-glides, his iridescent,
blue back striking like a brush
of Gauguin on the bare canvas of the air and then:
he flies! leaving behind him a small, perfect feather,
which I find shades from blue to brown—
my brother's color into mine.
Now in the space the diver and the booted fellow
left, my brother and I are there
fishing together, our poles glinting in the water.
My mouth moves. My eyes are alive!
I cry to my brother with joy.
For that bluejay was a messenger of what I want!

Gregory my friend and guide on this voyage seems benign.
He brushes my chest and my stretched,
naked arms open to the sun
with a branch of the fragrant pine.
"Be healed," he chants with each glancing
stroke. "Be healed." The needles prick my skin back into
    life,
and I go down to bathe my feet in the stream. The veins
form a light, mottled web along my white ankle.
I feel my kinship with the pine,
the jay, the luminescent stream
and with him—or is it with *her*,
the Mother? Gregory, my oracle, my teacher.
He leans there in the door of our tent by the river,
his face glowing, hair long and shining as a woman's,
his belly fat with life—pregnant with the two of us:
my brother and I, unborn twins who lie entangled
in each other's developing
limbs. Soon we will be born! He and I will taste of milk

for the very first time! And taste of strawberry pop
and of bright bananas. And we will eat, my brother
and I, a great, shining, autumn-red apple fallen
from our father's tree as if from the long sky, and *you*
too will taste this apple with us
for we all have the same mother, and her name is Grace.

UNDER DISCUSSION
Donald Hall, General Editor

Volumes in the Under Discussion series collect reviews
and essays about individual poets. The series is con-
cerned with contemporary American and English poets
about whom the consensus has not yet been formed and
the final vote has not been taken. Among those to be
considered are:

Elizabeth Bishop and Her Art
edited by Lloyd Schwartz and Sybil P. Estess
Richard Wilbur's Creation *edited by Wendy Salinger*
Adrienne Rich *edited by Jane Roberta Cooper*
Robert Bly *edited by Joyce Peseroff*
Allen Ginsberg *edited by Lewis Hyde*

*Please write for further information on available editions and
current prices.*

Ann Arbor   **The University of Michigan Press**

9087